Anne Thomas Soffee was born and raised in Richmond, Virginia. She was educated at the College of William and Mary and received an MFA from Virginia Commonwealth University. Her hips were educated at Scheherezade's, Sheva's and ZZ's Schools of Belly Dance. In the past, she has been employed as a bookseller, gas station attendant, heavy metal band wrangler, freelance music journalist, tattoo parlour lackey, and voiceover actress for kung fu movies. She now teaches special education.

SNAKE HIPS

BELLY DANCING
AND HOW I FOUND TRUE LOVE

Anne Thomas Soffee

BANTAM BOOKS

LONDON • NEW YORK • TORONTO • SYDNEY • AUCKLAND

SNAKE HIPS
A BANTAM BOOK: 0 553 81654 3

First publication in Great Britain
Originally published in the United States by Chicago Review Press

PRINTING HISTORY
Bantam edition published 2004

1 3 5 7 9 10 8 6 4 2

Set in 11/13pt Sabon by
Falcon Oast Graphic Art Ltd.

Bantam Books are published by Transworld Publishers,
61–63 Uxbridge Road, London W5 5SA,
a division of The Random House Group Ltd,
in Australia by Random House Australia (Pty) Ltd,
20 Alfred Street, Milsons Point, Sydney, NSW 2061, Australia,
in New Zealand by Random House New Zealand Ltd,
18 Poland Road, Glenfield, Auckland 10, New Zealand
and in South Africa by Random House (Pty) Ltd,
Endulini, 5a Jubilee Road, Parktown 2193, South Africa.

Printed and bound in Great Britain by
Cox & Wyman Ltd, Reading, Berkshire.

Papers used by Transworld Publishers are natural, recyclable
products made from wood grown in sustainable forests. The
manufacturing processes conform to the environmental
regulations of the country of origin.

To my parents

CONTENTS

ACKNOWLEDGMENTS

Needless to say, my first and most important acknowledgment goes to my family. Thanks for everything – and I do mean everything. I really do have the best family in the world. Extra special thanks go out to my Uncle Ronnie for always giving a damn.

I want to thank the coolest girls in the world, Karen Riddle, Melissa Burgess, and Sammie Griffin, for scraping me up off the ground and putting me back together when I fell apart. Thanks to everybody else who listened to me cry and whine that year, especially my L.A. buds because the time difference meant I could bug them in those miserable post-midnight hours. Thanks there to Wayne Pemberton, Tye Smith, and David and Margaret Perry.

Zaghareets and zils to all of my great dance teachers – Sheva, Lucy Smith, Susan Dodd, Fran Tribble, Janiece Bernardini, and Debbie West. Thanks to Tammy Keeler and Doris McCormick for the swell costumes, and thanks for welcoming me into the Corner. I am honored. Extra special *zil* trills also to Vicki Silver and Jen Willis for jogging my fuzzy memory and to Sabrina for moral support and commiseration.

On the publishing end, I owe a ton of thanks to Jane Dystel and Miriam Goderich for their enthusiasm and perseverance and, of course, to Cynthia Sherry, Lisa

Rosenthal, and the folks at Chicago Review Press. You guys are the greatest.

For moral support, advice, and general swellness, shout-outs go to Tom DeHaven, Lee Snavely, Randy Hallman, John Chapin (my one-man Sri Lanka rooting section), Mariane Matera, Vickie Holpe, Doctor Ducky Doolittle, Lisa Palac, and Erika Lopez. 'Mad props' to my students – especially the fine young men of the Genesis Treatment Agency. Thanks, keeds! For inspiration, a tip of the fez to Aladdin Express – the best hummus this side of the Mediterranean.

Finally, I am deeply grateful to Tad Hill for love, encouragement, acceptance, affection, and ammunition. Even though you refuse to take me to the Israeli-occupied territory on our honeymoon, I love you anyway.

For those of you keeping score at home, all of the events recounted herein are as I remember them. I know of at least one case where my recollection doesn't match up with another dancer's (and hers no doubt conflicts with someone else's). To those who would cry foul, I invite you to write your own book. I promise I'll be the first in line to buy it.

Hardcore glitter groupies and local insiders may notice that some names have been changed and some details have been altered. For the most part, who you see is who you get, but I shielded some dancers about whom I recounted backstage hearsay or general bad behavior (theirs or my own). In my effort to tell my story truthfully and completely, I'm sure I'll ruffle some maribou somewhere – but I tried to be fair.

INTRODUCTION

Behind
the Veil

Cairo Comes to the Holiday Inn

'I am telling you now, she will never dance in another one of my shows. *Never*.' Scheherezade, local belly dancer, Egyptian import maven, and all-around *Raks Sharki* impresario, is losing her shit. It is three minutes to curtain and Salina Asmin, the opening dancer, is nowhere to be found. Other belly dancers are crammed gauntlet to hip sash in the crowded hotel corridor. The air is thick with the smell of hair spray and exotic perfumes. Every performer for the first half of the show is lined up by number in order of appearance, starting with number two, Kamila Doumani, and trailing rhinestones all the way down the carpeted breezeway to number ten, Hadira Hizal. Only number one, Salina Asmin, is missing in action. No one is even sure if she checked into the hotel this afternoon. A messenger is dispatched to the front desk to find out. In the meantime, Scheherezade continues to fume.

For the past eight Wednesday nights, I have come to know Scheherezade as Lucy Smith, the instructor of the beginners' belly dancing class that I take at Dumbarton Elementary School. Lucy is a short, peasantlike woman with a frizzy halo of dark hair and an authoritative New York accent. In a Rakassah T-shirt and purple leggings, she demonstrates basic Middle Eastern techniques to the beat of a portable tape deck, following each new move with an encouraging nod and a 'Yah? See?' It always makes me feel like she is selling me some cool new gadget on a Manhattan street corner when she says that. 'Yah? See?' *Undulations, yours for just a buck. Hip shimmies, today only. Get your ribcage circles.* Tonight, though, the only thing Scheherezade is offering up is a world of hurt, and the recipient is going to be Salina if she doesn't get her sequin-covered ass to stage left in a hurry.

Tonight is the first night of Scheherezade's weekend-long gala Nadia Hamdi appearance, an event that takes place only once every two years and is undoubtedly the hottest belly dancing ticket on the East Coast. Nadia Hamdi's name might not mean much to the average American, but to belly dancers and their fans, there are few names that mean more. Nadia is one of just a handful of performing Cairo Greats left on the circuit, one of only four or five remaining superstars of the dance. Certainly, she is the only big-name Egyptian belly dancer you'll ever see on American soil. The Airport Holiday Inn is abuzz with anticipation. The banquet room is packed. Many of the attendees are belly dancers, in town for the all-day technique workshops that Nadia will be hosting, but there are also the 'glitter groupies,' hungry-looking single men, mostly older, some a little on the effete side, who turn up regularly at belly dancing events, their bespectacled eyes anxiously darting from sequined bra to chiffon veil but rarely meeting a dancer's kohl-lined gaze directly.

In addition to the Women Who Dance and the Men Who Love Them, there are, as always, several older

14

Middle Eastern men occupying the choicest seats along the edge of the dais. They greet passing dancers warmly, familiarly, and seem used to being treated with deference in these circles. I myself was indoctrinated just that evening, as I bravely manned the ticket counter when the doors opened. Lucy had handed me the stack of prepaid tickets, numbered and sealed in envelopes, and a stock roll of red paper tickets to be torn off and sold at the door. After showing me how to record the sales, she rattled off a list of names that blended into one long adjective – *ArtuniakhanalianhananianJibouniBalzikian* – and waved her hand as if to indicate that the explanation would be even longer than the names. 'If any of *those guys* show up and tell you they are on the list, just send them in and tell them their seats are reserved.'

'No problem.' I was eager to do this right, new as I was to belly dancing. I wanted to impress Scheherezade with my show-biz savvy, so that I might get asked to do this again some time. Tickets to Nadia Weekend run upward of a hundred bucks, but I had schmoozed my way into a coveted insider's position by, well, begging Lucy to let me help. I tried to use my experience as a Los Angeles heavy metal flack as a selling point, but I don't think that was what sold her. I think it was the shameless begging. Still, I wanted to do a good job, and now she was speaking my language. I knew how to work a guest list. Thinking that I was being extra-cool and Hollywood, I asked her if they should get a plus one. She looked at me blankly. I rephrased.

'Are they on the list as just themselves, for one ticket, or are they down for themselves plus one guest, for two tickets?'

Lucy blinked at me once, twice. She pointed to the folding table where she had just set the tickets and the cash box. It was otherwise empty.

'There is no guest list. Just tell them they're on one. They like that.'

This ain't no Mudd Club. I hiked up my caftan and opened the cash box. The fun was about to begin.

An hour later, the tickets distributed, the guests flattered, fawned over, and finally seated, I am called from my post at the front door to join the search party for Salina Asmin.

'Somebody's always gotta be a diva,' Lucy mutters, rolling her eyes and flipping frantically through a stack of index cards. 'It never fails. Carol,' she calls to a gold-clad woman in a Louise Brooks wig, 'go out there and tell the soundman we have a diva in our midst, and just screw it, we'll start with the second number.' Carol scurries toward the back of the banquet room, lamé shimmering in her wake, leaving Lucy to mumble and curse under her breath as the house lights dim and the opening strains of the intro music begin. Crossing herself briskly, Lucy clasps the stack of cards and turns to me as if she is about to entrust me with something very important and glamorous indeed. I am thrilled, simply thrilled, to be a part of it all. An international belly dancing extravaganza is on the line, and only I can save the day. I am ready.

'*Loooooo-seeeeeeeeeey*!' A singsongy little baby voice quivers up from behind dancer number seven. The sound of tiny bells tinkles closer, closer, closer. '*Loooooooooooo-seeeeeeeeey*!'

A small hooded creature hustles down the hallway toward us, jingling and chanting Lucy's name. When it reaches us, it stretches out its arms, golden cymbals strapped onto bony fingers. With one flick of a finger cymbal, it flips back its voluminous hood, revealing a shock of waffle-crimped ash-blonde hair cascading down over a leathery décolletage that belies the cutesy prepubescent voice. The creature blinks once, twice at Lucy, with eyes ringed by enough black kohl to sketch a landscape.

'Here I am,' it coos, crossing its wrists coyly across its outsized chest and chiming the cymbals perkily.

Lucy glares at the despicable thing that is Salina Asn and narrows her eyes. Thrusting the stack of cards at the offending diva, she shakes her head, jaw set, teeth clenched. Then, summoning all the restraint she can muster so as not to grab the still-chiming Salina by the beaded fringe and wring her sun-damaged little neck, Lucy shoves past her into the banquet room, all smiles and charming patter, resplendent in her royal blue caftan and Saudi gold, and welcomes the crowd to an Evening with Nadia Hamdi. Taking the mike, she enthuses that she is so glad they could all join us for this wonderful evening, it promises to be a truly memorable event, and this evening we are fortunate to have with us the star of the nightclub stage and party circuit, choreographer, and advisor to the stars, golden giver goddess who originally *brought* belly dance to the huddled masses of Norfolk, Virginia – the lovely, the talented, I am waiting for her to announce that this is her *absolute most favorite dancer in the whole wide world*, she hides her ire so well – the marvelous SALINA ASMIN!

Salina shucks her cloak and holds it out to me expectantly. Humbled in the presence of greatness, I take it with only a minimal amount of eyeball rolling. As she primes her finger cymbals and licks her teeth in preparation for serious smiling, a gold streak catches my eye in the banquet room. Having already adjusted the lineup to account for Salina's absence, Carol has less than fifteen seconds of leader tape to adjust for her presence. I look at Salina incredulously, projecting what I hope is a look-at-the-trouble-you've-caused guilt beam in her direction. She winks at me, all kohl and crow's feet, and purses her copper-frosted lips against a cymbal. Taking a deep breath, she inflates her already overflowing bosom to its fullest, most imposing capacity. She glances down appreciatively at her own assets and extends one arm out in front of herself and raises the other over her head. As

...mbeats of 'Laylet Hob' throb over the Holiday ... he squinches her eyes tightly and smiles so ... neck muscles strain. Then, to the delighted ... of the men on the guest list, she prances out onto the stage and starts to dance.

In the hallway, the dancers who have yet to perform primp and stretch under modest caftans. It is considered terribly, terribly gauche to be seen in costume when one isn't in the throes of performance. This is one of the cardinal rules of belly dancing, along with 'don't do a backbend with your crotch toward the audience' and 'don't touch yourself lasciviously while you dance.' Depending on the caliber of the lineup, at any given show you will see most of these rules broken in one way or another. Tonight, the only violation I see is the caftan edict. Lounging against a column at the far end of the hall, Princess Arabia in full regalia is dragging on a Misty Menthol (make that two violations), arguing with her boyfriend, costume completely uncovered but for a black satin Hooters jacket.

Princess Arabia had already won a special place in my heart of hearts that morning at registration. I was manning the table alone, bleary eyed and coffeeless – the things I do for the dance, I mean to tell you – when her royal Hooterness trotted up, long-haired boyfriend in tow, and demanded a registration packet for Princess Arabia.

'Real name?' The logistical complications of filing the packets under stage names would be endless. How many Leylas, how many Delilahs? And that didn't even take into account the crying scarcity of surnames. Princess Arabia flipped her dirty blonde bangs wearily and sighed.

'My *name* is Princess *Arabia*.'

Now it was my turn to sigh. 'Yes, but your registration is listed under your real name.' I riffled through the envelopes enticingly – *all this could be yours, honey, if you'd just come up off the goods and tell me your name.*

Princess Arabia rolled her eyes. She stood silently, as if waiting for me to come around. When this didn't happen, she restated her claim.

'It *should* be under Princess Arabia.' That was her story and she was sticking to it.

'But it's *not*.' Now that I had what I considered a license to get nasty, I could relate a little more to the registration game. My previous guest list experience, years ago during the hair-metal heyday of the L.A. scene, involved guys named Nasty and Ice, and between schmoozing the press and baby-sitting the bands, I was expected to screen out anyone wearing blatant gang colors and any groupies that the band had decided they were done with. Princess Arabia was about to find herself in a class with yesterday's blow job and a Crip named Li'l Mack. Fortunately for her, she saw things my way before I was forced to get Hollywood on her.

'Well, they might be under Amber Carver.'

I handed her the envelope with barely concealed arrogance. 'Here we are, Amber!' I sounded like a nurse about to hand her a paper smock. She snatched the envelope and stuffed it in the pocket of her satin jacket. As she huffed down the hallway toward the elevator, her denim-clad ass switching defiantly from side to side, I allowed myself one last irresistible indulgence.

'Thank you, AMBER! Have a great weekend, mmmmmkay?'

I really should not be allowed in polite society before ten a.m. Not without coffee, anyway. I giggled quietly to myself and crossed Amber Carver off the list.

Ninety minutes, twenty-odd dancers, and a thousand and one undulations later, the already dimmed houselights are extinguished in anticipation of the first act's finale, the *Raqsat Shemadan* ('Dance of the Candelabra'). Nadia Hamdi is Egypt's premier *shemadan* maven, and *raks shemadan* had been the subject of the afternoon's workshop – a workshop that found my classmate Nadine crouched in the stairwell hyperventilating, near hysterics, the three-tiered brass candelabra still strapped to her head. 'I just can't handle all this fuckin' *choreography*,' she wailed between gasping sobs. 'My brain ain't as functional as y'all's!'

While Carol goes to fetch Nadia from the dressing room, I stand vigilantly at my post, guarding the doorway against loitering dancers, zealous busboys, and over-enthusiastic Armenian men to ensure that Nadia and her *shemadan* will have a clear passage from the dressing room to the stage. My curiosity about Nadia's stage show is peaking. All day long I have been bottom lackey in the Nadia Hamdi entourage – a position I am all too used to after paying my dues on the Sunset Strip. At least Lucy didn't expect me to find Nadia clean needles. My duties so far have involved much more wholesome demands. We are to make sure Nadia has fresh orange juice within reach while teaching, and, when she isn't teaching, see that she is not disturbed while resting in her room enjoying her favorite pastime, watching American television. ('Oh, TV,' she had said when she checked in, fluttering her hand over her heart in anticipation. 'Bobhope. *Yalla*, Lucy! Turn on Bobhope!') Finally, I, like everyone else in the entourage, am to make absolutely sure she didn't run out of chewing gum.

I have never seen anyone chew gum as constantly or as enthusiastically as Nadia. The entire weekend, she keeps a piece of Wrigley's Juicy Fruit working, Violet Beauregarde–style, no matter what the occasion. In her chiffon quasi-tutu practice skirt and foofy white lace headband, she looks more like a chubby, mischievous little schoolgirl than an international belly dancing superstar – not to mention the mother of a grown son, a son whose protests had led her to end her performing career in Cairo at the height of her fame. More than anything else, it is the constant *chk-a-chk-a-chk* of the gum that seems incongruous with my glamorous expectations of Nadia Hamdi, Queen of the Dance. '*Akh*,' came the eye-rolling response when I mentioned the gum chewing at Soffee Family Dinner on Sunday. 'What did you expect? She's *Egyptian*.' Egyptians – renowned for their majestic pyramids, early civilizations, and incessant gum chewing. I made a note.

The gum-chomping, headband-wearing Nadia is nowhere in evidence as the music begins to build for the *Raqsat Shemadan*. Carol leads a glittering, sparkling, white-sequin-clad Nadia down the hall, elaborate candelabra perched atop cascading hennaed curls. On the candelabra, twelve white tapers flicker with actual live flames, a detail I had conveniently forgotten to consider while guarding my post, a wooden doorway festooned with gaily colored and highly flammable paper streamers. Frantically, I leap for their tails, pulling down as many of them as time and stature will allow as Nadia makes her way beatifically down the hall. I can envision the headlines: 'ONE HUNDRED BELLY DANCERS KILLED IN FREAK HOLIDAY INN *SHEMADAN* FIRE!' Yanking at the streamers as Nadia draws closer, I feel the same sense of serene resignation that I had felt at the Hollywood Palladium when I was sure I was about to be crushed to death in the front row of an Iggy Pop show – *these may be my last moments, but what a way to go*.

My fears, whether real or imagined, are apparently not shared by Nadia or Lucy or any of the dancers and fans who are left breathless in the wake of the *shemadan* as Nadia floats through the doorway. 'Thank-ayoo,' she chirps as she ducks gracefully under the remaining streamers without incident. God protects drunks, infants, and candelabra-wearing belly dancers. I sink wearily against the doorway and turn my attention to the *Raqsat Shemadan*.

Belly dancing, is, by definition, a dazzling display of pageantry and glitz. The hand-decorated Madam Abla costumes, dripping with bugle beads and huge sequined appliqués; the elaborate, painstaking makeup that reminds one as much of a Bally's showgirl as of Cleopatra; the requisite cascade of glossy, immaculately coiffed hair – and, of course, the moves. Would that every form of performance art included a four-minute drum solo as interpreted by a beautiful woman's hips. Few things can compare to a well-executed hip snap when the drummer is hot and the dancer is right on the money. Add a demi-tasse of Turkish coffee and a honey-soaked square of baklava and you will believe that your life, here in this room, watching this dancer, is the most glamorous, most decadent, most enviable life that has ever been lived. Watching a belly dancer is a sensual experience that cannot be surpassed . . . except by *Raqsat Shemadan*.

The only thing more captivating than watching a regular belly dancer is watching a belly dancer with a three-tiered candelabra on her head. Seeing Nadia shake, twirl, undulate, and prance underneath her crown of dancing lights is nothing short of hypnotic. When she lowers herself to the floor in a flawless split – *how* old did you say she was? – and performs a series of graceful, snakelike waves with her body, still balancing the candles seemingly without effort, even the hotel staff stand breathlessly still, caught in the spell of the *shemadan*. On the floor, Nadia smiles, winks, waves a little at the crowd as she moves. She has us where she wants us. It is a position she is used to.

Raqsat Shemadan is traditionally a part of the Egyptian wedding celebration. Watching Nadia, I have to wonder

22

how many couples have their first spat over the belly dancer? How must it feel to watch your husband of just a few minutes staring, open-mouthed, at a beautiful woman undulating on the floor of your reception hall? How many Egyptian husbands find themselves on the fold-out couch in the honeymoon suite of the Luxor Hilton? Looking around the banquet room, I decide that the grooms of Egypt are probably safe. There is no one, no man, no woman, who is not looking at Nadia and her *shemadan*. Wedding vows and covetous wishes are no contest for a belly dancer and a candelabra. With my eyes back on Nadia, I think for a moment that she will probably be done soon, that maybe I should find a chair and climb up and remove the remaining streamers from the doorway before her grand exit and inevitable curtain call. No, I decide. It isn't worth missing the rest of the show. And besides, the entire Holiday Inn could become a deadly inferno right now and none of us would care. *Why didn't you run?* Saint Peter would ask us at the gates. *For Christ's sake, why didn't one of you idiots pull the fire alarm?*

You didn't see her, Pete, we would answer, one after the other, black smoke wisping on our breath. *You had to be there.*

It's been five years, nearly to the day, since I originally set terrified half-Lebanese foot in my first belly dancing class. What began as a joke meant to take my mind off a bad case of heartbreak has turned into a way of life for me. Who would have thought the tattoo dude's old lady would end up shimmying for seniors and strutting on the midway with the likes of the Learned Dog of Wonder and Serpentina the Snake Girl? It's not exactly how I envisioned starting the new millennium.

When I first entertained the idea of belly dancing, I pictured something that would give me a clearer idea of my history. I imagined it as a personal pilgrimage, an investigation of my Lebanese heritage by way of music and dance. I guess if I had a little more willpower and culture, I could have pursued that scenario – but as is evidenced by history and the pages you are about to read, willpower and culture aren't my strong suits. While belly dancing – or *danse orientale*, as the culturati like to call it – has plenty to offer in the way of ethnic history and heritage, I chose instead to heed the call of rhinestones and sequins and follow Little Egypt into the tent for a show that shocks and amazes.

When I'm mugging my way through 'Istanbul (Not Constantinople)' at the county fair, in pink satin harem pants and a veiled pillbox hat, I'm not communing with my history. I'm not getting in touch with my heritage. And I'm not performing *Raks Sharki, danse orientale*, or any of the other names used to denote 'real' Middle Eastern dance. I'm breaking all the rules. When I swivel my head from side to side like a genie and wink, the Ethnic Police get their *thobes* all in a bunch. But I don't care, because I'm doing what I love.

I'm *belly dancin'*. I am doing things my ancestors would never have imagined in a million years. I am a fugitive from the Ethnic Police. And I am having the time of my life. This is the story of how belly dancing changed my life.

SNAKE HIPS

1

It's Gonna Be a Generation
Xmas . . . or Not

Farewell to the Tiki Lounge

'Is this yours?' a foot-high plastic statuette of the X-Men's Wolverine is held up for me to peruse. I nod mutely and it is carried out to the truck.

'How about these?' Melissa motions toward a set of Godzilla figurines marching across the top of the bookcase. Mothra, Gidjrah, Megalon, the Atomic Monster. I paid for all of them but I don't want to take them with me because they remind me too much of Chris, with his full-sleeve tattoo of Godzilla serving the severed head of Felix the Cat to a bound and gagged Bettie Page. I shake my head. She starts throwing Bettie Page magnets into a box, and I want to protest but I just don't have the energy to explain. I let her pack the magnets even though I never want to see them again. Damn Bettie Page. Damn Bettie and Felix and Ganesh and Elvis and every other super-hip icon in this stupid house. *Oooooh, we're just so cool, with our tattoo parlor and our black Volkswagen and our painfully ironic decor.* We were the coolest things in Winston-Salem for six glorious months – and that and

27

eighty bucks bought me a U-Haul ride back to Richmond to live with my parents, broke, brokenhearted, and too cool for words.

Two years ago, I moved in with Chris, when he was a short-order cook and I was a high school teacher at a psychiatric hospital. We met at the modern-day version of the soda shop – an AA meeting. His story was edgy and dramatic – art school at sixteen, time on the road with the rock band GWAR, a year in New York as an animator for a hip gross-out cartoon, a hitchhiking trip down south that left him in a ditch, OD'd in a hospital gown. It was such a good story that I never questioned the inconsistencies and contradictions that popped up each time he retold it. Besides, my own story was less interesting. My stint as a small-time heavy metal flack in hairband-era L.A. had left me with a propensity for other people's prescriptions and a drinking program that edged my freelance journalism work right off my schedule. I came skulking back to Richmond by way of rehab, bloated and broke, looking like a miniature Ozzy Osbourne and doomed to a future of glamorous Friday nights in church basements, making coffee and cleaning ashtrays after the Serenity Prayer.

By the time Chris showed up on my recovery radar, things were looking up. I had gone back to school and gotten my master's degree, lost the beer weight, and found that I had a gift for teaching hard-knock kids. In my English class, I had junior felons reading Shakespeare and runaway girls writing their anger out in epic poems. I might have lost my chance at heavy metal glory, but life was OK. And when I met Chris, it looked like it was getting even better.

Six months ago I had quit my job and moved with him to Winston-Salem, North Carolina, so that he could apprentice as a tattoo artist at the Ink Well. It had seemed like the perfect answer to the eternal artist's dilemma – how to make a living at your art. We thought that the apprenticeship would be our first step on the road to financial independence, artistic freedom, and, eventually, happily ever after. Two weeks ago, casually and coolly, with the Royal Crown Revue's 'Hey, Pachuco' playing in the background, he told me to go home. So, for the past two weeks, home has been my childhood room at my parents' house, where I huddled, tearstained and crushed, awaiting my thirtieth birthday . . . alone.

I never saw it coming, though by all accounts I should have. Business was great. After tattooing for only six months, Chris was already working by appointment only. Every multi-pierced hipster in town wanted custom work from the hot new artist. Everybody at the coffee shop, the small-town raves, and the Greensboro nightclubs knew who he was, and he ate it up. He started getting into the role. He cut his curly, shoulder-length hair into a slicked-down Caesar, bleached it out, and grew a goatee. He started smoking high-priced imported cigarettes ('They're part of my image'), wearing bowling shirts, and listening to Sinatra. Our living room was always full of twentysomething guys with shaved heads and their barely legal stripper girlfriends, playing Nintendo and eating our food. It was hard not to notice that, in my own house, I no longer fit in. More and more often, I was inventing reasons to retire to the spare room when company showed up – e-mails to return, auctions to monitor, any excuse not to sit on the floor watching my boyfriend bond with kids barely older than my former students over Tomb Raider and Korn. I had become the Cynthia Lennon of the Winston-Salem tattoo scene, a bespectacled, frumpy reminder of life before cool.

I tried, however weakly, to get with the program. I traded my passé round schoolteacher frames for saucy black cat's-eye specs. I thrift-shopped on weekends for just the right touches for our happy hipster home – a fleet of vintage chrome toasters, a Formica dinette, a curvaceous doublewide 1950s stove (though I drew the line at letting him paint flames on the sides). I even helped out at the tattoo parlor as much as I could, making runs to Bojangles' and Burger King for the artists, picking up Vaseline and gloves when supplies were low, and handing out tiny tubes of Bacitracin and care sheets to the satisfied customers. I cannot pretend that I enjoyed my job all of the time. More than once, while waiting in the Taco Bell drive-through lane for half an hour or more – only a few hours south of Richmond, the pace of everything in Winston-Salem is decidedly more *Suhth'n* – I caught myself thinking, *So this is why I got a master's degree? So that I can pick up tostadas for a former biker who, even as we speak, is sketching a Taz on some trailer bride's ass?*

Not that I didn't like Bishop, the owner of the shop and Chris's boss. In fact, one of the few things I enjoyed about spending twelve hours a day there was bantering with Bishop, who possessed that dry, languid wit that seems to come so naturally to beefy tough guys. Still, it was not lost on me that, in the hierarchy of the Ink Well, I was dead last on the roster, well below Bishop and Chris, not to mention Bishop's wife, Renée, a sulky former stripper with a tongue full of metal and a midriff-baring wardrobe left over from her pole-dancing days.

Renée was the shop piercer, a position that, unnervingly enough, can be filled by anyone who chooses to pick up a needle. The APA (American Piercing Association) offers weekend seminars in safety and procedure, but attendance at a seminar is above and beyond shop requirements and strictly up to the discretion of the piercer – if she has any. Due to certain nuances of credit and taxation, Renée was also listed as sole owner of the Ink Well, a detail that rarely escaped mention during her daily knock-down-drag-outs with Bishop in the back room.

From the start, my presence at the Ink Well had been somewhat uneasy. More than once I had been taken aside and reminded that it was not in the best interests of the shop for me to recommend that someone 'go home and think it over.' My inability to come up with a decent poker face had not gone unnoticed or uncommented on by Bishop and Renée. When a customer asked for a particularly ill-advised piece of work – a new girlfriend's name, the logo of a band destined for near-immediate 'where are they now' status, or a flaming marijuana leaf on the side of his neck, my rolling eyes and pursed lips inevitably made public my opinion and won me no points in the parlor. The tattoo business was about closing the sale fast, before the customer had a chance to think twice, and talking the customer up if possible – never down.

Chris's smooth patter and nice-boy good looks led more than one hapless female to leave the shop with more than she bargained for. One moony-eyed eighteen-year-old Chiclet, still schoolgirl homely in a retainer and halter top, was so taken with Chris and the attention he was lavishing on her that she allowed herself to be talked up from a dime-sized yin-yang symbol on the back of her shoulder to a five-inch-high full-color Virgin of Guadalupe between her smallish breasts. No ordinary Mother of God, this proud Mary had the ears and whiskers of a tabby cat under her halo, and floating above her clasped hands was a steaming cup of joe.

While Chris was tattooing, if there were no sales to be rung, fast food to fetch, or supplies to be purchased, I would spend my time lounging on the rented purple leather couch in the lobby, reading back issues of *Skin & Ink* and *Easyriders*. Having exhausted the thrift shopping possibilities, the one coffee shop, and the utter and complete banality of the Hanes Mall, I was finding Winston-Salem to be sadly lacking in entertainment value.

It is a city that runs on NASCAR, Goody Powder, and the smoke of numerous huge factories – Sara Lee, R. J. Reynolds, Hanes – and a far cry from any place I had lived before. In fact, I was finding about as much satisfaction in the city as I was in our new circle of 'friends.'

Chris's hangers-on from the tattoo parlor were, for the most part, young, white, and blandly trendy. Decked out in whatever was considered 'alternative' that week, the pink-haired girls and baggy-jeaned boys showed up at our door at all hours, wanting to bask in the glow of the Ink God. Chris never hesitated to humor them, occasionally throwing 'ink parties' in our living room where all of the local tattooists would, just for fun, treat each other to new tattoos on whatever blank patch of skin they could locate. 'Just surprise me' was a common request while rolling up a pants leg or doffing a shirt. In between rounds of PlayStation and Mountain Dew, they would add freehand, stream-of-consciousness sketches to their friends' already overcrowded extremities. A coffee cup. An evil insect. A bulldog in a top hat and tails juggling three bones. The challenge was to come up with the most ludicrous visual possible . . . and stick your friend with it for life.

I have one tattoo. It is a vestigial reminder of my heavy metal days, a faded tribute to the two years I spent in L.A., lurking backstage at Danzig shows and knocking back Jagermeister at the Frolic Room with would-be guitar gods. The tattoo is a crappy red-and-black tribal-style scorpion, its tail curling around my left nipple, the red claws now faded almost pink. In truth, it looks more like an anemic crawfish than anything else. It was a first-date present from a pretty-boy rehab biker whose Harley I hopped on the back of on Hollywood Boulevard. It was one of those decisions that would have been instantly regrettable if not for the anecdotal value. Of course, the story always carried that unspoken caveat: *Now, though, I am old enough to know better.*

When I fell in love with Chris, I never thought that being old enough to know better would become my fatal flaw. 'You're not any fun anymore,' he told me the night we broke up. These words stand out as the basic foundation beneath the litany of my sins he recited as he gave me my leave. Tattoo magazines and PlayStation cartridges littered the living room floor. A black-light poster of the Devil in a paisley smoking jacket loomed overhead. This was what our life together had become. This was the fun that I was not. I looked numbly at the flaming checkers etched on the side of his neck, 'King Me' inscribed underneath them on a curling scroll, and wondered how I came to get my heart broken by a man who could pass a double-A battery through his earlobe. Somehow the universe must have made a bad mistake. This, obviously, was never supposed to happen.

A year ago, we had been blissful in our tiny warehouse apartment in downtown Richmond, an achingly cute geek couple who spent quiet evenings listening to jazz, reading Bukowski, and drinking coffee. Our matching overalls and glasses led the Panda Garden deliveryman to mistake us for siblings. On my birthday, Chris had presented me with hand-drawn tributes, self-portraits of him serenading me with birthday songs of love, accompanied by good old Felix the Cat.

The main thing that had attracted me when I met him was his seriousness. He seemed unimpressed with the riot-grrrl waitresses who flirted with him as they poured his coffee at the diner. There was something unpretentious about him. I felt that I was finally reaping the rewards that AA's dusty Big Book promises those who trudge the path of happy destiny with nary a drop of assistance from John Barleycorn. This was the happily ever after that everyone was talking about. I didn't feel like I was asking for too much – I didn't need a doctor or lawyer for a beau, and I had no desire for a sprawling McMansion in the suburbs. NPR on the radio and a good cup of Colombian Supremo together in our tiny apartment were my personal gold ring.

When Chris proposed the idea of learning how to tattoo, it seemed the perfect solution to the problem he wrestled with daily – how to make a decent living without selling out. Tattooing, while not the most highbrow of the visual arts, paid well and would allow him to set his own hours and promote his own original work, both on the flesh and on the flash – the sheets of preprinted designs that are displayed on the walls of tattoo parlors. Sure, there would be the salad days, the humble beginnings where most of his time would be spent inking in another artist's flash, or the usual public domain designs – hearts, roses, and the omnipresent cover-any-ex-girlfriend's-name cure-all, the black panther. But I had faith in his talent, and I knew that if we could stick it out for the first few months, the investment would pay off.

The first shop to offer Chris an apprenticeship was in Greensboro, North Carolina. A block up from the site of the Woolworth's Civil Rights Movement sit-in, Forever Yours Tattoo occupied a run-down storefront in a run-down block of downtown Greensboro. Tic Toc, the shop's proprietor, was a beady-eyed pit bull of a kid, probably not much older than twenty. Decked out in Fubu baggy jeans and a Chicago Bulls cap, he looked like a redneck caricature of an L.A. street tough. Tic Toc kept a six-pack and a loaded nine-millimeter under the counter and laid down the rules as he shaded a grinning skull on a Marine's bicep.

'You run errands, clean the shop, make needles. If you do OK, in about a month you can start on grapefruits, then chickens, then your own legs. When 'em's full, we'll see if we can use you.'

Chris joined Tic Toc's cousin Dave on the bottom rung of the Forever Yours crew. Dave was apparently so dim he couldn't even be trusted to make needles, so his duties were mostly janitorial. He seemed thrilled just to be allowed to hang around the shop, fetching beers and stacking magazines. Dave was covered with samples of Tic Toc's dubious artistry, including a full-back illustration of an ample blonde in a string bikini seated atop a lifeguard's chair. Behind a pair of mirrored aviator shades, the blonde's face was a grinning skull, which seemed to be something of a *leitmotif* at Forever Yours. Then, as if any further embellishment was needed, above the blonde, across Dave's scrawny shoulders in two-inch-high block letters, was the subtle legend 'LIFEGUAD OF DEATH.'

'I already know he forgot the *r*,' Dave warned us, almost apologetically, as he raised his shirt to show us his prize. 'Cain't exactly erase it, though.'

Through all of this, Forever Yours' other artist, Bishop, sat stoically by, shaking his head and painstakingly lining up needles in groups to be welded together. Six-foot-four, bald, and perpetually shirtless, Bishop communicated in drawled asides and raised eyebrows. One night, when I had run out of magazines to pretend to read, I worked up the courage to ask to examine his tattoos. Checking out each other's art was a new etiquette ritual that I had picked up from watching Chris as he met and schmoozed with other artists. As far as I could tell, it was sort of a cross between the way Japanese businessmen bow to each other and the way dogs sniff each other's butts. Bishop patiently slid his stool back from the counter and lifted a beefy arm, turning it first one way and then the other.

'They ain't all that,' he drawled as he displayed one grinning skull after another, interspersed with the odd evil clown and one particularly fetching chromed motorcycle engine. 'They're mostly old, left over from when I was a Harley-ridin' redneck.' He rubbed his fingers fondly over the lines of the engine. 'Thet's as opposed to a regular redneck, like I am now.' Bishop had been tattooing for almost ten years, supporting a wife and two kids working at various East Coast parlors for kids who were still doing time in detention hall when he started inking. He was mainly a flash artist and had no pretensions about joining the big leagues – for Bishop, tattooing was a technical skill, not a means of expression. He recognized Chris's potential right away.

We had only been in North Carolina a few weeks when Bishop showed up at our door one Sunday night with a business proposition. He and Renée had found an investor and a building in Winston-Salem and were planning to branch out on their own. The shop he was looking to open would be more upscale than Forever Yours and would specialize in custom work and original artwork – so, of course, they would need an artist. He offered Chris a sixty-forty split to start and would pay half of the thousand-dollar licensing fee that North Carolina used to dissuade fly-by-night 'scratchers' from doing business in the state. It was a reprieve from grinning skulls and Tic Toc's less-than-benevolent guidance; it seemed that the better Chris got with the needle, the more grunt work he was given by his territorial instructor. We made the move to Winston-Salem quickly and gratefully.

Now, four months after the move to Winston-Salem and six months after the move to Carolina, I am headed back to Richmond. Melissa, my best friend since childhood, and Karen, my original AA sponsor whose return to her party-girl ways had ended the sponsorship but not our friendship, have commandeered a U-Haul and barreled down Route 360 posthaste on a mission of mercy. While I sit, shell-shocked, at the blue Formica dinette that had held so much promise for my life as a postmodern June Cleaver, Melissa and Karen load boxes with stereo equipment, dishes, books, and all of the kitsehy tchotchkes that Chris and I had collected together over the past two years. Fueled by can after can of Pabst Blue Ribbon, they are a two-woman repo crew, loading up everything that had been mine, mine and his, a gift from me to him, or a gift from him to me.

'I know you don't want it now,' Karen warns as she throws a wooden folk-art monkey Chris had given me into a box already brimming with painful memories, 'but later on you'll thank me.' She stuffs a deck of Annie Sprinkle pinup playing cards into the side of the box. 'When you stop cryin' you might want this stuff again.'

Melissa agrees. As she dumps handfuls of kitchen utensils into a grocery bag, she imparts the wisdom of her recent divorce. 'When I left, I just wanted to take the important things and get out as fast as I could. But—' and she waves a potato masher at me before throwing it into the bag, 'it's going to add insult to injury if you have to go out and buy stuff like *this* all over again.' She unplugs a chrome toaster and lowers it into the bag.

Sniffling, I nod in agreement though I remain unconvinced. I never want to see any of this stuff again. It's only going to remind me of what a sham the whole thing turned out to be. Happily ever after indeed. I found the one true soul mate the world had to offer me, and he sold out for a free latte and a backstage pass to Rage Against the Machine. I've been dumped, not to mention the fact that I'm six weeks away from thirty, ten pounds overweight, unemployed, and technically homeless. Potato mashers and wooden monkeys are the least of my worries.

'Heyyyyyyyyy . . .' I recognize Melissa's tone from fifteen years of scavenging flea markets together. A find. She reaches up gingerly and unhooks a stained glass Tiffany reproduction from the window. 'This is yours, right?'

'I guess.' She hands me the pane, and I dust it off glumly. 'Chris made it for me when he was working at the place that does these for museum shops. I don't want it, though.' I hand it back to her.

'You could sell it, though.' She holds it up to the light, peering through it with an appraising eye. 'How much do these things go for? A hundred bucks?'

I look at the pane and think about the hundred dollars I've spent already on Christmas presents for Chris – a Bettie Page lighter, a set of Mexican wrestling dolls, and three lounge CDs. I think about the deposit that I'm going to lose on the house we rented in Winston-Salem, the bills that are all still in my name thanks to his rotten credit history, and the new bills that surely await me in Richmond. Then I think of the day he had given me the pane, wrapped in tissue paper and tied with purple ribbons, accompanied by a handmade card that read 'something nice for you, because you deserve nice things.'

'Here, let me have that.' I stand up from the dinette, grab the pane, and stride out of the kitchen, clutching it in both hands. Melissa and Karen follow in shock, as I am displaying more energy now than I have in the two weeks since the dumping. 'Find me that Slinky,' I command, referring to the first present Chris had ever given me, packed earlier in the day by Karen. 'And bring me that cigar box from beside the desk.' Melissa scurries off to locate the Slinky. 'Oh!' I call after her. 'And bring a knife – a big knife!' She sticks her head back in the door briefly, her expression halfway between morbid curiosity and fear, then returns to her mission. Karen keeps a safe distance behind me as I proceed to the bedroom.

The room that Chris and I had shared is now empty. As was the case in most of the other rooms as well, everything had been mine. The bed, the dresser, the TV and VCR – all mine from before we had met. When Chris moved in with me, he brought a Hefty bag full of dirty clothes, his art supplies, and some comic books. It was an all-too-common phenomenon that we had discussed the night before around the kitchen table. 'I'm tired of being a port in a storm for vagabond artists and musicians,' Melissa had said over her fourth PBR, as Karen and I nodded sympathetically. 'I mean, I bust my ass to keep a comfortable house with food in the cupboard and the heating bill paid – and these losers act like it's a bed-and-breakfast where they can stop in and enjoy the amenities for a while, then move on.'

Matching their beers with endless cups of coffee, I was the amen corner, wordlessly accepting my thankless role as queen of the loser ex-boyfriends. Before Chris it had been Paul Bearer, lead singer for Philadelphia's legendary Serial Killers and part-time Lollapalooza roadie. His quick wit and groovy leather boots did little to compensate for a nagging heroin problem and a fiancée in Ohio. Paul's predecessor was Lewis Bucket of the local Richmond band Bucket. Lewis was a rock star by night and a weenie cart vendor by day. Bucket's songs were heartrendingly soulful, with plaintive lyrics full of tender phrasing and empathetic rhymes. Lewis gave me crabs and joked about it to his friends.

When I met Chris, I had put all of this behind me. I considered it a sign of growth that he didn't even play an instrument. The fact that he was already in recovery meant that drunken indiscretions and rent money spent on drugs would not be the issue as with my former parade of champions. Even the other teachers at work marveled over my great catch every day as I unpacked homemade vegetarian lunches, always with a little sketch and a love note enclosed in the brown bag. I was happy, content, and maybe even a little cocky. I had found a man who spoiled me, but I deserved to be spoiled. I knew this was true because he told me so every day. He loved me.

* * *

Stained glass does not sound particularly fancy when it's breaking. When dropped from a height of five feet onto a hardwood floor, it sounds similar to a dinner plate being dropped, or a teacup – not a dainty, gold-edged one but a thick, matronly one with dull edges and a wide mouth. The pieces of the Tiffany window spread out on the bedroom floor like puddles after a storm. With the instep of my Doc Martens, I push them into a little pile in the middle of the room.

'Give me the cigar box.' I reach for the box, full of letters, drawings, and photographs documenting Life Before Tattoos. Riffling through a thick stack of pictures, I pull out three of my former favorites: one of Chris asleep in a red union suit on the night before Christmas, one of the two of us standing triumphantly outside the Ink Well the day before it opened, and one of us sitting in our favorite diner, mugging for the camera over plates of pancakes and the omnipresent coffee cups. I hand the box back to Melissa and reach for the Slinky.

Setting the photographs to the side for the moment, I crouch carefully above the pile of broken stained glass. Stretching the Slinky out as far as I can reach, I twist the ends and fold it over on itself, making certain to link some of its coils for maximum tangling. Tangling a Slinky is one of those enigmatic occurrences that seem to come naturally exactly when you're not trying but never when you are, like a good hearty burp or a perfectly round smoke ring. After a couple of lame attempts, though, I come up with a fairly Gordian Slinkyknot. Slowly and deliberately, I lower the Slinkyknot onto the broken stained glass. Melissa and Karen are still watching cautiously from the doorway. The knife has not entered into my equation – yet.

I pick up the first photograph – the diner. Holding it up ceremoniously over the pile, I rip a clean line down the middle of the photo, separating Chris and me into two halves. Then, with a flourish, I tuck each half into the coils of the Slinkyknot. I do the same with the Ink Well photo. The photo of Chris alone I don't rip. I stick that one in a high coil, up above the others, in the hopes that maybe seeing a glimpse of his old self will trigger some recognition, some remorse, something real from this image-obsessed scene-ster who used to be my boyfriend.

Reaching back into the cigar box, I pull out a handful of tiny sketches of me that Chris had done on Post-it notes. He used to put them on the computer screen to surprise me when I got home from teaching school. I stick the pictures in the Slinkyknot, my own face peering at me from between the twisted metal coils. Melissa tips her beer can back and drains the last few swallows. I can only imagine the pain that my horrible attempt at abstract sculpture is causing her aesthetic eye. But I'm not finished yet.

I dig to the bottom of the cigar box, where I keep the mushy cards that Chris was prone to include with his frequent no-occasion gifts. Flipping each one open and scanning the empty words inside, I select the one that seems to be the most antithetical to what he had said two weeks ago to the beat of 'Hey, Pachucho.' The card depicts Curious George and the Man with the Yellow Hat. They are seated at a small table, gazing admiringly at each other with cartoon affection. Inside, in Chris's loopy artist's scrawl, is a purple-markered message penned two months prior:

'Thank you for everything you do for me. I couldn't have done it without you, and I wouldn't want to. You make life worth living. Having you in my life teaches me what gratitude really is – it's what I feel when I realize we might never have met. Love and Gratitude, Chris.'

THWAK! With a swift overhead motion, I bring the

knife down to the floor, stabbing into the card and the wood with one quick thrust. The card is now splayed open, tacked to the floor in front of the pile of broken glass, torn paper, and twisted metal. Karen nods approvingly. Melissa shakes her head and goes to the kitchen for another beer. I wipe away fresh tears – catharsis will only get you so far when you have to read nullified love notes to find it. Taking a long look at the shattered remains of happily ever after piled in the middle of my former bedroom, I close the cigar box and hand it to Karen.

'Let's get on the road. Tell Melissa to make sure she got my Jesus candles.'

'Were they on the same shelf as the Elvis bust?'

'Uh huh.'

'All clear, Annie. Let's get you home.'

Ten weeks after my unceremonious dumping and two months after my completely untriumphant return to Richmond, fortuna finds me spending yet another weepy Thursday night on Karen's couch, chain smoking and watching *ER*. It doesn't faze my parents that their youngest daughter shacked up with a tattoo artist, or traveled with rockabilly bands, or ended up in rehab three thousand miles from home – but even on the cusp of thirty, I am afraid to let them find out I smoke cigarettes. So, night after night, I white-knuckle it through dinner until I can slip over to Karen's for my requisite smoke-and-sobfest. Fortunately, it coincides perfectly with Karen's scheduled bong hit and ice cream ritual. So here we are again, a couple of white chicks sitting around smoking.

'Poor old Annie,' Karen drawls sympathetically, loading her bowl with another sticky clump of weed. 'We gotta find something to cheer you up.'

'I'm never going to cheer up,' I declare decisively,

staring at the ceiling as the sounds of fabricated life-and-death emergencies blare from the television. 'How am I supposed to be cheerful now that I know what a sham it all is? That's all it is, a big sham.' I pick up Sylvester, Karen's long-suffering black tomcat, and drape him across my belly. 'I mean, if something as perfect as what I had with Chris could turn out wrong, how am I supposed to believe in *anything* anymore?' I stroke Sylvester's head and mentally review my ever-growing list of nevers: I'll never fall in love again, I'll never get married, never have kids. I'll never trust anyone again. I'll never be happy. I'll never forget what it felt like to have everything I've ever wanted. I'll never get over having it all snatched away in a hot second. Never, never, never.

'You're gonna cheer up,' Karen insists. 'You just need to find something to take your mind off things. I'd offer you a hit, but, you know.' She shrugs and takes another hit herself. Neither of us take the offer seriously; even pre-AA, I've never been a fan of smoking pot. It's an awful lot of work and mess for a drug that has nothing more to offer me than sleepy and stupid. My disdain for the marijuana high is part of the reason that it has been so easy for us to stay friends since Karen went off the wagon. I could sit in a roomful of people smoking pot until the cows came home and went back out again and never feel the least bit tempted. Up the ante with a few nice warm opiates and you might have a problem, but as far as I'm concerned, pot is a nonissue – and both Karen and I know that it is far from the answer to my chronic weepiness. But what is?

In the months since I have been back, I have tried all of the usual solutions offered to the brokenhearted. I've started seeing a counselor, an understanding wisp of a woman whose overstuffed couch and endless supply of Kleenex give me a place to cry for an hour a week – but, aside from repeated assurances that I didn't deserve to be dumped, she has no quick fixes to offer me. I've upped my meeting schedule, double dipping at both AA and NA, puking out my sad tale of woe at every open discussion meeting in town, regardless of the topic. First step? Second step? Making amends? It doesn't matter, let me tell you about my ex. Fortunately I'm not the only one who abuses the captive audience that is the recovery community; most nights I fit right in. I even temporarily found myself the perfect rebound dating companion at one such meeting – an adorable Italian lawyer, always ready to hit the coffee shop or rent a movie on a Friday night. If it wasn't for his overweening clinical depression and a propensity for drag queen hookers, he would have been a true contender. Drag queen hookers notwithstanding, at the time he was just what the doctor ordered. I am even back at my old job, home-teaching teenagers who are too depressed to attend school. But, even surrounded by examples of real depressive disorders that make my own problems seem self-pitying and eminently fleeting, the only time I am able to turn off the endless reel of hurt is when I am asleep – and getting there still isn't getting any easier.

Tossing alone in my bed at night only reminds me of what it was like to have someone to press up against, and I dread waking up to that gut-wrenching moment of realization each morning when reality smacks me hard. There are always a good thirty seconds of foggy morning serenity before I remember *hey, I'm thirty years old, living with my parents, and the love of my life never wants to see me again because I'm not cool*. The anticipation of that early morning bitch slap keeps me awake night after night, when all I really want to do is fall asleep and stay that way until it doesn't matter anymore. It is during those long nights that I entertain my first serious thoughts in years of bagging the clean and sober lifestyle and snuggling up to a friendly, reassuring Percocet or twenty.

Fortunately that doesn't happen, which is good because I am about to find salvation in a much less obvious substance – the Department of Recreation and Parks' Continuing Education Program.

'I tell you what, Miss Annie.' Karen drapes the Recreation Program newsletter over her knees and runs down the page with her ice cream spoon. 'Let's take a class.'

'I'm in class all day,' I moan, lighting another cigarette. 'I don't see how more class is going to make anything any better.'

'Well, it will,' Karen says, blithely ignoring my water-tight rationale. 'How about we take a vegetarian cooking class?'

'Cooking reminds me of Chris,' I mutter. Granted, Chris was a great cook and we did spend a lot of time in the kitchen together, but how I think I'm going to get through the rest of my life without cooking is a logistical impossibility that I hope Karen will overlook. She does.

'Well, how about yoga?'

'See who teaches it. If it's that same guy who taught it when I was in high school, I don't want to take it, because he was always looking at us in the different positions and then touching himself.'

'What was his name?'

'I forgot.'

Karen rolls her eyes at me and flicks the page with her fingernail. 'OK, so much for yoga. Dancing, Annie! We can take ballroom dancing!'

'You need *men* for ballroom dancing. It's a partner dance.'

'Well, God and everybody knows we don't have men. How about country line dancing?'

'You've gotta be fucking *kidding*.'

'You never know! It could be fun.'

'Or it could be something like having your eyes plucked

out with hot tongs – in *Hell*.' I make a gargoyle face to emphasize my resistance. The effort is wasted; Karen doesn't look up.

'OK, Annie, here's exactly what we need.' She taps the paper with her spoon. 'Belly Dancing for Beginners.'

I roll over defiantly, quite done with entertaining options from the Recreation Program. Karen returns to her browsing and Cherry Garcia, and I lie there with my face in the couch, thinking. Not about Chris, but about the belly dancers I had seen at the Middle East Restaurant in Cambridge years ago, when I visited Melissa and her then-husband, Rick. How they tinkled their finger cymbals and fluttered their bellies and how they could do amazing, mesmerizing things with first one hip, then the other, then an arm, then a shoulder – all the while keeping the rest of their bodies completely and serenely motionless, as if they just happened to be standing there, minding their own business, when their right hip broke into this stunning display of muscle control and rhythm. I remembered, too, the snarling, beer-fueled fight Melissa and Rick had on the way home about just how impressed he was or was not by one of the dancers, a dark-eyed, round-hipped beauty who was fifty if she was a day.

Those were the only belly dancers I had ever seen in person. In my father's record collection, though, there were several belly dancing albums. He played them only rarely, bringing them out occasionally for cocktail parties where hummus and baba ghanouj and his own delicious home-made kibbe nayee shared space on the sideboard with less exotic delicacies like Smithfield ham, biscuits, and tiny butter cookies from Dot's Bakery. Save for nights like those, the albums were stashed under the receiver, behind Leon Redbone and Tony Orlando and Dawn. Recorded by Mohammed el-Bakkar 'and his Oriental Ensemble,' among others, the records boasted exotic titles – *Port Said*, *East of Suez*, and *Sultan of Bagdad* – and even more exotic covers.

When we were little, my brother, Robert, and I would dare each other to sneak peeks at the dancers on the covers; though it had never been expressly forbidden, it made us feel like we were doing something bold and naughty and usually sent us giggling to our rooms with brazen glee. My favorite one was Port Said because it featured Nejla Ates doing an almost crotch-baring twirl, flourishing a fuchsia veil behind her and topless but for a pair of silver-sequined pasties. Tiny in stature, with overly made-up elfin features, there was something compelling and almost eerie about Ates that made her all the more intriguing. Years later, I would see the album listed on ebay by a nondance enthusiast under the heading 'GOTTA SEE! WEIRD SEX MIDGET NUDE BELLY DANCE LP!'

'When?'

'When what?'

'When does it start?'

Karen puts down her spoon and eyes me suspiciously. 'When does what start?'

'Belly dancing class.'

'Annie, that time I really was kidding.'

'Well I'm not.' I sit up and reach for the program. 'I want to take a belly dancing class. When does it start?'

'Annie, you are *not* taking a belly dancing class!'

'Why not? It'll be fun. Shit! It doesn't start until February. Come on, Karen, let's do it.'

'Annie, you really are crazy. My crazy friend Annie.' Karen shakes her head and snatches the program back, placing it just out of my reach. She picks up her bong and loads it with another hit. 'My crazy, belly dancing friend Annie.' She inhales deeply, squints at me, and holds her breath for as long as she can before coughing out a cloud of sweet, hazy smoke and a long, hoarse laugh.

'Well, at least it'll give you something to do, even if it is crazy. I guess it ain't any crazier than datin' a little

47

gay lawyer, though. You do what you gotta do, Annie.'

I nod and lean across her for the recreation program, which I tuck safely into my knapsack with my secret stash of cigarettes. I know what I have to do. I'm not sure why, but I am absolutely sure that I have to learn how to belly dance. It's the first good thing I've been sure about in two months.

2

Blood Is Thicker
than Sand

Crawling Across the Desert in Search of Nejla Ates

Sunday night finds me, as always, eating dinner with my family. It's now been four months since Chris dumped me; I've moved into a quaint duplex, a steal at $370 a month, that I would love if every corner of it didn't remind me why I was living there . . . alone. I'm glad to be back at my job, though I feel a little sheepish to be back so soon and so single. At least the ever-rotating roster of incarcerated teens means it's only my coworkers who know this and not, God forbid, my students. Even my social life is booming, in spite of the little gay lawyer's less-than-suave exit – he showed up for our New Year's Eve dinner reservations with a date. The three of us ate Pad Thai in awkward silence, and I was at home alone by eleven. Date or no date, I am out most evenings – coffee shops, night-clubs, visiting friends – but I *always* reserve Sunday evenings for Soffee Family Dinner. That's just the way it is.

'Are you listening, Bobby?' My mother waves across the table at my father, who, true to form, stares straight past her as he continues his two-fisted attack on a heaping plate of meat loaf and mashed potatoes.

'Bobby! *Bobby!*' She raises her voice until finally he looks up wearily, a forkful of potatoes hovering in mid-bite.

'Your *daughter* just said she's taking *belly dancing* lessons.' She pauses dramatically, eyebrows raised. I recognize the pause – it is the same one that always follows the 'your daughter says' news flashes. From 'your daughter says all her friends are going to see the Dead Kennedys' to 'your daughter says she's spending her junior year in China' to 'your daughter says she's going to follow the Rolling Stones on tour,' the look and the pause remain the same. The standard reaction is equally predictable – a hunch of the shoulders, a shake of the head, and a blunt denial that any such thing is going to happen – always preceded by 'Now, why in the shit.'

'Now, why in the shit would anybody take belly dancing lessons?' He speaks around a mouthful of potatoes, adding another bite before he continues. 'I didn't even think they had belly dancers anymore. They used to have 'em up the Phoenicia all the time.' The Phoenicia was a Lebanese restaurant that my parents and their friends had frequented in the 1970s. I vaguely remember being taken there one time. The main things I remember about it are that I got to stay up past my bedtime, and that my siblings and I were afraid to eat the *kibbe* because we suspected it might be made the traditional way – that is, with lamb – as opposed to the Americanized way we were used to, with beef. I don't remember seeing a belly dancer.

'Well, are you *surprised* at all?' My mother continues to press for some kind of reaction, a declaration of either approval or disapproval, anything other than vague disbelief. It is a losing battle she has been fighting for thirty-odd years. My father has always been a man of few words, and the few, when uttered, are usually blunt and more than a little sarcastic. My brother is the same, and, from what I can remember of my grandfather, I can say that it is a tradition that has been with Soffee men for at least three generations.

Daddy Fats, as we called my grandfather Ghiddis Soffee, was a stocky, olive-skinned man with hooded brown eyes and a perpetual half-smile that seemed to imply that the joke was on you, which, in the presence of my grand-father, it usually was. He was not above pranking his own grandchildren and always seemed gratified and mildly amused at our constant gullibility. One of his favorite stunts involved a commercial for Creomulsion Cough Syrup that featured an eerie mime, an image that always sent all three of us into shrieking fits of apprehension. Flipping the knob back and forth, seemingly changing the channels but, as we figured out later when we were older, wiser, and psychologically traumatized, merely flipping from static to the same channel again and again, he would say, with exaggerated fear in his voice, 'Oh, no! Look! He's done come on all the channels! He's on all the channels, I can't turn him off!' By the time he tired of this game, we would all be cowering behind the kitchen door, whimpering and sobbing. Our fear didn't seem to trigger any sort of grandfatherly sympathy in him whatsoever; rather, when the commercial ended, he would plop back down in his chair, chuckling over our terror and grateful for a chance to have the television to himself, however briefly.

Asking Daddy Fats for advice on anything only brought more pranking. I remember my brother, Robert, all of five years old, approaching Daddy Fats with a carefully folded comic book ad for Sea Monkeys. 'Amazing Live Sea Monkeys!' blared the headline above a cartoon illustration of several pink smiling Sea Monkeys frolicking in a goldfish bowl. Long-limbed and toothsome, the Sea Monkeys looked like tiny naked people with pointed heads. The female Sea Monkey wore her thick blonde hair in a beribboned bouffant, and one of the males was wearing horn-rims and a bow tie. Robert was diligently saving up for Sea Monkeys and had some questions regarding their abilities.

'Why, *sho*' they can, Robbie,' Daddy Fats would answer reassuringly each time my brother asked if they could perform a desired task. They could do tricks, they could come when called, they could leave the bowl for as long as you wished. By the time Daddy Fats had finished singing their praises, Robert was looking forward to having the Sea Monkeys clean his room for him, bring him candy from the store, and serve him Franken Berry in bed every morning. Last year, looking through a box of old toys and baby dolls in my parents' attic, I found a yellowed form letter tucked beneath a pile of Pez dispensers and battered action figures. 'Dear Sea Monkey Customer,' it began. 'We are sorry you were disappointed with your batch of AMAZING LIVE SEA MONKEYS!' It went on to deny any misrepresentation in the ad and reiterate the caveat emptor 'No Sea Monkey Refund' policy. I think my grandfather's favorite part of the Sea Monkey episode was when Robert tried to make the best of things and take his Sea Monkeys to school for show-and-tell. The homeroom mother mistook the entire Sea Monkey village for a jar of dirty water and poured them down the drain. Sea Monkey genocide. My brother has attachment issues to this day.

Unlikely though it may seem, I have always been grateful to have come from a line of smart-ass men. I think it toughened my hide and quickened my tongue, two qualities that can never be underestimated. And, though neither my father nor my grandfather were very demonstrative toward me when I was small, I always understood that I was in on the joke, even when it was on me. Thanks to my family's sarcastic heritage, my siblings and I were always a step ahead of our peers in the smart-mouthed kid playground wars, and, as jaded teenagers, we were always a little quicker on the draw with the comebacks. I have kept sarcasm in my back pocket as my defensive ace when things got tough, and it has served me well. I owe that to my father and my Daddy Fats.

Soffee women inevitably took up the slack for Soffee men, both verbally and emotionally. As Daddy Fats sat stoically in his easy chair, contemplating another game of poker, glass of whiskey, or pack of smokes, my female relatives swarmed around him, fluttering from room to room, a constant blur of waving arms, flowered housedresses, and high-pitched Arabic chatter – usually interspersed with more than a few English profanities. You never knew what to expect from my Mama Izzy and her sisters – they would grab you and smother you with red-lipsticked kisses one second and chase you from room to room with your unfinished bowl of *m'joudra* the next, screeching, 'You come back here and finish this, you little shit!' And, in my grandmother's house, there was no escape – it was always full. I might as well have had a dozen grandparents.

In keeping with family tradition, the house where I grew up was less than a mile from the duplex that my grandparents shared with my grandmother's sister Ida and her husband, Friday, and just two doors down from my grandparents, Aunt Ida's daughter Virginia and her husband, Howard, occupied a brick row house. My grandmother's brother Gimmel, his wife, Beverly, and their children were one house over from that. Next door to Gimmel and Beverly there was another sister, Frances, and her three children. Staying within shouting distance of one's family was expected, if not tacitly required. I have been the only member of my immediate family to break this rule with any kind of severity, and the consequences were predictable. In 1987, when I moved to Beijing, my father took to his room and refused to come out for my farewell dinner. In 1990, when I moved to Los Angeles, he left for work an hour early to avoid being present for my departure. I can only imagine what my grandparents' reaction would have been had they lived to see such a flagrant display of daughterly disobedience. Growing up, though, I stayed close and was rewarded with a childhood full of doting relatives and full plates.

My memories of growing up in the shadow of my father's family are vivid and marked largely by exotic smells. In almost all of my memories of my Mama Izzy, she is in the kitchen, stirring a pot of *yukhnee*, a hearty stew made with carrots, potatoes, and lamb or, in my grandparents' house, beef. Although I know this is not the case, it seems as though I must have spent every waking moment of my childhood at my grandparents' seated at the Formica table in their tiny upstairs kitchen, eating bowl after bowl of *yukhnee*. It is that prevalent in my memory. I can remember the pink Melmac bowl full of huge chunks of potato and beef cooked almost to the point of dissolving, so tender you could separate it with a spoon. I remember my grandmother, touches of gray showing at the temples of her dyed red hair, shuffling back to the stove to stir the pot and skim the layer of *wubbid* from the top as it cooked. The more I ate, the more she spooned into my bowl, with an approving '*Sukhthange*' – 'Eat up.'

Food and its hearty consumption have been a constant in my family life, as it seems to be for all families of Mediterranean descent – Jewish, Italian, and Arab. And, even though the meals in my parents' house lean more

54

toward pot roast and meat loaf, bowing to the traditional mainly on special occasions, the quantities are always generous, an unspoken demonstration of love. My father shows his love for us by piling our plates with food, and we showed our love for him by finishing every bite. Every uneaten morsel is an affront. A diet is a slap in the face to the person who feeds you. When I announced on my first visit home from Los Angeles that I had become a vegetarian, my father was livid. 'You're going to miss the *kibbe* and the *fatayer* and everything else we're having for Christmas,' he warned, 'and when this little kick of yours is over, you'll be sorry!' Ten meatless years later, he still reminds me at every family dinner that it's time I 'got off that kick.' As strong as my resolve not to eat meat has been, the knowledge that it hurts my father's feelings has almost broken it many times. Is it any wonder Lebanese girls look so *healthy*?

So, as my father ignores my mother's repeated announcements about my impending belly dancing lessons, I help myself to more mashed potatoes and peas and try to remember if I had seen any belly dancing that one night at the Phoenicia. I don't expect my father to have any opinion about belly dancing any more than I expect him to show an interest in my boyfriends, my hairstyle, or my job. It's just not him. After dinner, he and I will retire to the family room, where he'll pass me miniature candy bars and macaroons from the stash he keeps beside his La-Z-Boy. We won't talk, except to comment on the relative freshness or tastiness of our snacks. I used to do the same thing with Daddy Fats, only instead of macaroons it was Goldenberg's peanut chews.

As my father unwraps yet another sesame candy, I wander to the back of the family room to flip through the stack of albums that still remain under the long-silent stereo. Since sending in my registration for belly dancing class, I have become obsessed with all things sequined and undulating. My addictive personality has resurfaced with a vengeance, and every free minute is spent researching, reading, and planning for the moment when I will finally learn how to belly dance. I have visited countless Web sites, scoured Middle Eastern travel guides for photos, and checked out and rechecked out the public library's only belly dancing manual – *The Compleat Belly Dancer*, an earthy 1973 tome illustrated with black-and-white photos of a dark-haired hippie chick in a coin bra and peasant skirt. The book's quaint *Cosmo*-style writing, with headers like 'Belly Dancing for the Everybody' and 'The Ladies' Home Cabaret,' has given me some basic technical terms to go on and an idea of what some of the moves look like step-by-step, but little else – other than the promise that I will 'get and stay slim!' and will be able to throw away my 'confining elastic girdle.'

The night before – the morning actually, those wee hours that always find one typing in increasingly inane keyboard searches as the monitor glare starts to sear your corneas – I had realized that I needed a sound track for my research, something more exotic than Wanda Jackson to listen to as I drew closer and closer to BD Day. I haven't seen my father's albums in years, but I am sure they're still around. Ours is not a family that discards. We still have Freakies (that really bad cereal with really good prizes) in our pantry. So I know they're here somewhere. I flip past Ray Charles, Barbra Streisand, and a wealth of Brothers Four albums before I hit pay dirt. *East of Suez* by the 101 Strings, recorded in Stereophonic sound – 'The entire sound spectrum: all the human ear can sense and hear!' The cover depicts a view through the ubiquitous keyhole-shaped doorway, where a veiled, brown-skinned harem girl wearing a bra made of two coiled gold serpents peers invitingly at the camera. Beside her are several tasseled floor cushions and a *shisha*, or Middle Eastern water pipe. The *shisha* is traditionally used to smoke a sweet, fruity molasses-and-tobacco blend, and there is a lot of pageantry and ceremony associated with the sharing of it, but in our house the family *shisha* always stood idly by the hearth, gathering dust and looking woefully out of place among my mother's early American knickknacks and tole-painted boxes. The only other function it ever served was to break the ice with my high school boyfriends, who would invariably begin to chortle à la Beavis and Butthead as soon as they spotted it. '*Huh-huh. Huh-huh*. Your mom and dad have a *bong* in their living room. *Huh-huh*.' I slide the album out of the stereo cabinet and set it aside.

Past a few more old chestnuts (Mitch Miller, anyone?) I find *Sultan of Baghdad*, its gatefold cover held tentatively together with crispy brown cellophane tape. This one has portly, rubber-faced *oud* player Mohammed el-Bakkar reclining at the feet of two whirling belly dancers, a cheesy Bugs Bunny-style turban with a huge pink feather barely balanced above his beefy, grinning face. The belly dancers are fairly anemic looking, in nondescript bandeau tops and simple flowing skirts. The only thing that draws my eye is the fact that they are each wearing finger cymbals on one hand only. From my obsessive research, I know that this is not the norm. I decide that perhaps they had only one set of finger cymbals available for the photo shoot and decided to share them. I study the girls carefully and find little resemblance to the actual belly dancers I have found represented in my studies so far. They seem to have more in common with Herb Alpert's 'Whipped Cream' girl than with Mona Said or Fifi Abdou. All the same, I am excited to see the album again after so many years.

I open it gingerly, the tape crackling and falling off in tiny translucent flakes in my lap. I am disappointed to find that almost the entire gatefold is devoted to a detailed description of the wonders of Stereophonic sound – 'each loudspeaker brings you a different part of the total sound, so the program – orchestra, jazz ensemble, railroad train, or what-have-you reassembles itself in your living room.' The description is illustrated with a number of graphs, diagrams, and magnified drawings of record grooves. I am momentarily distracted from my quest by the sheer bizarreness of the implications contained in this unassuming belly dancing record. Apparently, 1950s audiophiles were so taken with the concept of stereo that they were actually driven to purchase and play stereophonic recordings of railroad trains or what-have-you in their living rooms as a leisure activity! I ask you!

My reverie is interrupted when I find several paragraphs of fine print mixed in with the treatise on stereo. These paragraphs, apparently intended to set the mood for the listener, are a garbled, anonymous mishmash of stereotypes and stock images, camels and sheiks and misguided references to the 'Mohammedan religion.' The story whiplashes back and forth, from Baghdad to the Nile, from *felahin* to pharaoh, with little regard for clarity or accuracy. But throughout the story, time and again, they come back to what I was looking for: the belly dancers.

'In Baghdad one savors the perfumes of Araby and marvels at the frail modern vials that contain them. Here in dimly-lit retreats the world comes to watch voluptuousness. There are dark-eyed dancing girls who perform ritualistically as they have for ages . . . supple bodies veiled in shimmering silk dance in time to music that imparts an imperishable glamor to the subtlety of this art.'

I am thrilled and flattered to be a part of it all. Imperishable glamour and subtlety, indeed! Tattoo *that*! I feel vindicated already, and voluptuous, and supple. Not to mention very, very Lebanese – in a 1950s stereophonic kind of way. Sliding the album carefully out of its cover, I glance over the titles in the hopes that I will recognize a song, a rhythm, something that I have read about during my late-night research sessions. I don't, but I do recognize one word, in the title of the first song, and that is all the encouragement I need. I flip the receiver on and place the album on the turntable.

As soon as the needle touches the vinyl I am greeted with a stereophonic reverie of hisses, crackles, and what-have-you. I am immediately comforted, transported back to the carefree days before tattoos and heartbreak. The sound of scratchy vinyl always gives me a heady rush of teenaged nostalgia, and I half expect to hear Joey Ramone chanting 'Hey, ho, let's go' when the track begins. Instead, the plinking of a xylophone echoes through the family room, and Mohammed el-Bakkar wails over the din of xylophone and hissing. '*Ya habib O ya habibi, something something something.*' A group of cheerfully off-key women join in behind him. '*Ya habib O ya habibi, some-thing something something . . . ya habibi ya habibi!*'

'Hey, what in the shit? Turn that down; I'm looking at *Sixty Minutes.*'

I turn the volume down slightly and lean into the speaker, listening intently, trying to imagine what kind of belly dancing moves one would do to the pleasings of a xylophone. I have not seen xylophones mentioned in any of the literature. I can also pick out the sound of finger cymbals in the background, and the insistent plodding beat of the *derbickie.*

'I remember this one.' My mother comes in and perches on the edge of the sofa, tapping her foot along with the *derbickie.* 'Remember this, Bobby?' My father replies with something between a snort and a shrug, which does nothing to dissuade her. She picks up a Martha Stewart magazine and starts flipping through it absently. '*Ya habibi, ya habibi*,' she sings as she examines a wreath made from antique buttons, adding one more off-key woman to the reverie. '*Ya habibi, ya habibi*.'

'Do y'all *mind*,' he mutters, rolling his eyes and turning Andy Rooney up a notch. I lift the needle off the record and switch the stereo off. I am pleased with my haul but not entirely satisfied. There is one album that is still missing, and it is the one I was the most eager to find – *Port Said*. After having flipped through the cabinet twice, forward and back, I have found no sign of the bare-breasted Nejla Ates. I've found the 101 Strings, which I suspect will be a wash in spite of the cool cover, and *Sultan of Baghdad*, which is volume two to *Port Said*'s volume one – but I have seen neither veil nor *zil* of *Port Said*. Still, I've got two more belly dancing records than I had yesterday, which is two more than anyone I know, so I count myself lucky, something I've been doing more and more since sending in my belly dancing registration. Lucky to find albums, lucky to have stumbled on the class, lucky to be half Lebanese. It's refreshing to feel lucky again. I've even revived my Lucky Seven rockabilly dice necklace from the 'bad juju box' in the back of my closet, where I keep the few reminders of Chris that I didn't tear up.

'You're not *takin'* those, are you?' Robert points possessively at the belly dancing records. In true Arab tradition, Robert, the only son, has grown up with an air of entitlement that was cosigned wholeheartedly by my parents. In twenty-eight years he has been denied absolutely nothing. My older sister, Christy, and I spent our teenaged years in a perpetual state of bitter indignance over Robert's status in our household. Years later, her eyes still narrow when she talks about her perceived teenage persecution – which she never misses an opportunity to do. Having found myself in the position of Robert Advocate since high school, I am now worse than my parents when it comes to bending over backward for him. I look mournfully at the records.

'Well, not if you want them.' He picks them up and scowls at the scantily clad dancers, turning them over in his huge hands, reading the song titles, shaking his head.

'I was sampling some stuff off one of them, but I don't think it was one of these.' He hands them back and I breathe my silent thanks. Since high school, sampling has taken up most of Robert's waking hours. He used to drive us all crazy, playing the same loop over and over in his makeshift studio on the side porch, following that innate Soffee drive to get it just right. I still can't listen to Foreigner without cringing at the memory of an entire weekend of a single line from 'Jukebox Hero' played non-stop at top volume. Now he has a mysterious recording studio across town. No one is really sure what he does there, only that it involves sampling, of course, and MIDI, and late-night phone calls from smooth-voiced black men with names like Mario and Antoine. I can't imagine what he would need with a handful of scratchy belly dancing records – but then, I couldn't imagine what he needed with one line from 'Jukebox Hero' fifteen years ago. Following a hunch, I ask him which album he was sampling if it wasn't one of these.

'I dunno . . . Something Port. I think I left it at my studio.'

Port Said?

'Probably. I dunno.' Typical Robert.

'Do you think I could get it?'

'I'm not *done* with it yet.' Not a good sign. He probably isn't done with 'Jukebox Hero,' either. If I wait for him to be done with *Port Said*, I will be well past my belly dancing prime before I ever see Nejla and her pasties again – and this is a possibility I'm not prepared to face.

'How about if I just borrow it for a couple of days and return it to you?'

Robert is taken aback, but my status as heartbroken sister still carries a little weight. Even though my conversations with Robert are even more circumspect than my conversations with my father, I know he is a Soffee man at heart, and that means he would crawl across the desert for me – albeit grumbling all the way – if it would cheer me up a tiny bit.

Crawling across the desert is a specialty of Lebanese men, or so one would think to hear the stories. When I was in high school, there was a huge media blitz in Richmond about Leo Koury. He was a local Lebanese softball umpire and gambler who was wanted for the murder of a doorman at the Cha Cha Palace, a Richmond bar that was in competition with Koury's own string of gay bars, the Dialtone, the Mailbox, and the 409. For some reason, we have a historical monopoly on the gay bar scene in Richmond; Babe's, our local 'wimmen's bar' where I used to dance the night away with my Rugby-playing college roommates, is named for Babe Shulleeta, the sister of my great-grandmother, Sadie Shulleeta Soffee. It's under new ownership now, but the name remains. It adds a whole new facet to that lame old 'Lesbian/Lebanese' wordplay that people somehow still think is clever.

Koury's solution to friendly competition was to kill Charles R. Kernaghan, Jr., and dump his body in the Rappahannock River. Somehow none of this was ever mentioned to me when 'the Cha' became the hip hangout for new wave teenyboppers, and Melissa and I patronized it as faithfully as fourteen-year-olds can patronize an after-hours shot house. What was mentioned to me, regularly and repeatedly, was that Leo Koury, despite his laundry list of racketeering and murder charges, had a heart of gold. Even as the FBI was posting Most Wanted billboards of Leo's mug shots, my father never missed an opportunity to remind us, 'Leo Koury is a good man. If one of you was sick, and Leo had to crawl across the desert to get you medicine, he would do it.' Having seen the lengths my father had gone to for practically anyone who asked, I never doubted it. If Leo was anything like my father – and murder and racketeering charges aside, I'm sure he was – then there was no desert he would not have crossed for me. With Robert, though, things are a little bit dicier. He would cross in the end, but there would have to be negotiations. Such is the nature of sibling dynamics.

'How about if I buy you a box of recordable CDs? You could record it, and keep the rest.'

'I already *have* three boxes.' He knows and I know that he's going to give me the album, but I have to come up with a viable trade so that it doesn't look like he's giving in. I try again.

'Do you need any disks?' He shakes his head scornfully. Disks – *pah*! Trinkets! I feel like a dust-covered trader in a second-rate souk. What do you offer the man who has everything?

'Buy you a coffee? You could bring the record to me at Starbucks.'

'I don't go to Starbucks any more. That blue-haired girl is a *jerk*.' It's like my childhood all over again. Model rockets, Legos, Lancelot Link – I never could keep up with Robert's likes and dislikes. I do still have one ace in the whole, though, more precious than coffee, more valuable than recordable CDs.

'I'll lend you Man Frozen Solid.'

This offer requires no response, because I know it is a done deal. Man Frozen Solid is the creation of one of my students at the residential facility where I teach. It is so bizarre that, when I pulled it from my in box, I had no idea what assignment the fourteen-year-old artist had intended it to fulfill. It is a magic marker drawing of a wobbly blue ice cube with a silhouetted human figure hovering in the center of it. Across the top of the page, in crooked red sideshow letters an inch high, he had written 'MAN – frozen solid!' and added his name with a flourish in the bottom corner. Man Frozen Solid has hung over my stereo ever since, and Robert has coveted it mightily. For *Port Said* it is a fair trade, I feel. Art begets art. We make plans to make the swap at my Uncle Ronnie's house later on that night, which inspires a new round of 'why in the shit' from my father: 'Why in the shit are you going over there? He's crazy. You should *ostracize* him.' This about his only brother. It sounds awful but it's all smoke, and I know that, so I begin gathering my records to head to Ronnie's.

Any mention of Ronnie throws my father into a frenzy of warnings and disclaimers, all of which belie the fact that, were Ronnie ever in need, desert crawling would be the order of the day, posthaste. In fact, it is more than likely that a number of deserts have already been crawled on his behalf. But that doesn't stop my father from insisting, implausibly, whenever anyone asks if they're related, that he has heard of Ronnie and thinks he 'might be a distant cousin.' I ignore his rant, having already triumphed in my own sibling psychodrama, and run upstairs to fetch Man Frozen Solid. Then, belly dancing records and artwork in hand, I trot out to the car to head to Ronnie's, singing '*Ya habibi*' as I go.

Reclining on an array of Moroccan cushions in front of a wide-screen television, Ronnie sets down the remote control long enough to pick up one of several Qur'ans from the coffee table. He is the bizarro-world version of my father, somehow his polar opposite and yet disturbingly similar as well. He wants to read me a passage that, in his mind, summarizes the problem that led Chris to dump me. Though not a practicing Muslim, or a practicing anything for that matter, he peppers his conversation with references to Islam and the Qur'an, to the chagrin of my Maronite Catholic father. He finds the passage and jabs at it repeatedly.

"Do not strut about arrogantly on the earth; Allah does not love anyone who is vain or boastful.' Right there, see? You know what that means? It means he's a no-good *motherfucker*, that's what it means.' I question whether this was Mohammad's intended interpretation, but I keep my doubts to myself. Even the slightest comment in this situation will lead to a lengthy lecture of dubious theological accuracy and extreme profanity. I nod sagely and try to look as though it is sinking in. Then I change the subject.

'You know, I start belly dancing class in a couple of weeks.'

His eyes widen, even though I know I've told him about it before. 'Well, that's *great*,' he enthuses. He really means it. Somehow, as part and parcel of his bizarro Soffee personality, he's lost the gene that precludes interest in outside goings-on. When I was in high school, I was constantly fabricating reasons why I had to spend this night or that night at Ronnie's house – closer to school, on the bus line, near the mall – because at Ronnie's, I was always part of the equation, no matter what was going on. Everyone's opinions counted – my sixteen-year-old ones, my Aunt Ida's eighty-year-old ones, my cousin Holly's twelve-year-old ones. This means Ronnie's house is always full of strange extra bodies and curious visitors, some who just drop by for a few hours and some who stay for days, months, years. If you're there, you're part of the family and you are extended the same Soffee hospitality as those of us who were born to it. Lead us to the desert and let us crawl.

'You should let her hear that CD you bought.' Dot wanders in from the kitchen, a glass of wine and a

65

Virginia Slim clutched in her hand. One of the ones who's stayed for years, Dot has been part of the equation at Ronnie's since shortly after my aunt Mary Ellen moved out. Though Mary Ellen and Ronnie have been separated for almost two decades, they remain married, and she has free rein to come and go as she pleases with the same house keys she's always had. Her status as a member of the family has never been questioned. This is not so with Dot, even though she lives with Ronnie. Although I consider her my aunt, as do Christy and George, and always refer to her as such, my father cannot seem to get past the minor detail of Dot's skin color, which is almost imperceptibly darker than his own. My father obstinately refuses to acknowledge her presence in our family, much in the same way he refuses to acknowledge everything else that goes on around him. Ronnie pushed the issue once, insisting that my father verbalize why he didn't want Dot to be invited to Thanksgiving dinner. My father grumbled something about propriety and appropriateness and inter-racial relationships, giving Ronnie precisely the straight line he was hoping for.

'Look who's talking about interracial relationships,' he retorted. 'You married a *white* woman!'

My dad does this great thing where every muscle in his face freezes with absolutely no expression but his eyes bug out so far that your head jerks back reflexively when he looks at you. I bet Leo Koury did that, and I bet that, when he did, someone was about to die.

'Oh, yeah, lemme play you this.' Any visit to Ronnie's will always involve a forced listening session. Ever since I was little, he's been sitting me in front of the stereo and making me listen to everything from the Bonzo Dog Band to Eminem. For a while, during the 1970s, he co-owned Bohannon's, a chain of record stores that sold more plexiglass bongs than actual records. Those days, he would just hand me stacks of records with instructions to take them home and listen to them. Now, though, we're back to supervised sessions.

He pushes some buttons on the CD player and hands me a sepia-toned booklet. *The Music of Arab Americans*. The two men in the photo look like all of the men in my dad's old family photos – hawk noses, fedora hats, and more than a touch of street smart in their smiles. The man on the left could have been my Daddy Fats. The music starts, and Ronnie turns up the volume.

'What do you think?' As always, he gives me roughly ten seconds to form an opinion.

'It's scratchy.'

'Your ass would be scratchy, too, if you were up in the fucking attic for seventy years,' he barked. 'Now listen to it!'

'*Il-bulbul nagha ghusn il-ban, Ah ya shaqiq al-nu'-mani!*' The singer's nasal wail is reminiscent of Mohammed el-Bakkar. I surmise from the liner notes that *al-nu'mani* is Arabic for 'anemone.' I am quite sure this is the first song I have ever heard about an anemone. Ronnie skips impatiently through the tracks. He stops on one featuring the Off-Key Women's Chorus, apparently a constant in Arabic music. I scan the liner notes to see what they're saying. Something about the bride's father being angry because the groom doesn't own a house. '*Wa ana khayif yisibni da' i-jnun*,' they sing.

'I am worried about going crazy,' I translate aloud from the liner notes.

'I'm not,' says Ronnie, 'I'm already crazy. You heard anything from that piece of shit?' He means Chris. 'That piece of shit' is what he calls all my boyfriends. This time, though it's hardly new, it's remarkably appropriate. I shake my head.

'Well, you know what I've been saying about him all along. *Ya'ha sit'ti.*'

I nod. *Ya'ha sit'ti* is another mantle that Ronnie has endowed on all of my boyfriends. He says it's something my grandmother used to say and that it means something like 'may his future be brighter,' with the implication that it won't be. A less complicated translation would be 'that piece of shit.' I don't recall my grandmother saying this, but I don't doubt that she did; my Aunt Ida has a fouler mouth than any of my delinquent students, and in more languages. I do, however, doubt the phrase's authenticity and pronunciation. My relatives spoke a bastardized, colloquial Arabic that seemed to be part street slang and part half-remembered Lebanese dialect. Whatever it is, it doesn't get me very far with Arab merchants, who usually look at me quizzically when I try to order oddly pronounced variations on *m'joudra* and *fatayer*.

'*Ya'ha sit'ti*, right?' he repeats, and I nod again, more emphatically. 'Three hundred dollars would put him in the canal.'

'Three hundred dollars?' Such a bargain.

'Well, that's what my daddy used to say. I don't think the price has changed too much since then.'

One of the things I've always enjoyed about going to Ronnie's is hearing the stories about my family that my father won't tell me. I suppose he wants me to remember his father, our grandfather, in a positive light, which he doesn't have to worry about, because I do. I remember muggy summer afternoons spent barefoot at my grandfather's produce market on Jefferson Davis Highway, sipping Brownie drinks from the cooler as he weighed and bagged huge Hanover tomatoes in the dark cinderblock shelter. And of course I remember the pranks, and the smile, and the endless boxes of Goldenberg's peanut chews.

But thanks to Ronnie, I know another side of my grandfather, too. I know that when he was young he could knock a man across the street with one punch. I know that he got in a fight with a cousin named Mouni and Mouni beat him with a chain, but in the end it was Mouni who ended up in the hospital. And now I know that he could either put you in the canal or get in touch with someone who could. My father vehemently denies any of these things ever took place. He insists that Ronnie has invented them or misremembered them. I hope that he hasn't. I *like* having a badass for a grandfather.

My mother's father was a Methodist minister, a tall quiet man with a subscription to *Guideposts* and a Norman Rockwell profile. When I spent weekends in the country with him, he would play the Jew's harp for me on the porch and take me on walks in the woods, where we would identify trees by their leaves and pull sassafras roots that my grandmother would brew into tea. Somehow it appeals to me to also have a grandfather who you could beat with a chain and he would still kick your ass. I like the balance.

'That's not even the one I'm talking about.' Dot reaches across us and pulls another CD out of the cabinet. 'That's just scratchy old *historic* shit. I mean the *belly dancing* one you got.' She shakes it in his face. *Best of Bellydance from Morocco, Egypt, Lebanon, Turkey*. The cover features a real belly dancer. I can tell by the belly.

'Oh, yeah!' Ronnie grabs the CD from Dot and hands it to me. 'I bought this last week, but it's not what I wanted. You can have it.' I flip it open and dive into the liner notes. Chalf Hassan! Mostafa Sax! Emad Sayyah! *Hossam Ramzy!* I recognize these names from my research! This is not your father's 101 Strings! I can't believe my luck. It's raining belly dancing music. I wonder what the poor white girls who are obsessed with belly dancing do for music? Nobody's throwing castoff Hossam Ramzy CDs at them, that's for sure. I feel blessed to be a part of this crazy Lebanese family.

Just as I am thinking that my good fortune has surely reached its bounds, Robert skulks into the room with a brown paper bag under his arm. I hand him Man Frozen Solid and he slips me the bag. Somehow every transaction he makes, regardless of its innocence, winds up looking like a drug deal. We almost got arrested at the mall one day because he gave me some flea drops to take home to the cat. What's in this bag is better than drugs, though. It's better than drugs or tattoos or little gay lawyers or flea drops. I reach in and pull it out, reverently, gratefully, and hold it up for all to see. *Port Said.* The holy grail of belly dancing records. The Rosebud to my Citizen Kane, the oft-remembered link to my belly dancing heritage. And now it's mine. I read the cover.

'A study in high fidelity sound – Mohammed El-Bakkar and his Oriental Ensemble. PORT SAID, Music of the Middle East.' There is Nejla, good old Nejla, in all her pastied, foreshortened glory. All fuchsias and aquas, the photo is even more garish than I remember. I feel like I'm looking at a long-lost picture of an old friend – a half-naked stereophonic old friend.

Ronnie and Robert immediately dive into a discussion of some new type of ridiculously expensive speakers they've heard about and whether or not they'll be an improvement over the ridiculously expensive speakers they both already have. Dot inspects Nejla Ates and dismisses her with a disapproving 'huh' before heading into the kitchen for more wine. I try to play *Port Said* but I can't figure out which of the 473 buttons powers the turntable. No matter, I'll play it when I get home. For now, I'm content to look at the cover and listen to the *Music of Arab Americans*, still playing on the CD. I let it play through to the very last line. '*Tartaji min yawmika l-ati s-alah, W-al-amani fil-a'ali ta'irah.*' I check the liner notes. 'You expect goodness from your coming day and the hopes are soaring high.' I smile. Lebanese fortune cookie. (Fortune Mamoul?) Seventeen days to BD Day. Life is good. I gather up my wealth of belly dancing music and let myself out.

3

'Your Daddy Ought to Smack Your Face'

Nice Girls Don't Undulate

'What do you call that thing?' Karen puffs on her cigarette and looks skeptically at the coin-covered sash I have wrapped around my hips.

'I don't know. A tail cover?' I shake my hips gamely. *Chk-a-chk-a-chk!* The coins bounce against each other, sounding like a pocketful of loose change. The tail cover is my first purchase from Scheherezade Imports, a belly dancing costume company run by Scheherezade, otherwise known as Lucy Smith, Henrico Recreation and Parks' belly dancing teacher. *My* belly dancing teacher.

BD Day had come at last. Earlier that evening, I gamely donned a pair of leggings and a black velvet bodysuit left over from my hair-metal days and made my way out to the West End for my first class with Lucy Smith. Unsure of what to expect, I was relieved to see my fellow hopefuls clustered in the hallway, dressed in everything from torn sweats to chiffon skirts and looking decidedly unintimidating.

Ponytails and no makeup seemed to be the order of the day, and not a supermodel among them. Off to a good start, I thought. Peering into the auditorium at the advanced class, I was even more relieved to see that the pros, the big-time advanced belly dancers who met before our class to study choreographies and finger cymbals, just looked like a bunch of chicks having a boisterously good time. Sporting flowing skirts and ample figures and not a one under forty, these ladies were cracking each other up in between choreographed hip movements and seemed, in a word, saucy.

Emboldened by their approachability, I had stuck my head in the door and peered up front to see what Lucy herself looked like. I wasn't sure what I had been expecting – a lithe blonde yoga type, a kohl-wearing taskmaster from the old country, or maybe a Nejla Ates-style nymph in tassels and jewels? In my endless obsessions about BD Day, my concept of Lucy had been vague at best. As I scrutinized the scene from the doorway, I was encouraged to see not a New Age diva or an Egyptian matron but a short, fortyish woman with wild dark curls and no makeup, wearing a T-shirt over a purple leotard and laughing along with her students. Any lingering fears I was harboring about my first class vanished as I watched Lucy jibe and banter with the advanced class – and my comfort level increased even more as more of my beginner classmates arrived. Whispers and self-conscious grins were exchanged as we slipped in past the departing advanced students and took our places in the elementary school auditorium.

I positioned myself in the second row, behind a tall girl with a grapevine tattooed across the small of her back. If I had noticed the tattoo earlier, I would have chosen another spot. The anticipation of BD Day had provided a welcome distraction from my heartbreak, but it was far from complete – and tattoos were a constant reminder of what was gone. I focused my attention on Lucy and kept my eyes up. This wasn't hard to do, as Lucy led us through the basic movements – snake arms, shoulder shimmies, ribcage slides, and an array of hip movements – accompanied by what she called a 'quick and dirty' history of Middle Eastern dance. The hour flew past as Lucy introduced new movements and provided running historical commentary in a brusque patter that made everything seem familiar.

'Good,' nodded Lucy, pointing out a tiny redheaded girl as we worked on our forward hips. 'Notice how she's leading with her hip, not her heinie.'

'That's because she doesn't *have* a heinie,' whispered a woman behind me. But her comment was good-natured, not insulting, and soon we were all leading with our hips, even those of us with plenty of heinie.

'Don't forget to lift your chest,' Lucy reminded us as we tried the next move, the hip circle. With grim determination, we awkwardly moved our hips in tiny circles where we stood, tracing 360 degrees on the ground. 'This may be a hip movement, but if you try to move your hips and your chest isn't lifted, you're gonna get *bupkis*!'

My chest was lifted, but I was still getting *bupkis*. My hips didn't seem to want to make the graceful little motions that Lucy was demonstrating; my circles seemed to have two settings – vulgar and undetectable. There was a subtlety to it that I guessed would come in time.

My class is conveniently located at Dumbarton Elementary School, right down the road from Karen's apartment. After my indoctrination into the lexicon and mechanics of belly dancing, I rush straight to Karen's for ice cream and a debriefing. My head is still spinning. I feel a buzzing somewhere in my brain, like a furnace about to ignite. It's something like I felt after my first AA meeting. It's hard to explain.

'Well, what did you learn?'

'I'm not sure. A lot. Hey, there's a show this weekend if you want to go. I'm definitely going.' The show, sponsored by Lucy's troupe, the Women of Selket, had been announced after class.

'A belly dancin' show? Sure, why not?' She stubs her cigarette out and shakes her head. 'I can't believe you're really doin' this, Annie. What do your parents think?'

I'm not sure about that, either. My father has remained inscrutable, and my mother has wavered between relief that I'm finally starting to act like myself again and bemused embarrassment. 'This is just great,' she muttered to her neighbor Cindy when I raved about my impending class over dinner on Sunday. 'I've already got one daughter who's a Hooters Girl, and now my other daughter wants to be a belly dancer.' I didn't even try to point out the obvious differences to her – or mention that my sister had moved up the ranks to *Winston* girl – it would have been hard to do, anyway, without insulting my sister further. In any case, no one in my family seemed particularly thrilled that I was making what I felt was an honest attempt at exploring the culture of my father's family – least of all my father's family. I had mentioned it during a holiday gathering with less than approving results.

'Belly dancing?' My great-aunt Frances turned up her prodigious nose and glared at me. 'Your daddy ought to smack your face!'

'Why?' I thought sure they'd be as excited as Ronnie was about my undertaking. After all, outside of Ronnie's infamous lounge band, the Scariens, who perform 1960s covers in phony Arabic (gibberish with an occasional real word thrown in), no one in our family is doing anything at all to preserve our Lebanese heritage. We don't even attend the Maronite church regularly anymore, and the church started in my great-grandfather's living room. Aside from the occasional platter of *kibbe nayee*, we are about as Lebanese as Andy Griffith. I saw my belly dancing as an important step toward reclaiming our family's status as not just Lebanese Americans, but as prominent, visible members of the local Lebanese community. Apparently, aside from Ronnie, who was visible enough to make up for a lot of us, I was alone in this view.

'Well, my daddy would have smacked my face.' She shook her head and frowned at me. I looked incredulously at my Aunt Ida for support.

'Daddy Howard was a good man.' At eighty-nine, Aunt Ida is the matriarch of our family. Hers is usually the last word on family matters. Still, I couldn't help but doubt this proclamation about her stepfather, my great-grandmother's second husband. All of the stories I'd heard about him make him out to be the quintessential wicked stepfather – fearsome, philandering, and violent. A 'street-corner Muslim,' according to family legend, he had mistresses of various races and faiths all over Richmond – yet he was a pious enough Muslim to beat his Christian stepdaughters black and blue when he caught them frying bacon. According to a story Ida used to tell, the sisters would post a lookout in the front window and sizzle away. More than once, a pan of searing hot bacon and grease was pitched out the kitchen window in the nick of time. The smell always gave them away, though.

'He was a good man?' Ronnie interjected between bites of his Smithfield ham biscuit – thank Allah Daddy Howard died decades ago. 'I thought he kicked my mama in the stomach when she was pregnant because daddy was a Catholic.'

'Well,' Ida says unapologetically, 'that's because he was a *bastard*.' Have I mentioned how much I love my family? Self-contradiction is the rule rather than the exception where I come from. It can be confusing, but the freedom it affords is awesome. Indeed, what other option is there in a Muslim Catholic Jewish Methodist household? I've been to bar mitzvahs and first communions, *bris milahs* and baptisms. I grew up eating matzo crackers, which halfway reminded me of really big host wafers. And this is two generations down the road. I can only imagine what it was like when it was all still under one roof.

As it stands, our family is split into branches, all of whom ascribe to one particular faith, albeit for the most part half-assedly. All of Frances's children were raised Jewish, but her grandchildren go to Catholic schools. My grandparents raised their children Maronite Catholic, but, of all of their descendants, my father is the only one who still attends Saint Anthony's. Ronnie won't even set foot on church property for the annual food festival. '*Self-haters*,' he dubs the parishioners. 'They all think they're white.' My great-uncle Gimmel's children are so Jewish that they had me convinced *I* was Jewish when I was a kid. How could they be my cousins otherwise? See what I mean about self-contradiction? It's a survival tactic.

'I dunno what my parents think. You know how they are about stuff.' I crane over my shoulder as I shake, trying to see what the coins look like as they move. 'They didn't really say anything. I mean,' *chk-a-chk-a-chk*, 'they know I'm taking it and all, but they don't really talk about it.'

Karen nods. She knows just how they are. Karen knows my father well enough to use him against me in theological arguments when I'm so depressed that I'm convinced there is no God – and there have been many such arguments over the past few months.

'*Look* at you,' she'll say, shaking her head disgustedly. 'What if your daddy promised you somethin' rilly great, but he told you thet you had to wait for it? An' what if he

77

tol' you thet it might take a long time, but thet he *promised* it'd be worth it? Would you b'lieve him? *Course* you would! So how come you don't b'lieve it when *God* says it?' Karen's theological arguments are about as sound as Ronnie's, and sometimes as profane. It was Karen who explained to me why it's important to kneel down when praying: 'Cos thet way, you don't get *distracted*. If you're on your knees, and you ain't got nobody's dick in your mouth, you *must* be prayin'.'

I plant my feet about six inches apart, butt under, shoulders up, just as Lucy instructed. 'OK, here's about the main thing we learned tonight.' Gritting my teeth in concentration, I step forward with one foot, then bring the other leg forward with a snap! of the hip, up and out like someone is pulling it on a leash. Step, *snap!* Step, *snap!* Step, *snap!* I jerk my way around Karen's tiny living room with a look of grim determination on my face.

'Well, whadda they call that? The Toot Uncommon Trot?'

'*No.*' Corny jokes aside, I'm already starting to gall at what I see as a distinctly Egyptcentric view of the Middle East among belly dancers and dance enthusiasts. I know from Lucy's first-night lecture that Cairo is currently the heart of the belly dancing scene, and that much of what is taught in the United States is Egyptian-style belly dancing. But hello, *Lebanon*? There's a whole series of CDs entitled *Modern Bellydance from Lebanon*, so I know that Lebanese belly dancing at least exists. I hope that eventually we will learn some distinctively Lebanese belly dancing . . . and I know if I see one more pyramid or Eye of Horus, I'm gonna scream. But nothing short of the mummy's curse will put me off belly dancing at this point. I'm in.

'Is that it? You learned to walk? Thet didn't have nuthin' to do with your belly.'

I consider attempting to show her the ribcage circles we learned, which are at least a little geographically closer to

belly dancing, but I decide against it. The moves themselves, isolated from the context and framework of the
dance, are unimpressive. It would be like showing people
a picture of your grandchild and expecting them to be as
infatuated as you are. It just doesn't translate. I can't sit in
Karen's smoky living room and tell her about intercostal
muscles and the Indus Valley and keeping energy in your
arms and expect her to be as excited about it as I am. I just
know that my first belly dancing class was everything I
had hoped it would be – and that when we tested out our
new walk in a big lopsided circle around the gymnasium
at Dumbarton Elementary School, step, *snap*, step, *snap*,
and Lucy yelled from the center of the circle, 'Look! Like
the swans from *Swan Lake*! Are we elegant or what?' I may
have looked like or what but I felt elegant – and Lebanese,
and happy, and eager to learn more.

'Oh, my *God*. I can't believe they're having it here.' The
nondescript name of the West End Community Center
hadn't rung any bells when Scheherezade announced it in
class, but as we make the slow left in front of the
Tuckahoe Shopping Center, I realize where we are headed.
The community center, small, unpretentious, and looking
for all the world like a Sunday school building, is tucked
just behind some houses on Ridge Road, not far from the
Country Club of Virginia. Back in Chris's pre-hipster
days, when I first met him, he used to sweep the
community center and stack the folding chairs after events
in exchange for room and board from the couple who
used to be the caretakers. I never knew exactly what kind
of events took place there. I always imagined small, tightly
budgeted cake-and-punch wedding receptions, or garden
club meetings. Maybe Parents Without Partners. Not belly
dancing shows, though.

'Well, Miss Annie, here we are.' Karen straightens her

omnipresent ball cap and pops her eyes at me. 'Ah am now ready to experience *belly dancin'*!' We climb out of the car and join the trickle of attendees filing into the building. Once inside, we take our places in line at the folding card table just inside the door. It's five dollars each – such a bargain, I think, wishing that I had known my whole life that right here, in staid old Richmond, I could experience the exotic delights of Middle Eastern dance for a mere five dollars and a trip to the West End Community Center! Imagine!

It's a thought I have entertained repeatedly since signing up for class – if only I'd known about this before. *If only I'd started taking lessons when I was small. Thirty years old is almost too old already. If I'd started young and worked hard, I could be a professional belly dancer by now. If I'd taken belly dancing in high school, I wouldn't have felt like such a reject. If I'd been a belly dancer when I was still going to church, the kids who were full Lebanese might have accepted me.* And the omnipresent, nagging one that played itself over and over in my head – *If I started belly dancing sooner, I would have been so cool that Chris never would have dumped me.*

It's been almost six months since I left Winston-Salem; the first three were spent crying and the second three gearing up to start belly dancing. I look around the community center, remembering so many promising evenings that started here, with Chris giving the floors a quick once-over before we headed out to diners, to meetings, to coffeehouses. I remember being so happy I was bordering on smug – I had the best apartment, the best boyfriend, the best life. I felt like I had found my place in the world, and it was an enviable one. Little did I know I'd be starting from scratch before the year was out, with no apartment, no boyfriend, no life. Little did I know that in a year's time I'd be a single belly dancer in this very room. But here I am.

The chairs are set up in a semicircle, only about forty in all, and there are women in stage makeup and caftans scurrying around, still sliding chairs and backdrops into position as the audience members find their seats. I scan the room to see if I recognize anyone from my class. Although her artwork is fully covered up, I recognize the tattooed girl who stood in front of me from her biker-style bilevel hairdo and elaborately pierced ears. I also notice the seventy-ish woman with flame orange hair who had been practicing her cane moves with Lucy's advanced class. Though seated, she's wearing a caftan and an elaborate headdress with dangling beaded fringe. Finally I see the white-haired lady named Irene who had worn a purple chiffon skirt and told us about her upcoming trip to Russia. She is sitting in the back row . . . and she's talking to Nadine.

Nadine was the first person I spotted when I arrived at Lucy's class on BD Day. Clad in a voluminous black shawl, black stiletto spikes, and a Bedouin headdress, she looked every bit the belly dancer – intriguing, exotic, mysterious, and sexy. And I knew it wasn't a put-on because I'd seen her dressed the same way at the public library years ago. I had surreptitiously followed her in and out of the stacks, trying to sneak peeks at what she was reading. I couldn't figure out how a creature like this could exist in the mundane world of Henrico County, and, if she could, how it could be that I had never seen her before? Where did she come from? What was she about? And most important, *what was she reading*?

I wave at Nadine and she waves back from her hip, like it's a big secret. She's not wearing the Bedouin headdress today, but she is wearing a midriff-baring ensemble made up of layer after drapy layer of black gauzy fabric. Her necklace and earrings are made up of what appear to be the bones of small animals, or maybe human fingers. And, again, she's wearing black stiletto heels. This time they have studded ankle straps.

'Good common sense! Who is *that* woman?' Karen has her head tipped back and is peering unsubtly at Nadine from beneath the bill of her cap.

'That's Nadine. She's in my class. She's really nice.'

'It's a wonder that little old lady ain't runnin' in terror!' Irene is chatting animatedly with Nadine, probably about the Russia trip. Her pink peasant skirt and yellow cardigan contrast weirdly with Nadine's morbid attire. It looks like they're having a great time.

'Nadine travels all over the world. So does Irene. I think they already took the class before, too.'

'Well, I'm scared a' her.' Karen squints toward Nadine and frowns. 'She might wanna make a l'il hat outta my kneecap or somethin'.'

'No, really, she's *nice*,' I insist. 'She came up and introduced herself and everything. Besides, I don't think kneecaps are really shaped like caps. It's a misnomer.'

'A miss what?' Karen snaps her brim down and leans against the wall. 'You're a crazy ole belly dancin' English teacher,' she muses, 'thet runs around with *savages*.'

Savages? Sounds like fun. I wonder what she thinks is so bad about this. I thought I was moving up. I pose a question. 'Are savages better or worse than tattoo artists?'

'Better.'

'Better or worse than little gay lawyers?'

'Better. At least they ain't in a *risk* category.'

'Depends on what kind of risk you're talking about.'

'You got that right. Do they serve food at these things? Wine?'

'Oh, because I've been to so many of them.' I was actually hoping for some hummus, myself, or at the very least a cup of coffee. But, aside from an empty table draped hopefully with a paper tablecloth, I don't see any refreshments. 'Let's grab some seats.'

We find two empty seats on the end of a row and plop

down. Karen is continuing her blatant scoping out of the audience. 'So these women are all belly dancers,' she mutters, not quite low enough. It is not for nothing that my mother has come to refer to her as my 'loud friend.' She moves her eyes appraisingly over a black-haired woman I haven't seen before. The woman is exotic and self-assured as she cruises between the chairs in her requisite caftan. Her heavily lined eyes sparkle and she has an appealing smile with just a touch of an overbite. She also weighs at least two hundred and fifty pounds. I know what Karen is going to say even before she says it, and I wince in anticipation.

'They right *big*.' To a word. She sees my wince and immediately starts to backtrack. 'I mean, for dancers.' She thinks for more disclaimers. 'I just expected them to look smaller, thet's all. Not that I'm small, myself.' She bounces her thighs on the chair. 'But then, I'm not gonna get up there in a genie suit.' She turns around in her chair, checking out the dancers who are setting up the coffeepot in the back of the hall. 'They ain't all big. But,' and she says it again, just in case there was someone who was not offended yet, 'most of 'em are right *big*.'

I look around. She has a point, and then again she doesn't. Yes, many of the dancers would be considered large by American standards. By dance standards, meaning, say, oh, I don't know, let's take ballet – they would be considered morbidly obese. But then, so would I, and I wear a size ten (and even that is baggy given the always effective heartbreak diet plan: *Lose ten pounds fast by pacing, crying all the time, and never eating! Here's how!*). However, the dancers in the house tonight would be considered beautiful in the Middle East, with their wide hips, round faces, and generous thighs. The pictures I've found on-line of Egypt's top dancers, Nadia Hamdi and Lucy and Fifi Abdou, are conspicuous in their lack of washboard abs and concave tummies. These are women

83

of substance, women who are shaped like women, not waifs or twelve-year-old boys. And, from what I've read in my research, this is what the audience wants. These women are mega-celebrities in Cairo, commanding four and five figures for a performance – and this without arugula salad and mineral water for lunch. Did you ever? The more I learn about belly dancing, the more I love it.

I wonder, though, how much of the Middle Eastern appreciation for ample flesh came about through necessity? I mean, we've all heard the old saws about how the wide hips foretold an ability to bear many fine sons, and how soft fleshy bodies were a symbol of opulence and wealth and therefore considered more attractive than muscular, lean ones, but I can't help but wonder if there might not also be just a touch of 'might as well learn to love it' justification? In the 1980s, my father used to joke that the Widettes sketch on *Saturday Night Live*, the one with the family who all had comically huge behinds, must have been filmed at Saint Anthony's. Even the smaller women in the congregation had unbelievably wide hips, ballooning out like great round bustles under their demure church dresses. The Widette gene is apparently dominant, too; although I didn't inherit the glossy back hair or olive skin I always coveted on the full Lebanese kids at Saint Anthony's, I was blessed with a 100 percent Lebanese ass. From my first pair of Toughskin Huskies, my butt would not be ignored. In middle school, Roger Wright first paid me the backhanded compliment that I would hear repeated more than once over the years: 'You know, you got a nice ass—' (meaningful pause) 'for a *white* girl.'

I feel relieved to see that tonight's dancers are pretty much representative of what I have come to expect from my limited belly dancing experience – many older, some younger, a few thin, most average to generous. I feel like I did when I walked into Lucy's class on Wednesday, which is the opposite of what I've felt every time I've ever walked into a health club, aerobics class, or gym: *Hey, these chicks look like me. I think I could hang here.* Belly dancing class was proving to be one of the few places I'd been where I didn't feel 'not something enough' – not cool enough, not blonde enough, not thin enough, not Lebanese enough. At belly dancing class, not only do I feel enough, but I feel like I have a secret ace up my sleeve by being an undercover Arab. My half-Lebanese pedigree makes me feel somehow protected, as if no one can tell me I don't belong in belly dancing class.

The threat of having some faceless avatar find me out is a running fear of mine – in graduate school, backstage at concerts, at the tattoo parlor, and at all my teaching jobs, I always half expected some guy with a suit and a clipboard to walk in and say, 'There's been a mistake. It's come to our attention that *you* are not qualified to be here. We are going to have to ask you to leave.' In belly dancing class, I don't feel that. I think part of it is due to my sheer enthusiasm for what I'm learning; there is absolutely no doubt that I want to belly dance, and I couldn't say that about graduate school, or a White Lion concert, or the tattoo parlor. Even more than that, though, I think that I have found the first and possibly only place where being half Lebanese is a big fat plus. If I were any more obviously Lebanese, I'd feel pressured to get all the moves right on the first try. I'd be thinking that everyone was expecting me to break into a flawless *debke* on the first day of class. But as an undercover Arab, my secret is hidden beneath my pale skin and green eyes. I imagine this is how I would have felt at the tattoo parlor if I'd been hiding an elaborate full back piece under my flannel shirt instead of just my puny biker scorpion. No one else knows it, but it makes me walk a little taller, hold my head a little higher, snap my hip a little sharper. It's purely psychological, but it's just the boost I need right now.

But there is really no way I can explain this to Karen, or anyone else for that matter. The only people I know who could even identify with what I'm feeling might be my siblings, and I don't think either of them would be open to taking up belly dancing as a journey of ethnic self-discovery any time soon. My brother is absorbed in his recording business and doesn't seem to give too much thought to what being half Lebanese does or doesn't make him. He's listed on the Scariens CD as Jidis Safi, an Arabicized version of his own name, but I know this is purely Ronnie's doing and doubt that Robert cares anything about it one way or the other. And my sister has done her best to carefully excise any remnants of ethnicity from her life in the years since she danced the *debke* onstage as part of the Maroniteens dance troupe. Her Mechanicsville tract house is decorated with country knickknacks and homey Americana, and she drives to her corporate sales job in a shiny red pickup truck with the stereo permanently tuned to K95 contemporary country. On the weekends, she dances with cowboys and firemen at nightclubs with names like Little Texas and Mulligan's, and on Sundays, she plays the piano at church. Not at Saint Anthony's, Allah forbid – but at a little white Protestant church in a clearing that she chose 'because it looks just like a picture.'

I can only imagine what my sister would think about the first dancer, whose red-sequined *bedlah* frames a convex stomach that quivers unashamedly with every shimmy. Quivering and shaking, she raises her arms above her head triumphantly, *shimmyshimmyshimmyshimmyshimmy*, beads and fringe and stomach blurring in an impressive display of stamina and motion. Then she does the thing that will come to be my personal favorite belly dancing stage tactic – she looks down at her stomach, then at us, then at her stomach again, as if to say '*oh, my goodness! Will you look at that! I was just minding my own business, just standing here in this* bedlah*, and, why, my stomach just started moving!*' Then she kind of halfway winks at us and crinkles her nose – '*gotcha! I was doing it on purpose all along, ha ha*,' and breaks into a sailing travel that takes her once, twice around the floor and off the stage. She leaves me breathless, wanting more. I want a red-sequined *bedlah*. I want to be able to play the finger cymbals in groovy syncopation to the music. I want a tummy that pooches out like a quivering little dome.

Christy would be scandalized. A poochy tummy would be a fate worse than death for my aerobicized sister, who is forever scolding me for wearing roomy jeans that make me 'look big.' Her own painted-on clothes leave no room for error – you can practically make out the outline of her internal organs through the fabric, she is encased so tightly. She would probably see my burgeoning desire for a poochy stomach dome as one more way I'm trying to embarrass her. Throughout our years together at William and Mary, my parents received repeated tearful phone calls about how I was 'trying to ruin her good name.' To her credit, she usually didn't elaborate, so my nose ring, leather bustier, and boyfriends of various races and political affiliations all escaped my parents' scrutiny, if not my hapless sister's. The tummy dome would hit closer to home than boyfriends and bustiers, though, as my refusal to share in her obsession about weight has always galled her more than anything else. 'They call them models for a *reason*,' she once lectured me, shoving a copy of *Glamour* into my slightly-wider-than-acceptable lap. 'You're supposed to *model* yourself after them.' A word to the wise was not sufficient. I have never made any effort, before or since, to model myself after a nineteen-year-old anorexic millionaire with a vacuous stare and a heroin problem. Now, though, I know exactly who I want to model myself after, and she is on stage right now.

Aegela is the headlining dancer for the evening, a

87

redheaded, blue-eyed fireball from Stone Mountain, Georgia. She wears a gorgeous green costume that sets off her red curls and glints gaily with every hip drop she does. Aegela is a fantastic dancer, that's for sure, but I'm so new to all of this that I don't know a fantastic dancer from chopped tabouli. To me, every one of the dancers I've seen tonight has been show-stoppingly fabulous, blindingly awesome, ready to headline at the Cairo Hilton at a moment's notice. I'm just thrilled and flattered to be a part of it all. But even to my untrained eye, I know there is something that puts Aegela in a class by herself. It's an elusive quality, nothing that I can specifically define, but it's strong. I guess the closest I can come to describing it is that what makes Aegela better is *her* certainty that she is the best dancer we've ever seen – and not only that, but that *we* are the best audience she's ever had. She smiles, and winks, and undulates, and shimmies, and most of all, she likes us, she really likes us! Aegela's performance makes me feel invigorated, euphoric. I can't believe that I have lived for thirty years without this. What was I thinking? How did I ever survive?

After the show, Karen and I convene at Dot's Back Inn, a side street bar near her Northside apartment. Over a greasy plate of nachos, Karen gives her assessment of the show.

'I don't know, Annie. I kin see how you're all inta it and everything, but it all jes' about looked the same to me after a while. A whole lot of shakin' and a whole lot of sparklin'.' I sip my Coke quietly and think how grateful I am that Karen backed out of taking the class with me. As hyped as I am about belly dancing, I think it would probably kill at least some of my enthusiasm to have a nay-saying partner along for the ride. Sort of like why I insisted on following the Rolling Stones tour alone –

because I was convinced that *no one* liked the Rolling Stones as much as I did, and therefore *no one* was worthy of accompanying me to the concerts. Being obsessive is a lonely job, but somebody's gotta do it – and they've gotta do it alone. Which is how I usually end up. I'm getting used to it.

Karen is going on and on, speculating now about whether or not belly dancing *makes* your stomach pooch out like that, but I'm not listening. Instead I'm wondering if maybe this is how Chris felt about me in the end. Were my lukewarm emotions about tattooing what undid us? Would he eventually find some pink-haired, nose-ringed *grrrlie* who could share his love of needles and ink? Could I have faked it if I'd known? I'm gratified to realize that it doesn't matter to me anymore, at least not as much as it used to. If Chris hadn't dumped me, I wouldn't have been crying on Karen's couch, and she wouldn't have suggested belly dancing lessons. Six months down the road the hurt is still fresh enough that I'm not ready to say it was worth it – but somewhere, deep down, I know that it was.

'*Psst . . . Annie!* Look! There's one of 'em right now!' Karen leans over the nachos, her stage whisper about as quiet as she's able to get. She bugs her eyeballs to the right.

'One of what?' I try not to let on that I had stopped listening about five nachos ago.

'One of *what*! *Belly dancers, silly Annie*!' I look where her eyes are motioning and I see a blonde woman with a 1960s shag hairdo and big blue eyes seated with a Marlboro Man over in a corner booth. They're sharing a tall pitcher of draft beer, and the woman is puffing on a long skinny cigarette. She looks like she belongs in a Virginia Slims ad except that the bar is too dingy and depressing to really photograph all that well. She's pretty, actress pretty, and she looks out of place here. But I don't recognize her.

'You're kidding. That's not a belly dancer. What would a belly dancer be doing *here*?' I want to believe that they all go somewhere glamorous and exotic when they leave the West End Community Center – not to some greasy watering hole on a Lakeside side street.

'It *is* one, Annie. Remember, she had the silver costume? And the gloves? And she did that cowboy move where she looked like she was shootin' us with her fingers.' Karen points at me with her index fingers to illustrate her description. I look at the blonde again, not caring that I am definitely staring at her now. She glances warily around the bar and doesn't show any sign of recognition when her eyes pass me. I think, *if that was Aegela, she would recognize me*. But Aegela would never be in Dot's Back Inn.

The harder I stare, the harder it is for me to deny that she is, in fact, the belly dancer in the silver costume. She's wearing a black turtleneck now, and simple gold jewelry, and she doesn't look at all glamorous or belly dancery. She looks like a fortyish woman in a bar. An attractive fortyish woman, for sure, and somewhat out of place among the barflies and regulars at this seedy bar, but without her silver veil and finger cymbals, she's nothing special to me.

I avert my eyes and shrug off the image of her sitting in the corner booth. I don't want to see a belly dancer in Dot's Back Inn. I want to see belly dancers on stages and on Oriental carpets and in exotic nightclubs where I sit on cushions on the floor. I want them to twinkle and shine and smell of sandalwood and musk, and I want them to wink at me like I'm their best friend in the world when they dance past the low brass table where my Lebanese coffee cools in a tiny blue cup. I don't want my waitress to freshen their ashtrays before she brings me the check for my nachos. I don't want them to wear turtlenecks, and I don't want to think about them going home to Lakeside because then I have to admit that they are regular people just like me.

For now, I want to think that belly dancers are removed from all of this. I want to believe that they don't have day jobs or ex-husbands or credit card debt or any of those other troublesome details of human life. I want to believe that, if they even live in houses, they have palatial mansions somewhere on the outskirts of town, where huge empty rooms are covered in wall-to-wall mirrors so they can practice belly dancing all day long, between drinking Lebanese coffee and snacking on dates. I know how ridiculous this is, and wrong, and implausible. But I want to believe that belly dancing is going to fix me, and I can't believe that if I admit that belly dancers have real lives. I want them to live in a perpetual 101 Strings fantasy of keyhole-shaped doors and hanging lanterns, because that's where I want to live.

I steal another peek over my shoulder at the blonde. She's getting up from her booth and making her way to the ladies' room, where she waits patiently for the non-keyhole-shaped door to open so she can pee. I sigh and lay down five dollars for my nachos. I've seen enough. I feel the need to go home and get out my Mohammed el-Bakkar records so I can look at Nejla Ates for a while to erase the image of the belly dancer waiting to use the bathroom at Dot's Back Inn.

The details are sketchy, the history incomplete, and there is absolutely no data to support this . . . but I feel almost certain that Nejla Ates never had to wait in line to pee.

4

'Sheeeeeeeeva!'

Sequins and Sheet Cake
at the Lakeside Moose Lodge

Three months into my new life as a student of
Scheherezade, I catch wind via Nadine of an upcoming
show of unprecedented proportions. Sheva, who I
suppose could be called my 'grand-teacher,' is celebrating
her twenty-fifth anniversary as a teacher of the *danse
orientale*. Sheva, teacher of teachers, the one to whom all
local belly dancers can trace their hip circles, Sheva who
taught the Women of Selket how to shimmy, still teaches
three classes a week in the clubhouse of the Hunt Club
apartments. Nadine is one of her students, and she invites
me to come along to the show. She doesn't have to ask me
twice. I am literally counting down the days until my next
chance to see belly dancing. I am so there.

We pull into the parking lot of the Lakeside Moose
Lodge just after eight. Tanker-sized luxury sedans sit jowl
to jowl with flashy, low-slung sports cars and the odd
pickup truck. Nadine flicks her Marlboro out of the car
window and squints at the low, bunkerlike building, her
lip twitching as she twists a lock of hair around her finger.

She checks her lipstick in my rearview once, makes an unsuccessful attempt to readjust the mirror, then compulsively snatches it back around and peers in it again, this time leaving it twisted around toward the passenger seat, useless.

'I don't know why she gotta have it *here*,' she mutters under her breath as she stuffs her cigarettes, lighter, and lipstick into the black fringed pocketbook she holds between her stiletto-heeled boots. 'I been here before. Buncha old men, buncha Bubbas. I think I might know that guy – yeah, I seen that guy before. Prob'ly lotsa guys I know here. Prob'ly drunk. Ohhhhh, man.' She fishes the cigarettes back out of the bag and crosses herself with the pack. 'Well, anyway, we're here now,' she says to me, plucking another Marlboro out with two vermilion nails and motioning for me to turn off the engine. 'Might as well. Come on.'

I've never been in a Moose Lodge before, but I could have picked this one out of a lineup with no trouble. The smell of stale smoke hits us as soon as we walk through the looming steel doors. In the lobby, two geriatric Naugahyde couches compete for attention with a very big, very tatty moose head mounted on the wall, its glass eyes clouded with a thin film of nicotine and dust. The requisite wood paneling is complemented by clusters of framed faded photographs, some eight by tens of middle-aged men in 1950s horn-rims, some staged promo shots of children being handed wrapped packages by unseen benefactors whose arms loom in from the corners of the photos like the arms of God, if God looked like Fred MacMurray from the elbows down.

There is another set of doors just inside the lobby, and a card table is set up beside them, draped with black fabric printed with tiny gold ankhs. Arranged carefully on the table are a bowl of Starlite mints, a silk flower arrangement, a stack of Xeroxed programs, and a foot-high plaster figurine of a freckle-faced, chubby moppet – the type of figurine that usually bears some sort of legend at the bottom, à la 'I Love You This Much!' This statuette is distinguished from its smaller brethren by the fact that it is wearing a lavender *bedlah* and holding a purple veil high above its outsized head. Its round plaster stomach pokes out from beneath a puritanically flat chest, and I have to resist the temptation to rub it for luck. I take a program and look up to see the same curvy blonde who had manned the door at the Nadia Hamdi show working the table. Apparently there is some overlap in the local belly dancer camps. Nadine introduces her – Susan, Sheva's assistant – and compliments her on her hieroglyph sweater; she smiles and compliments Nadine back on her skeleton shawl clasp. The line begins to pile up behind us, though, so she takes our money distractedly and waves us in.

Inside the main hall of the Lakeside Moose Lodge, long folding banquet tables have been set up in deep rows, filling all but one corner of the room. Each table is filled, nay, *crammed* with women – some men, some children, but mostly women, and most of them elaborately made up and dressed in evening outfits involving various patterns of sequins and rhinestones. I look down at my own black pullover and jeans, and at Nadine's black stretch minidress and boots. Nadine leans in and mutters her own peculiar brand of reassurance. 'They're gonna think you're weird anyway, 'cos you're here with me,' she says, tugging at the hem of her dress, 'but next time you see 'em you'll be all made up and won't nobody remember who you are. You got the kinda face blends in good.' Yeah, I think to myself, a white face. Central casting, stock American girl. Fucking great. Who am I kidding with this belly dancing crap? As if it's going to somehow solve my Anglo problem. *Instant Arab, just add sequins!*

My pity party is interrupted by a jingling behind us. I

turn and find myself face to face with the anti-me. A tall, sinewy black woman in aviator sunglasses and cornrows, wearing a gold-striped caftan and a red-sequined headband, pops her chewing gum and smiles at us from behind her mirrored lenses. Tiny flecks of red glitter sparkle on her brown arms, and between the sparkles, on her left bicep, faded blue letters spell out *JAKE*. The jingling I hear is emanating from beneath the caftan somewhere, a faint tinkling sound, like keys to a faraway castle. She looks me up and down, slowly, indifferently, then turns and nods at Nadine, saying her name calmly and evenly under her breath, as if it were a password. Nadine leans up toward the Amazon's ear, steadying herself by grasping my shoulder.

'This is Anne,' she says, twitching her head in my direction. 'She's one of Lucy's new students.'

The Amazon responds with something that sounds suspiciously like 'ten four,' claps me heartily on my free shoulder, and eases through the crowd and into a back room. As always, Nadine provides the debriefing. 'That was Rosie – she's in Sheva's class. She drives an eighteen wheeler.' Aha. Ten-four indeed. I look at my program and see that Rosie is in the show – is, in fact, first in the lineup, a lineup due to start any minute. I suggest that we may want to look for a seat, then glance around and realize that there are none. I see that several of the children and younger adults are seated on the grubby tile floor, a concept that I could deal with, but Nadine couldn't – not in that skirt, anyway. Scrutinizing the room, I see a hand waving at us from one of the farthest tables on the other side. Pulling Nadine through the crowd, I realize it's Lucy herself, almost unrecognizable in an elaborate headdress and deeply kohled eyes.

'You guys can share our table. We probably won't all be sitting down at once, anyway, depending on who's dancing.' I thank her and perch on the edge of the one vacant chair, and Nadine joins me. We look around the table and then at each other, nervously, as we realize that we're seated at the Women of Selket's table. I feel like a middle schooler crashing the senior prom. Lucy immediately returns to her conversation, speaking to a short, redheaded woman in hushed tones about some business deal gone sour. I recognize the blonde woman across from us as the dancer featured on the television commercials for the one Lebanese restaurant in town – the restaurant that charges nine dollars for *m'joudra*, a poor man's supper of lentils and rice. Oblivious to my stare, she sips her beer and puffs absently on a cigarette. To her left, two older women I remember from Selket's last show are also drinking beer and plucking greasy breaded shrimp from a red plastic basket. And, of course, there is the woman from Dot's Back Inn, who once again looks at me without a glimmer of recognition.

I watch the women eat the shrimp, rapt with fascination and horror. If I were about to dance for a crowd this size, I wouldn't be able to eat anything, much less greasy fried shrimp. I would probably not be able to eat for days beforehand, and here they are about to go on any minute now, in their costumes, and eating shrimp! The Women of Selket are my new heroes, I decide. Their cool indifference reminds me of a clip I saw on MTV years ago, when I was in the throes of my teenaged obsession with the Rolling Stones. The clip was of video shot backstage at a Stones concert, and MTV reporter Kurt Loder was talking to Keith Richards and eating an apple. An apple! With Keith Richards standing right there! The nerve! *One day*, I had told myself then, *I will be as cool as Kurt Loder*. And tonight, at the Moose Lodge, I tell myself, *One day I will be as cool as the Women of Selket*.

The houselights go down, which is a good thing because I realize that I'm staring, anyway, and a wobbly blue spotlight is trained on the one corner of the room where the floor is clear. The MC, by the looks of his burgundy dinner jacket and tinted Foster Grants, could possibly have come with the room. He taps on the head of the microphone a few times, welcomes us in a gravelly voice, and asks us in turn to welcome our gracious hostess, Sheva – only he pronounces it 'Sheever.'

If I was staring at the Women of Selket, I am gawking at Sheva. She glides through the crowd as if she is on wheels, her red-sequined evening gown reflecting the spotlight as she steps confidently up to the microphone. She moves with the grace and assurance of someone who has been belly dancing for the better part of three decades, smiling benevolently at the crowd as if to say *yes, yes, how fortunate for all of you, here I am!* She waves to the crowd, diamonds glinting from every finger, nails perfectly manicured in the same glittery red as her gown. Her lipstick, again, perfectly matched, outlines a practiced, just-the-right-amount-of-teeth smile, the kind of smile that has seen a thousand publicity shots. But what has me truly captivated is Sheva's hair.

Her hair sits out a good six inches from her head on all sides, an awesome shellacked superstructure, perfectly symmetrical and frozen in time and space. It is a deep glossy brown, and so precisely shaped, so utterly spherical, that it defies logic. Sheva's hair is at the same time old-fashioned and futuristic, like something from the 1950s or the 2050s. It is hair that would make Judy Jetson proud, hair that Priscilla Presley would die for. Sheva's hair is the hippest hair on wheels. I think of the Bettie Page wannabe girls who hung out at the tattoo parlor, how painstakingly they maintained their retro hairstyles – bumper bangs, beehives, various shades of pink and blue and the perennial peroxide rinse. Not one of them could hold a curling wand to Sheva. Her hair is for real.

Sheva introduces Rosie as 'Little Egypt,' and Rosie comes out sans caftan and shades and does her thing to a

Turkish drum number, cornrows flying and glitter sparkling. As she lifts and drops one hip, and then the other – *up-down, up-down* – she stares out over the massive crowd as if she is staring out over just so much open highway, her eyes fixed on some point in the far back of the Lakeside Moose. Her dancing is different from most of the other belly dancing I've seen – it's earthier, more forceful, and somehow familiar. It isn't until later that Nadine explains that Rosie also dances at Native American powwows and I realize that's the influence that I see in her belly dancing, with its heavy footfalls and jutting elbows. The song ends and Rosie raises one red-gloved hand high over her head, dipping her chin ever so slightly in thanks for the applause. I almost expect to hear a 'ten-four, ten-two' as she strides offstage.

Dancer after dancer takes the stage – Shamara, Razia, Zahira Adia. I notice that *Sheever* shares the MC's fondness for the inserted r – 'Janeeta' becomes 'Janeeter,' 'Alinda' is introduced as 'Alinder,' and one dancer is even described as being from 'Canader.' I watch each dancer, fascinated, making mental notes about costumes, choreography, accents. Sheva's dancers are less intimidating than the dancers I've seen at restaurants and at the Selket show. Instead of the pricey imported costumes that seem *de rigeur* at the other shows, many of these women wear obviously home-stitched outfits – simple chiffon skirts, belts decorated with fake pearls and stretch sequins, bras covered in gold lamé and rhinestones. Granted, some of the costumes are less than flattering, and as a whole, without the flashy fringe and bugle beads, the numbers lack the gee-whiz factor that counts for some of the appeal that belly dancing holds for me. But still, with each dancer who takes the stage, each hesitant teenager, each pair of giggly coworkers, each Rubenesque diva, I feel a little less like I'm doomed to the sidelines forevermore. When a bespectacled, fortyish woman comes out holding two candles and proceeds to stand stock-still as she circles the candles in front of her, I think *I could do that*. When a meticulously painted Cosmo blonde essentially spends four minutes shaking her ta-tas at the crowd without regard to timing or rhythm, I think *I sure as hell could do that*. When a dozen dancers crowd into the tiny spotlight to do a Middle Eastern rendition of the Macarena, I think *well, technically, I could do that, but I'll be damned if I want to*. And when a big-eyed nine-year-old in pink chiffon harem pants lies down on the floor, arches her back, and starts frantically vibrating her pelvis, I think *I can see the headlines now – LOCAL TEACHER INDICTED IN CHILD SEX SHOW RAID*.

Although my experience is still meager – twelve weekly classes do not an avatar make – I find that I am beginning to differentiate between impressive dancers and average dancers. I am like the wannabe at the art gallery with the pretentious turtleneck and a glass of cheap white wine – 'I may not know art, but I know what I like!' Zitana's flashy cabaret number with a high-slit skirt and syncopated *zils* impresses me. Alisa's drum solo captivates me. The folky numbers, with drapy layers of costumes and stiff choreographed steps, do not. I feel a little guilty, like a traitor to my heritage, but I can't help my tastes. I've always preferred the midway over the museum. I'm tacky like that.

After fifteen numbers, intermission is announced – a good thing, I figure, since I think we could all use some air after the nine-year-old's act. Nadine and I stand up from our shared seat, but our escape route is blocked by a giant sheet cake being wheeled in on yet another table, as if the room could hold one more. The monstrous confection is the size of four cakes; it is a dessert that could be measured by the yard. Red flowers and elaborate swirls dance across its thickly frosted top, surrounding iced cursive letters spelling out *SHEVA'S SCHOOL OF DANCE*

– 25 YEARS. Perched in the center of the cake is a tiny plastic doll. In stark contrast to the doll in the lobby, she is intimidatingly endowed, her plastic breasts jutting precariously close to the candles. Her tiny arms are raised behind her head, and her hands are hidden by her flowing black hair. On her face is a look of dazed ecstasy, inasmuch as ecstasy is possible for a plastic doll; in any case, her eyes are heavily lidded, her cheeks flushed, and her mouth open in a perpetual 'oh.' The combination of her expression and her proportions makes me wonder if she doesn't have a possible sideline gig as a cake topper for bachelor parties, and I can imagine her looking very much at home reclining nude in some poor groom's icing – but here she is dressed for the occasion in a red-and-gold *bedlah*, her chiffon-covered ass planted firmly in the white sugar frosting.

We decide to forgo the cake and sneak out a side door so Nadine can have a smoke. Squatting in the gravel behind the Lakeside Moose we find Rosie, back in the caftan, eyes closed, hands arched around her temples, breathing deeply. When she hears the door open, she looks up and smiles.

'Hey, guys, what's up? Just getting centered before the next number.' She stands up, returning to her full imposing height, and pulls her cornrows back with one hand. Nadine nods, busily searching for a cigarette, and Rosie turns to me, smiling, casual, as if she's known me way longer than two hours. 'Anne, right? Anne. How long you been dancing?'

'Just a couple of months.' Something about Rosie's easy manner makes me feel like blabbing out the whole story, but I manage to keep it to basics. Had boyfriend, dumped by boyfriend, heart broken, crying, friend suggests belly dancing, tried it, liked it. Rosie takes this in, nods thoughtfully, and leans in, motioning Nadine over as well.

'People always want to get married,' she says, as if she

100

has given this a lot of thought. 'Especially women. Always want to get married. Like that's the big prize or something, the answer to all their problems. But I've been married twice,' she pauses for emphasis and nods at us, her jaw set. 'I've had two husbands, and I'll probably have another one. Don't get me wrong, I like it! But the thing is,' she says, raising one palm as if taking an oath, 'you have to be strong. You have to stand up for yourself and never compromise. I make a point of that now. I don't compromise on anything! Do it on your own if you have to, and don't take any crap off anybody. I mean it! No man is worth crawling for.' She puts her hand down, manifesto delivered, mission complete. She turns to walk back into the Moose Lodge, then slowly, thoughtfully, stops and turns around. 'Except Robert Urich,' she adds thoughtfully. A wistful smile plays across her face as she twists a fingerful of cornrows. 'You know. Dan Tanna.' Then she is gone.

I stare blankly at the door behind her, then at Nadine, who stares back at me quizzically, as if I might be the strange one here, as if what we've just witnessed is perfectly and unquestionably normal. Certainly if you had told me a year ago that I would soon find myself behind a Moose Lodge, getting a lecture on life, love, and Robert Urich by a truck-driving, belly dancing, cornrow-wearing Amazon, that would have been expected, would it not? Maybe this kind of stuff happens all the time to people like Nadine, but I'm new to this particular brand of weirdness and it's freaking me out just a little. Rock 'n' roll decadence I can handle; give me a rock-bottom junkie or a violent teenaged sex offender and I'm good to go. But belly dancer bonding is a new one on me. It's kind of cool, though. I like it.

Nadine grinds out her cigarette in the gravel and we slip back inside for the second half. There are another fifteen acts, and even with my new sense of oneness and belly dancer sisterhood wrapped around me like a chiffon veil, I have to admit that even I am getting a teensy bit sick of belly dancing. My head hurts from the smoke and the drums, one of my butt cheeks is asleep, and I am suffering from a bad case of undulation overkill. I stop counting after a dozen more numbers, and I have long since lost my place in the program. I am almost ready to ask Nadine if she wants to go ahead and leave – but, before I do, I want to see what the next number is like. It's a good thing, because I wouldn't have believed it if I hadn't stayed to see it. Some things just have to be witnessed.

For the grand finale, a round dozen dancers troop out in two lines to the twangy intro of a country song. In addition to full *bedlah*, they are wearing ten-gallon hats – how Moose Lodge! How sheet cake! How patently uncool! The song unfolds as a cracker version of the Ethnic Police's anathema, the 'noony noo noo noo' snake charmer ditty that every drunken loser you'll ever meet will sing to you when you say you're a belly dancer. Played on a twangy guitar, it's even less authentic, if that's possible, and I suppress a smirk as I watch the Women of Selket squirm in their seats and try to smile politely. I've come to know the Women of Selket as the local agents of the Ethnic Police, ready to take heretics to task for doing a *Saidi* number in a Saudi costume, or pairing Persian hands with Turkish hips. I can only imagine what they think of what is onstage right now.

This number is almost too tacky even for me, a burlesque of belly dancing played out to a country western sound track. The choreography is cliché after cliché, camel walks and Pharaoh arms and *I Dream of Jeannie* head slides. As Pam Tillis belts out 'Just call me Cleopatra, baby, 'cos I'm the queen of denial,' I notice Rosie is in this number too, way in the back, her cornrows hidden beneath her ten-gallon hat. The dancers weave in and out of their rows, never losing their stride, arms jutting out in front of them like paintings on a wall. As I watch Rosie grapevine first to the left, then to the right, *step-back-step-over-step-back*, working a piece of Bazooka Joe while her gold fringe sways, the other dancers fade into sequined nothingness for me. It's all about Rosie, a modern-day truck-stop Cleopatra, pointing a ruby-frosted toe as she spins in beautiful bored circles against the wood-paneled backdrop of the Lakeside Moose Lodge. I don't want to leave. I want to stay here at this Moose Lodge with Rosie forever and ever.

Unfortunately, or maybe by the grace of God, the show does end, and, after a final curtain call as the MC belts out Sheva's signature song ('Sheeeeeeeeeeeeva! Lighter than light, fairer than fair! Floating as if she's walking on aaaaaaiiiiirrr!'), the dancers take their bows and leave the floor. As the crowd files out, Nadine pushes me through the crowd and introduces me to Sheva herself as a potential new student. Sheva, a vision of Moose Lodge glamour, not the least bit faded even after four hours under the lights, reaches out and digs into my arm with her scarlet nails. 'Well, for goodness' sake, *hurry up* and sign up for class,' she admonishes. 'We're going to need more girls for the veil number!' After I disengage my arm and we make our escape, Nadine explains that the veil number is one of the choreographies that Sheva's students perform every year at the county fair, which will be coming up in a couple of months. My stage debut . . . so soon? 'It ain't that bad,' Nadine assures me, with a combination wave and hair flip. 'Last year the tent was half empty. Everybody was over at the pig race.'

The pig race. I unlock the car and let Nadine in, contemplating my potential as a county fair belly dancer. It's not exactly ethnically authentic, but something about performing in a tent appeals to the leftover hipster in me, the side of me that sees sideshows and midways as something deliciously sleazy and cool. 'AMAZING BELLY

DANCING GIRL! ALIVE! WHY? HALF-LEBANESE, HALF-???' I can almost see the red and yellow canvas banners now. Who needs tattoo parlors? The sideshow is where the real grit is, and I'm going to be an exhibit. Who says the best revenge is living well? That might work for regular people, but when it comes down to who can outdo whom in the hipster irony department, the best revenge is shaking your butt in a tent next door to the bearded lady while the Tilt-a-Whirl zings past in the foreground. Deep down, the idea terrifies me as much as it thrills me, and in fact I can't imagine going through with it at this stage of the game, but I set aside realism and dwell in the glorious possibility of being cooler than Chris for the rest of the ride home.

Some things are so hip they can only be accessed through secret Moose Lodge meetings with bubble-haired women long after the sheet cake is gone. I just wish Chris could see me in my new, privileged, in-the-loop position. If he were here right now, I would tell him exactly how it was. *You can buy your bowling shirts*, I would say to him, and *you can serve Spam and Cheez-Whiz to your cocktail party friends while you groove to swinging lounge tunes and think that you're all so kitschy and hip. But you're just faking something you can't have.* Then I would grab the handle on that big steel door, point to the sign up above it, and say, I *got news for you, baby . . . the Moose Lodge is members only.* Then I would slam the door, leaving him out in the cold with nothing but his bowling shirts and his lucky dice tattoos to keep him company, while inside the members-only Moose Lodge Sheva, Rosie, Nadine, the Women of Selket, and I would laugh and dance and eat plate after plate of deep-fried shrimp, on the house.

5

Peeking Under the Tent

Big Day on the Midway

At Nadine's urging, I add Sheva's Monday night class to my weekly belly dancing schedule. It is as far removed from Lucy's class as the Moose Lodge is from Mecca. In contrast to the spacious gymnasium where Lucy instructs us in hip circles and chest lifts, Sheva's class meets in the clubhouse at the Hunt Club Apartments, one of those ubiquitous complexes for 'young single professionals,' where Jonathans and Lisas are lured into leases with the promise of Friday night happy hour in the clubhouse with *'people just like you!'*

Some twenty-odd dancers maneuver gingerly between the bland floral couches and coffee tables as Sheva trills instructions over the blare of an el-Bakkar-era phonograph. 'Come on, ladies!' she cries in a high, warbling voice. 'Put some *hips* into it!' As we weave around the room, dodging furniture and elbows, we try our best to put some hips into it without knocking anyone else's hips out of it. And, as if I didn't already feel enough like an extra in a second-rate Fellini knockoff, we also have live accompaniment in the form of Dr Manuel Mendez, a semiretired gynecologist for the state women's prison who moonlights as a *doumbek* player for Sheva's class. Dr Mendez ambles around the room, absently tapping his *doumbek* and grinning at the dancers from behind his huge square spectacles. Nadine, Sheva, two dozen belly dancers, and me – and now Dr Mendez. All he needs is a fez to make this the absolute most surreal experience I have ever had.

After my first class at Sheva's I have to go home and lie down for an hour to get my wits back. I am used to Lucy's class – peaceful, regimented, and meticulous – where we will sometimes spend the entire hour going over one new move until we all have it just so, not to mention the time spent putting each move in its proper historical and geographical context. At Sheva's, we switch moves as often as Sheva switches albums, which is constantly. She slaps records on the turntable like so many blackjack cards, then drags the ancient tone arm across the vinyl without a second thought – 'Snake arms, ladies!' *Screeeeeeeech!* 'Sidestep!' *Screeeeeech!* 'Everybody shimmy!' Then, just in case I am not already traumatized enough, she utters the phrase that sends my pulse skyrocketing and almost single-handedly keeps me from ever returning to her class: '*All right, ladies – now do what you feel!*'

I suppose now would be as good a time as any to mention that I have spent most of my life avoiding any situation that might require me to dance. From preteen mixers at Thomas H. Henderson Middle School to the Whisky à Go Go on Sunset Boulevard, I was always the girl on the back wall, or at the bar, or riding the edge of the stage, just past the wooden sawhorses – anything to avoid facing the shame and humiliation of the dance floor. I don't think

I'm the worst dancer in the world – but then again I might be, because I've never tried. There's no evidence pointing one way or the other. Regardless of the veracity of my fears, though, they have always been there and they have always been strong. I'm terrified of dancing. Just the thought of setting foot on a nightclub floor makes me weak with panic.

For some unknown reason, yet another mysterious piece in the puzzle that led me to belly dancing, my fear of dancing went into total remission when Karen mentioned belly dancing classes. I cannot even begin to describe how total the remission was, except to say that being scared to belly dance never even entered my mind. In retrospect, it's amazing to me how absolutely *not* scared I was, which brings us to another mysterious piece of the puzzle: Did I somehow psychically know that Lucy's class would leave nothing to improvisation? Was there some intuitive factor at work telling me I had nothing to fear? If Lucy had told me 'do what you feel,' the results might have been disastrous. But Lucy doesn't *care* how we feel as long as we get the moves right, and that means one, two, three, four, left, right, left. It's rote, and measured, and very, very reassuring to the dancing impaired. I don't think I could have handled it any other way.

Still, though, there must have been some other factor at work in my momentary ability to stifle my danceophobia. Even basic steps and precise instructions did nothing for me in the past – why now? Was it that I somehow felt some deep-down innate spark for belly dancing because I'm half Lebanese? As much as I want to think so, I know that wasn't it either. Witness my steadfast refusal to learn the *debke* when I was in the Maroniteens. For the un-initiated, the *debke* barely even qualifies as dancing, it's so basic; it's little more than walking sideways, with the occasional stomp thrown in for good measure. Even my sister gamely put on the pink satin harem pants and rehearsed the *debke* weekend after weekend in preparation for the International Food Festival each year. I, however, remained true to my post as official soundperson for the afternoon rehearsals, hitting 'rewind' every time '*Hadouni Hadouni*' came to an end. From my perch on the picnic table, beside the boom box, I learned the steps to the *debke* as well as any of the girls who were dancing it in the show. In my head, I could do a perfect *debke* – but that was the only place I could do it. Somewhere in this story there is a very pithy AA-related metaphor about how just thinking about the steps is not enough, but I will spare you that particular bit of florid prose. Suffice to say that a mental *debke* and fifty cents will get you a cup of Lebanese coffee.

It takes every speck of courage I have to return to Sheva's class the next week. I tell myself that no one is looking at me, that we are all beginners, that I don't *have* to be good, I only have to enjoy myself – but the truth is, I am not enjoying myself at all. Even during the parts of the class where she is teaching us new moves, or screeching out the names of moves that I already know, I am still waiting for, dreading, imagining the moment when she's going to say 'do what you feel,' because, when that happens, what I'm going to feel is like crawling under the ratty flowered couch against the back wall. I feel like I have absolutely no sense of what is supposed to go with the music. I do snake arms, and I look around and everyone else is doing camels. I do a hip circle and the girl beside me is doing a shimmy. I want to give up, but at the same time, I want desperately to get it. I *want* to feel the music, to know intuitively when to shimmy my shoulders and when to slide my ribcage. And, as important as it is to learn the steps by themselves, I know that one day I'm going to have to face the belly dancing music and improvise. So, teeth clenched and pits unglamorously sweaty, I persevere.

Fortunately, Sheva has made allowances for the improvisation impaired by employing several assistants. Janiece, Debbie, and Susan – the same Susan with the hieroglyph sweater – mingle among the dancers, offering encouragement, correction, and, most important for me, moves to copy. When the edict comes down to do what I feel, I soon find I can avoid the inevitable panic attack by doing what Janiece feels or Susan feels. Whatever it is that Debbie feels is apparently quite complex and involved and, to my barely trained eye, absolutely inscrutable, and I cannot begin to imitate it – but no matter. As long as I can spot Janiece or Susan in the crowd, I am safe for the moment. I know that I'm cheating, and I vow that I won't do it forever, but for now it keeps me from fleeing to the parking lot, never to return.

The other thing that keeps me coming back to Sheva's is the enterprising way she's scheduled her classes. Just like Lucy's class, Sheva has the advanced and intermediate classes first, then the beginners' class. Also just like at Lucy's, I overcome my lifelong record of tardiness because I know that the earlier I get to class, the more belly dancing I'll get to watch. Lucy's advanced class is interesting, and I've gotten to witness her students learning *ghawazee* cane tricks, twirling sequined dowels in the air and balancing them on their heads with aplomb. I've gotten to listen to them practice their *zil* patterns, clanking out *tek a tek a tek a tek* on their brass finger cymbals. I've seen *Zar* head twirls and *Saidi* combinations and elegant Persian hand gestures. At Sheva's, though, I've gotten to watch advanced belly dancers, many of them the same dancers I've seen at local restaurants and at the Selket Workshop, doing what they feel. It's almost like getting a free belly dancing show every single Monday night. I get there earlier and earlier each week, taking my place on the couch between the dance bags and water bottles, and watch the dancers.

My punctuality proves to be my undoing – or maybe my doing; it's all in the perspective, as usual. I am sitting there, minding my own business. No, actually, I am minding the business of Julijana, the beautiful German belly dancer who looks like Sandra Bullock and dances like it's the only thing she was made for. Julijana carries her dance things to class in an open wicker basket and wears short, flouncy sundresses over bare legs and clunky European shoes. She can get away with it because she is tall and gorgeous and looks twenty-five, even though I know she has teenaged children. I have a new hero. I watch her shamelessly every week, like a movie, eagerly awaiting each new installment of the weekly Julijana Belly Dancing Show. And that's what I'm doing when Sheva sneaks up on me and grabs me by the arm.

'*Anne*. You do have a veil, don't you?'

I nod and begin rummaging in my bag for my ragged piece of window sheer that passes for a veil. I assume she wants it for someone, some real belly dancer who has misplaced her veil or is maybe planning to do some of the super-impressive *double* veil moves that I have seen only the best dancers use. I hold the veil out to her and wait for her to take it. She nods and pats it, like it was a small animal.

'I want you to learn the veil number with the intermediate class.' She makes this proclamation casually, then glides away toward the phonograph.

Obviously there has been a mistake. Sure, she mentioned it back at the Moose Lodge, but now that she's seen me dance, one would think she would know better. One would think. I leap up and follow her, tugging desperately at her leopard-printed sleeve.

'Sheva, I'm in the *beginners*' class.'

She blinks at me, her expression never wavering from the serene half-smile that usually means she can't hear you. I begin to panic.

110

'I've only been dancing since February!' I take it up a couple of decibels, hoping to cut through the scratchy *taqsim* and Dr Mendez's incessant tapping. Has she not seen me stumbling through the beginner moves? Maybe she has me confused with somebody else. It doesn't matter. You can't argue with Sheva. Especially if she can't hear you.

'You'll do fine. It's a basic routine.' She pats the veil that I am clutching in a death grip and smiles. 'Just learn it.'

I walk numbly back to my seat, uncertain as to whether I have been granted a reprieve or not. *Just learn it.* What does that mean? If I am just learning it, will I have to dance at the fair? If I am just learning it, am I actually *in* the choreography or can I stand off to the side, where my inevitable missteps will not affect the rest of the performers? I dodge my way across the room to where Susan is shimmying around a dusty ficus.

'She wants me to learn the veil number,' I hiss, hoping that Susan will be shocked and horrified and race over and tell Sheva that she is making a terrible mistake.

'That's nice.' She smiles at the ficus, beckons to it, tosses her blonde hair at it. The ficus is a prominent member of our imaginary audience. Sheva is always reminding us, 'dance to your people,' our people being the ficus, the lamp, the framed print of the Tour de France. I get between Susan and her person, my eyes wild with fear.

'She just wants me to *learn* it, right? I mean, I don't actually have to *do* it, I just have to *learn* it, right?'

Susan stops dancing and tilts her head ever so slightly. In the face of my blind panic, she remains her usual blasé self. Except when she is dancing, Susan seems bored with the world. Her perfectly painted eyelids are perpetually at half-mast, her lips pursed in a seen-it-all pout. She speaks in a lock-jawed monotone that implies that she is already tired of the discussion, has had it too many times, regardless of the topic. She would make a great cowgirl, or card

111

shark. And she has the greatest hips of anyone in town.

'If she told you to learn it, then *learn* it,' she says without a hint of irony. 'I don't *know* what she wants. *Nobody* does. That's *Sheva*.' She gives a halfway shrug and starts shimmying around the ficus again. I decide to try Janiece.

I creep between the couch and the coffee table to the Corner of the Room. Like that edge of the schoolyard where all the cool seniors hang out and smoke, the Corner of the Room is where all the cool belly dancers hang around and do what they feel – gossip, look at dancewear catalogs, swap accessories. Tammy, Janiece, and Doris are rummaging through a shopping bag, holding bits of fabric up against a length of silver beaded fringe. I stand meekly behind them, waiting for them to notice me. When they finally do, I feel like the dorkiest middle schooler on earth, with my stupid, middle-school-level problem. Thirty years old and afraid some lady in a leopardskin leotard is going to make me wave a veil around where people can see. The idea.

'Ummmm . . . sorry to bother you guys.' Doris tucks the fabric back in the bag, and Janiece turns to face me. It doesn't help that Janiece, with her shoulder-length crimped hair and bright red Trans-Am with her name on the plates, reminds me just a little bit of the eighth-grade girls who wore Candies to school and smacked me in the head on the school bus. Nor does it help to know that Janiece, at thirty-four, has been performing in Sheva's shows for over twenty years and that the traumatic experience that I am going through right now is something that she had conquered by the age of eleven. But that is Janiece, not me. I take a deep breath and spill the entire story, word for word, down to Susan's response. Then I wait for them to save me.

But they don't save me. They don't help me at all. Instead, they look at each other and *laugh*. It's not a mocking laugh, but more of an inside-joke kind of laugh, as if maybe I am not the first one who has come to them with this problem. Janiece shakes her head, still laughing, and leans against the wall.

'Sheva's kind of famous for casually adding people to the numbers as we go along,' she explains. 'If you happen to be in her line of sight, it doesn't matter if it's the week before the show. She'll throw you in there.'

'But I'm only a *beginner*,' I remind her, still hoping that someone besides me will eventually realize what a mistake this is.

'No matter,' Doris interjects, her deep dimples still lingering. 'Hey, you're lucky. At least she got you *early* – you'll have time to learn the steps.'

'You can tell her if you don't want to do it,' Janiece says, and my hopes soar for just a moment. Then she adds, 'I mean, she's not going to take no for an answer, but you can *tell* her.' And she and Doris laugh again, as if this is the best joke ever. I want to ask if there is any secret, any tried-and-true way to get out of a group number once Sheva has tapped you in – but before I can ask, I am pulled onto the floor by Sheva herself. It is time to learn the veil number.

For the next two months the veil number is my life. I hear the veil music in my head all the time, even when I'm sleeping. This would not be so bad except that the veil music is 'Never on Sunday' performed on the vibraphone – whiny, schlocky, and sickeningly sweet. 'Doopy doopy doop-a *doop-doop a doop-doop a doop-doop* a doopy doopy doo . . .' I buy myself a tape so I can practice at home; the only version I can find is a vocal rendition by the Chordettes, who sound not unlike a whitewashed version of the El-Bakkar squawkers. 'Oh, you can kiss me on a *bleak* day, a *freak* day, a *week* day . . .' I find myself singing it along with the hum of the copier at work, the thumping of the washing machine, the utility poles swooshing by on the highway. Since I have taken up belly dancing, everything rhythmic is now an eight count for me to practice hip circles, snake arms, shoulder shimmies, too. If I had a sex life, things could get interesting. As it is I have to settle for quizzical glances from the other teachers when they catch me doing hip drops in the copy room.

On the weekend, I trek to the local fabric store to find a sheet of gold lamé to make my performance veil. Wandering blindly through the bolts of fabric, it occurs to me that, had someone told me I would be shopping for a veil at the age of thirty, I would have assumed they meant a *wedding* veil. The irony does not cheer me. Though I miss Chris less with each passing day and each new class, I am still angry at him for disrupting my up-until-now smoothly running timetable. Finish college at twenty-one, sow wild oats, twenty-one to twenty-five, grad school twenty-five to twenty-seven, find job, settle in, get married at thirty, have kids by thirty-five. I am stalled! Stalled at the next-to-last step! Chris's refusal to get with the program leaves me with little time to find a suitable replacement for the final act. I note that 'become belly dancer' was not originally on the schedule; neither was 'go to rehab,' 'work in tattoo parlor,' or 'move to China.' One must allow for variations. Besides, Wendy Wasserstein never got married and had a kid at forty-eight, and how cool is *she*? I select a lovely tissue lamé and tell myself that wedding veils are a symbol of an oppressive patriarchy anyway.

Although I didn't feel lucky when Doris originally informed me that I was, eventually I begin to feel a level of gratitude for the two months between my addition to the veil number and the fair itself. One would think that eight weeks of practice would be more than sufficient to learn a simple number. One would think. However, in the bizarro universe in which Sheva's class exists, instead of buckling down and focusing up as performance time draws near, the weekly sessions become more chaotic, less organized, and more crowded – as if that were even a possibility. Classes rarely start on schedule, the choreographies change from week to week, and, true to Janiece's prediction, Sheva tosses new dancers into each number at whim. Additionally, each lineup is further augmented by the addition of a number of heretofore unseen babealicious babes, some of whom have been augmented themselves. They arrive fashionably late, kiss Sheva on both cheeks, fawn over Dr Mendez, then jump right into the front rows of previously arranged lineups with abandon. I notice the Corner of the Room becoming a festival of eye rolling and whispering, and I use my best inconspicuous hip-variation sidestep to position myself for eavesdropping.

'Looks like somebody's *grown* since the recital.'

'Wonder who paid for those?'

'I wonder if she's going to wear that purple thong again this year – and that chiffon skirt so you can see it?'

'Well, I don't know where she's been, but I can tell you where she hasn't been – takin' dance lessons. Look at those *hands*.'

I try to sneak a casual peek at the hands in question. They belong to a sultry brunette with a pierced navel (big Ethnic Police no-no) and several visible tattoos (ditto). Her fingers are splayed and her hands circle wildly from the wrist as she undulates. They are what Susan calls 'stupid hands.' Hands should be graceful, held straight and still, middle two fingers together. The objective is to avoid drawing attention away from your hips – or chest, or belly, or whatever you're *really* moving. 'All right, ladies, I don't want to see any *stupid hands*,' Susan often reminds us in that bored, just-slip-it-under-the-door voice. I glance quickly at my own hands. They are a little stupid. They could be smarter.

'Hey,' I interject casually, hoping to sound as if I haven't been eavesdropping. 'Who are all these *new* people?'

Doris shakes her head as she watches the blonde with the new boobs grapevine the wrong way and take out the entire front row of the drum number. 'They're not new. They always show up just before we have a show.' Her dimples start to show as the blonde attempts a shimmy but ends up with something more like a full-body seizure. 'I don't think they really care too much for belly dancin' – but they love to strut their stuff in a show.'

So. *Showgirls!* Thinking back, I do remember seeing all of them at the Moose Lodge but not since. I mostly remember their costumes and their hairdos, both quite elaborate, and their centerfold figures. I don't recall being particularly impressed by their dancing – not like I was with Doris's, or Monica's, or Joyce's, all three of whom are looking back on forty and size five like mile markers in a rearview mirror.

After ten years of rock 'n' roll scene-making, it is a relief to be part of a subculture where younger and thinner do not automatically equal better. Looking around, I note that I actually am younger and thinner than most people in the room – something that was never true at the tattoo parlor or on the Sunset Strip. But I know that I am also one of the worst dancers in the room, and that is not modesty but simple fact. As a beginner, I can't hold a Pharaonic candle to ninety percent of those present – and thank God for the babealicious babes, or my stats would be even more dismal – but for the first time, I feel like there's hope. The feeling that the clock is ticking ever faster and my best years are behind me fades every time I watch a thirtysomething, fortysomething, fiftysomething woman take the stage and seduce everyone in the audience. Gone, too, is the omnipresent loop of 'If I could just lose ten pounds . . .' Ten pounds? I need those ten pounds to put the push in my tush push, the hip in my hip drop. I watch the brunette, her meticulously painted acrylic nails clawing frenzied circles in the air above her head, and I feel suddenly serene. I wish I could bottle the feeling. I have a notion I'm going to need it come the fair.

The smell of rosewater and musk oil, wafting from the diaphanous silver veil drawn just below my eyes, is barely perceptible, though each breath brings the veil flush against my face. As I try my best to keep the delicate fabric from brushing against my vermilion-painted lips, I am overwhelmed by the competing aromas arriving on each bracing gust of the September night – cotton candy, Italian sausage, onion rings, and, when the direction of the breeze turns just so, the faintest whiff of horse manure.

Dating back to the days of Little Egypt, belly dancers and carnival midways have been inevitable if unlikely bedfellows. 'She walks! She talks! She crawls on her belly like a reptile!' In most cases, she also gets dressed behind the tent, and tonight I am paying my dues in the grand tradition. I wriggle tentatively out of my T-shirt under the almost modest cover of a parti-colored array of veils, held in front of me by my sister dancers. It probably would have been much easier to arrive in costume, but rides are rides, and cotton candy is cotton candy, and I've been a fair whore since way back. No sense wasting free admission. Once I'm in costume, I'll be expected to hold the veils for other dancers who need to change, some into costume, some out of costume, some from one costume to another. Most of the dancers have already been onstage once, and, in eleven minutes, they'll be expected onstage again to do the grand finale, which, for reasons that defy logic but are never questioned, always requires a full costume change. Somewhere between this moment and that finale lies the three minutes fifty that I have worked toward for the past two months – the veil number.

I can feel the mud oozing between my bare toes as I adjust my costume – at least, I hope it's mud. So much for the pedicure in any case. I roll the waistband of my chiffon skirt twice to raise the hem, just to ensure that I don't trail any organics onstage with me – *quelle glamour!* My hardware, Nadine's silver beaded bra and hip belt that make up the ten pounds of borrowed glitz that is my debut outfit, are laid out on a nearby bale of hay, shimmering atop the straw, Bob Mackie comes to Mayberry. I dart a glitter- and goosebump-covered arm and probably a good portion of bare breast out from under the veil to grab the belt. Fastened around my hips, it covers the rolled waistband nicely. I turn toward the bale to grab the bra and find it being handed to me by a grimy, beefy fist that is definitely not attached to a belly dancer.

'There yuh go, harem girl!' My new friend, a coveralled, NASCAR-capped carny, has somehow edged his way past the makeshift security squad of belly dancers and joined me, and my bare breasts, in my open-air dressing room. I cross one arm over myself and snatch the bra from his greasy clutches.

'Uh, thanks.' I peer over the veil at the other belly dancers, who, already having been no help whatsoever, are now staring open-mouthed in horror at my predicament. Some friends. 'You know,' I offer, with what I hope is an encouraging nod toward the stage, 'the show is still going on! You're missing all the fun back here.'

'They ain't nuthin," he replies eagerly, waving a dismissive mitt at the stage. 'Yew gon' be the best one up there. 'At cos-tume yew wearin' is sumthin' else.' Has he not noticed, I wonder, that I'm wearing exactly one half of a costume? I try to scramble into my bra without moving my arm, an ergonomic impossibility that I somehow almost manage. 'Yew need enny help with 'at?'

I stick my head over the veil again, hissing for someone, anyone, to bounce Cletus from the vicinity. Janiece, a seasoned pro to her fingertips, sets her corndog down on the corner of her makeup case and jingles over.

'Well, hello there! How are you enjoying the show?' She gives the situation a bemused once-over and rubs a stray dab of mustard from the corner of her mouth with a jeweled nail.

Cletus takes his cap off and runs his fingers nervously through his sweaty bangs. 'Y'all ladies are sumthin' else! I ain't never seen no belly dancin' before, 'cept in movies.' He waves his cap at me but stares fixedly at Janiece – or, rather, at Janiece's breasts, which are magnificently displayed in a purple-and-silver sequined bra. 'She's aw-right, but you was muh fav'rit. Them cymbals you was playin' sounded mighty purty.'

'Yes, well, thank you! I'm glad you enjoyed my cymbals.' This draws snickers from the veil-holding dancers, but poor Cletus is oblivious. All the while Janiece is talking, she is positioning herself between Cletus and me so that I can finish putting my bra on without being seen. 'In fact, I'm going to play them again in just a minute, and you need to hurry on back to the tent so you don't miss a second!' In case he somehow missed the point, she grasps him firmly by the wrist and guides him back around the tent toward the front. As he rounds the corner, I hear a chorus of hoots and applause from a pack of carnies, coconspirators, waiting for the report, which booms through the night seconds later:

'Yeah, man, they're *all* back'are – an' thuh li'l one is *nekkid*!'

I have just enough time to fasten my clasps and make it onstage for the veil number. Eight weeks of sweat and practice for three minutes fifty of glory in the Chesterfield County Fair Community Events tent. Our stage, archly titled the Back Porch Stage, is between the Tuckahoe

Volunteer Rescue Squad booth and the Amelia County 4-H Chicken Coop. I swoop my veil flawlessly; Nadine executes her spins with tooth-grinding precision. Except for Blonde Babe getting her fall tangled in her veil during a tricky over-the-head maneuver, we look like seasoned pros. Kind of like the Mermettes, only dry. Indeed, if we were being observed from above, the veil number would look a *lot* like the Mermettes – a lot of walking in circles with veils overhead, cute 'pinwheel' segments where we all touch fingers, arms straight, veils floating, and a lot of Red Rover–type crossover moves, where two lines of belly dancers become one and then two again. It's pretty, with the chiffon veils and all, but we're hardly the Women of Selket. We're basically just walking around with pretty pieces of fabric fluttering behind us.

Besides, the Community Events Tent is hardly the Casbah, and I feel the tiniest bit sheepish as I peer through my veil at the few dozen people who have gathered to watch us. Even my parents have abandoned their 'don't ask, don't tell' stance on my passion for belly dancing to come out to the Community Events Tent for my debut. Perched uncomfortably on a bale of hay, they smile politely as we twirl our way across the stage. I know they mean well, but it only adds to my niggling self-doubts. I'm thirty years old and my parents are watching me perform in a *recital* for my *dance class*. Shouldn't I have done this when I was five? Years ago, when a couple of my fellow teachers took tap dancing lessons and twittered over lunch about their upcoming recital, I had thought, smugly, *how pathetic. May I never become a middle-class mommy*. At the time, my idea of fun was still crawling between seedy night spots and seedier men. I was convinced that I was too edgy and hip for something as strip-mall mundane as *dancing lessons*. Now they are the highlight of my week. How the mighty have fallen.

This is different, I tell myself every time that strip-mall feeling creeps in. *I am celebrating my heritage as a Lebanese American.* But I can only convince myself of this for so long. Then, inevitably, something – be it a glimpse of Blondie's thong under her pink chiffon peekaboo skirt, an ethnically incorrect rhinestone gaudily plopped in a middle-aged navel, or Sheva's suggestion that we flirtatiously untie an audience member's shoe after executing the ever-empowering 'crawl to your Sultan' move – reminds me that most of what I am learning is about as Lebanese as Arthur Murray. Tonight it's the poster hanging behind us. With every graceful twirl, I am reminded that at three o'clock on Saturday there will be a Pudding Eating Contest on this very stage.

Pig race or no pig race, there is victory in this evening for me. That's *my* non-dancing ass up there, dancing in front of an audience. That's *my* hardly-washboard thirty-year-old belly on display for all the world to see. And, when our three minutes fifty in the limelight of the Back Porch Stage are over, that's me (and Nadine) posing for snapshots in front of the sideshow banner, immortalized for all time as Tent Performers on the midway at the Chesterfield County Fair.

My belly dancing debut fails to sway my parents from their standard responses to my never-standard passions. Whether I am en route to Beijing or returning triumphantly from the Rolling Stones tour, they maintain the status quo. Tonight is no exception – my mom says something snide about the blonde's implants, and my dad offers me a bite of his funnel cake. There are some things that even the spectacle of your thirty-year-old daughter in *bedlah* can't change.

Later on that night, as we ride the Tilt-a-Whirl for free over and over, this will all seem funny. At the moment, though, as I kick up sawdust and picture Cletus's gap-toothed leer, I wonder if this is really the cultural pilgrimage I had envisioned when I became a belly dancer.

121

Do they even have carnies in Lebanon? 4-H? I am quite certain that, even if they have pudding, they do not eat it in contests. Later on, I push down my feelings of Arab inadequacy with mind-numbing mouthfuls of cotton candy, funnel cakes, and fried onions as we take advantage of performers' carte blanche on the midway. Just when the sugar and the lights have almost succeeded in making me forget what a lousy Lebanese girl I am, I spot two blue and gold . . . *minarets*? Towering over the carousel canopy, they defy the surrounding Americana, each of them topped with a small gold moon. Leaving Nadine and Janiece standing in line at the Blooming Onion stand, I shove my way through the crowd toward the crescent-topped towers.

It is not a mirage. Flanked by the minarets, a gargantuan fiberglass rendition of an oriental carpet swoops up, and over, and back down, under the watchful eyes of the monstrous Sultans and hawk-nosed villains painted on the backdrop. Above the Sultans, a bevy of buxom harem girls cast sultry glances at the riders as they sail past before making their descent. Blinking overhead, in giant blue letters made up of hundreds of tiny bulbs, are the words *ALI BABA'S FLYING CARPET*.

My Cleopatra eye makeup is running from the g forces, but I don't care. It's the closest I'm going to get to Middle Eastern culture tonight, so I'm going to ride it until they make me stop – and besides, it's free. I wave away the greasy-haired boy who comes to release my lap bar. I want to ride it again. As I sail over the midway, bits of body glitter blow off my arms and shimmer in the air before me. I look down, toward the teacups, and I see Janiece and Nadine looking for me. I wave my arms, sending more glitter flying, but they can't see me. My carpet is flying too high. I lean back in the seat and close my eyes. I'm lost, but I'm having fun here on my own little pilgrimage at the Chesterfield County Fair. I might as well enjoy the ride.

6

Putting It On and Taking It Off

*Or How My Belly Ended Up in the
Mall's Lost-and-Found*

Now that it looks like I'm going to be hanging around awhile, and, more important, that some of my hanging around is going to take place onstage, I decide it is time to invest in a costume of my own and come up with a 'dance name.' The name part is easy for a word nerd like me. After a few evenings of on-line research, I settle on Samira. I don't know of any other Samiras in the area, and the translation feels appropriate – 'she who tells stories in the night.' Never content to leave well enough alone, I tack on *el-Safi*, wishing as I often have that the folks at Ellis Island hadn't been so clumsy when they phoneticized my great-grandfather's name. *Safi* looks exotic, foreign, mysterious. *Soffee* just looks funny and begs to be mispronounced as 'Sophie.' Oh, well. At least they let him through.

The costume won't be as easy as the name. Two years of middle school home ec notwithstanding, I can't tie a decent knot, much less sew, which leaves homemade costumes out of the question. To be honest, I am not disappointed about this at all. I know that since I can't sew and I am still intimidated enough by Doris and Tammy and the other Girls in the Corner that I can't very well commission *them* to design my costume as many of Sheva's girls do. I have only one option left. As the woman herself would say, 'it's a sad story, but a true story.' That's right. I'm going to buy a real Egyptian belly dancing costume from Scheherezade.

The good fortune of being home to the country's biggest wholesaler of belly dancing supplies is not lost on the Richmond belly dancing community. We are one of the best-dressed scenes this side of Cairo. Any beginner with a pocketful of U.S. dollars can be the proud owner of a Madame Abla original within weeks of her first shimmy . . . and this is to say nothing of the seasoned dancers, Lucy's troupe mates and traveling companions, who frequently turn up at the Selket *haflas* in eye-popping painted-on concoctions that are actually stitched on their bodies by Cairo's hottest designers. Pity the poor non-Virginia dancers who must mail-order, or wait for Lucy to vend at a workshop near them. All we have to do is wait for the next Selket show, or one of Lucy's open house sales. And should the need for a *shemadan* hit on the odd Tuesday afternoon, one has only to phone ahead for a private visit to Lucy's boutique, conveniently located in the basement of her Rockville home.

By sheer providence, my costume craving has the good manners to coincide with Lucy's winter clearance sale. Nadine and I stop at Starbucks to fuel up for the inevitable feeding frenzy that will occur when a houseful of belly dancers meets with a tableful of half-priced *bedlah*. Ignoring the usual curious stares that her voluminous black cape, stiletto boots, and Tuareg jewelry attract, Nadine selects an adorable teddy bear from a shelf of tchotchkes and presents it to me as a gift – 'for puttin' up with me an' all; I know I ain't right.' As we sip our coffee and nibble on brownies at the counter, I glare back protectively at every passing shopper who does a double-take at Nadine's attire. I feel empathy for Nadine, surrounded as she is in class by housewives and office girls. The stares she gets at Sheva's are worse than the ones I used to get in St Anthony's religion class, a lone white city kid in a sea of buttoned-down Americanized Lebanese. Any thought that the belly dance community would somehow be more open-minded, more exotic, more accepting of the alternative runs up against a brick wall when confronted with the Regis-and-Rosie reality of the average suburban belly dancer. Ethnically speaking, Nadine's Berber necklaces run rings around Debbie's rhinestone choker – but somehow the other dancers perceive *Nadine* as the odd one out. Go figure.

If other belly dancers think Nadine is odd, I wonder what other Rockvillians think of Lucy. Twenty minutes west of Richmond, as we drive past the Food Lion, the riding tack store, and several tiny farmhouses set back from the road, it strikes me that most of the residents of this quiet little town have no idea what lurks down that dirt road off State Route 771.

We pull up to the front yard of Lucy's house, already crowded with cars sporting plates from Maryland, North Carolina, even Georgia. The swingset on the lawn and the house's homey exterior belie what waits inside. To the tune of *Wash ya Wash*, dozens of belly dancers sip hibiscus tea, nibble on triangles of pita smeared with baba ghanouj, and shop. Tables laden with *bedlah*, *beledi* dresses, veils, and caftans line every wall of the first floor, and the sound of excited chatter can be heard coming from the basement as well. Dancers in various states of undress are running up and down the stairs to the makeshift dressing room on the second floor with arm-loads of costumes to try and to buy. In the middle of it all, seated at a cluttered telephone table with a receipt pad and a credit card scanner, Lucy directs traffic and racks up the sales.

'There is a veil that goes with that!' She is calling to a tiny redheaded woman who is already halfway up the stairs. 'The peach costume, the one with the cutouts – it has a peach veil, a circular one, that got mixed in with the skirts!' Then, to an African American woman directly behind her that I don't know how she sees: 'Those harem pants are twenty percent off! Only the lurex ones! Not the chiffon!' The whole time she's supervising and shouting, she is writing up a receipt for three complete costumes, absolutely gorgeous bra and belt sets – one green, one red, and one baby pink – that are being purchased by Vicki, sister of Laura with the grapevine tattoo. 'I'm spending my equity,' she says nonchalantly as she makes out a check for eight hundred dollars. In line behind her is an entire troupe from the beach, all buying eighty-dollar flying skirts and matching *choli* tops. I begin adding figures in my head. The amount of money in just the present line alone is daunting. I immediately begin to wish I was in the belly dancing costume business. The sale from one full costume alone would gross more than I make in a week teaching. It's overwhelming.

I help myself to a cup of hibiscus tea and get down to the business of browsing. I know that the amount of time I have to shop is going to depend largely on Nadine's mental health at any given moment. She doesn't generally do well with crowds, and there are certain dancers who, for reasons that are not entirely clear, make her even more skittish than usual. Then again, there are a couple of dancers – Rosie and Susan, in particular – who have a calming effect on her. There is something to be said for an unshakeable air of blasé serenity. It can be catching. I hope for the best and begin leafing through a tableful of Lurex veils.

It occurs to me that I have absolutely no idea what I am

looking for – a daunting realization, to say the least. I feel like one of the awestruck newbies we used to get in the tattoo shop. They would stand in the lobby and gape at the hundreds of flash designs on the wall, flummoxed, unable to choose. Inevitably, they would leave with something incredibly ludicrous, instantly regrettable, and altogether permanent etched in their flesh – a dancing carrot, a flying cat, a naked lady straddling a hot dog. I tell myself that I am lucky that *bedlah* are removable by nature. As if on cue, an Asian girl strolls past wearing a low-cut beaded number the color of a highway cone. I try not to grimace and keep browsing.

I'm able to rule about half of the costumes right out on the 'my cup will inevitably runneth over' theory. If I can't fit my closed fist comfortably in a cup, then I'm not going to be able to fit my boob in it, either. This means good-bye for almost all of the silver bras, two red ones, a number of pretty rhinestone ones, and an absolutely eye-popping black one with gold fringe and epaulets. I follow a busty older lady around for about fifteen minutes, hoping she'll put down the gorgeous emerald set she's got draped over her arm, but no luck. After rounding up several videos, a few CDs, and a *ghawazee* dress, she heads for Lucy's checkout line with the green costume still hanging at her elbow.

Nadine comes up from the basement sporting a metal cage bra with multicolored rhinestones. It's fantastic. It looks like it was made from pieces from a carnival ride – just my style. Of course, I would probably line it with opaque fabric or wear it over something besides my bare skin, which is the look Nadine has chosen, but no matter. Without even trying, I can tell that it won't pass the cup test – and if sequins and fabric are unforgiving, I know a metal cage is not going to offer any give at all. I sigh and go back to the table of costumes, figuring that perhaps a few more have rotated down from the dressing room.

I find a white one that looks to be my size, but I can't even bring myself to try it on. Forget Lebanese; I'm pale for a *white* girl. Casper the Friendly Belly Dancer isn't exactly the look I'm going for. Carol comes down from the dressing room with an armload of rejects, and I scoop up a red one and a seafoam green one that is saved from being downright annoying by a slightly iridescent sheen that makes it look almost like mermaid scales. I locate the belts that match them and head up the stairs.

In the dressing room, which actually looks to be a guest room, ten or so mostly nude women wriggle in and out of beaded bras, velvet *beledi* dresses, and sequined gowns. Redheaded Joyce from Lucy's class is inspecting her reflection in the mirror; she is wearing a forest green form-fitting dress with strategically placed designs made of sheer netting down the front. Next to her, a woman who appears to be about her age or maybe even older is wriggling into a black bra hung with multicolored strands of beads. I am sick with envy. Such a bra! And it has a belt to match! I want it. Surely she won't actually buy it.

'Ooh, Mary,' says Joyce, shaking her head at the bra. 'That is just the tackiest thing I ever saw!'

'I know,' Mary says, peering through her pink-framed glasses at the mirror. She shimmies her shoulders gamely and watches the multicolored fringe sway to and fro. 'It's tacky and disgusting, isn't it?'

'Mmmm-hmmm,' Joyce nods, and though I'd like to hope this means I'll get a shot at the bra, it doesn't sound at all like they don't like it. In fact, the tackier they declare it to be, the more it sounds like they absolutely love it. I am learning something very important about belly dancer fashion, I think. Apparently subtlety is not a plus. Fine by me. But too bad I didn't see that tacky bra first.

I slip out of my T-shirt and sports bra and position the red costume bra over my chest. It fits, sort of, but it does absolutely nothing for me. No lift, no push, no va-va-voom. Besides, the cups have a weird elliptical shape to them, sort of crunched down and narrow. My boobs look like a couple of disinterested gravy boats in drag. I take it off quickly. I hoist the green one up and position my boobs inside the cups. It takes a little smooshing, but it fits pretty well. The cups are nice and close together, so there is a forced cleavage thing going on that's pretty flattering, too. I turn sideways and check the profile. Not too bad. This could work. It's a start, I tell myself. Your first costume doesn't have to set any records. Good enough is good enough.

The price for the set, bra and belt together, is $235 on sale. It's quite a deal, considering, but not such a bargain considering the limits imposed by the color. Seafoam green? What color skirt will I need? Baby pink might work, I think, or something in lavender . . . it's not exactly versatile . . . maybe Carol would know? I look around, hoping to see someone like Susan or Vicki, someone safe and familiar who might be willing to tell me what would look really tacky and disgusting with a seafoam fringed bra. I decide to venture downstairs.

Seafoam doesn't know from tacky and disgusting compared to what I see when I step into the hall. A skinny blonde girl is scurrying up the stairs, her lithe form practically swimming in a *bedlah* that would be three sizes too big for her at least – that is, if *bedlah* ran in sizes. She is holding the belt together at the side, but there are a good eight inches of overlap to contend with. The cups of the bra are smooshed under her arm, but it's easy to see that beneath the smoosh there is nothing holding them up. It's quite obviously not for her . . . and it's just as obviously for me.

I suppose now would be the time to mention that this costume is multicolored. It doesn't have multicolored *fringe* like the one Mary is trying on; it doesn't have multicolored *rhinestones* like Nadine's cage – it's *multicolored*. Each color of the rainbow, and then some, claims equal space in the color scheme of this bra and belt. It is a red-and-blue-and-green-and-yellow-and-pink-and-purple costume. There is absolutely no dominant color. It is encrusted with sequins and dripping with fringe. It looks like the fair, like rides and sideshows and candy apples and cotton candy all smashed together and made into a bra and belt. It is the tackiest, most disgusting costume in the entire world. I must have it.

I unsubtly block the door and make the girl promise to give me next dibs on the costume before I let her come in to get her clothes. I hover around her as she pulls it off, hopping expectantly in my sock feet and underwear. I know I look like a total freak, but I don't care. I absolutely have to have that costume. Wrapping the belt around my hips, I'm met with roughly five inches of extra belt, but that's fixable; even a nonsewing dancer like myself knows that too much can be fixed much more easily than too little. Then the moment of truth. Wriggling my arms into the straps, I give a quick shrug and a shimmy to adjust my boobs in the cups. They fit with a little extra jiggling room – nothing a couple of push-up pads won't fix, and that's something I can do with mere safety pins. Reaching around back, I feel for the clasps. Again, we've got some overlap, but it's nothing a little altering can't cure. I resolve to get over my fear of Doris within the week. This costume makes me feel like the queen of the midway. All I need is a canvas banner.

'Well, I declare! If that isn't the tackiest thing I ever saw.' Mary has her hand to her forehead like my costume hurts her to look at. She turns her head as if she's seen something disturbing. I am ecstatic.

Joyce crosses her arms and makes a *tsk*ing sound. 'That thing is just a terrible eyesore.' She shakes her head from side to side. 'Look at all those colors.' I turn around, once, twice, beaming in my gaudy armor. 'You're not actually going to buy that awful thing, are you?'

I nod, grinning like an idiot. This costume isn't even on sale; it's one of the new ones. I don't care. I have to have it.

'Well, *phoo*,' she says, scooping up the green cutout dress and stamping her foot. 'You think of me if you ever decide to sell it!'

'And you leave it to me in your will when you do get it,' Mary tells Joyce. 'Along with your orange one and that one with the taxicabs on it.' *Taxicabs?* Mary and Joyce, climbing back into their unassuming slacks and sweaters, look like two soignée grandmothers on their way to Miss Morton's Tea Room for cucumber sandwiches. It's hard to picture either of them shimmying the night away in a taxicab *bedlah*. I wonder how many times I've been sitting right next to a belly dancer and didn't even know it? My dental hygienist could be a belly dancer. My third-grade teacher. The nice lady I always see at World Cup doing crosswords. And me. There's not a keyhole-shaped doorway or a low table in sight, but I don't mind. I think these ladies could hold their own with Nejla just fine.

I have to admire myself in the rainbow *bedlah* just a little more before I take it off. In Lucy's guest room mirror, I look absolutely ridiculous, in this too-big rainbow contraption, my cotton underpants, and cat's-eye glasses. But I feel fantastic. I feel like a glamorous and yet slightly seedy carnival midway dancer, decked out to rival the Flying Bobs just outside the tent. I feel like Little Egypt, not the real one from way, way back but the one from the Coasters song, with a ruby on her tummy and a diamond as big as Texas on her toe. I beam at my reflection. Now all I need is a picture of a cowboy tattooed on my spine saying 'Phoenix, Arizona, 1949' and I'll be loaded for bear. I practically skip downstairs to give Lucy my check for four hundred dollars. It's more than my rent, but I consider it an investment in my future happiness – and it's already paying off in spades.

'That's it, that's it, you're perfect. Now lift your arm just a little.' I am standing in front of a pale purple canvas backdrop beneath an array of lights and reflective umbrellas. Several enormous graduation and wedding portraits loom on the opposite wall, where Nadine is standing and chomping on her fingers as she waits her turn. We are here at the portrait studio in Chesterfield Towne Center Mall having our publicity portraits done. Stan the photographer had been recruited to do the on-location shots at Sheva's show, and, sensing a good thing when he saw it, offered a special deal to any of Sheva's students who stopped by the studio on this particular evening for more 'formal' shots – in other words, shots taken *not* with a line of edgy belly dancers tapping their feet behind you and eleven minutes until your next costume change. It sounded like a winner to me, so I packed up my new costume and headed to the mall – and here I am now, posing my little heart out.

'Flip your hair off your shoulder. There you go. That's it.' Debbie jumps into frame long enough to straighten the fingers on my right hand and fluff my hip scarves out a little. Thank God for Debbie or I would be standing here like I was posing for my driver's license photo. Every pose I've struck has been her idea. Debbie has already posed for her shots; Nadine is going to go after me. While Stan is snapping away, Lexie arrives with an armload of costume changes as well. There are enough of us here to feel like an event, but not enough to necessitate rushing – a perfect turnout.

As he snaps, Stan tells us how much more interesting we are than his usual subjects – babies, graduates, and prize-winning show dogs. He clicks a few frames and tells us he never wanted to be a studio photographer. *Click*. *Click*. He mentions an ex-wife who left him heavily in debt after running off with another woman. *Click*. They had a pineapple farm in Hawaii, but it was in her name; he was unceremoniously given a plane ticket to the mainland and left with the clothes on his back. *Click*. *Click*. *Click*. Perhaps we'd heard of her. She's a moderately famous television actress. *Click*. I grow more uncomfortable with each detail. After years of AA meetings, you'd think I would have gotten over 'too much information anxiety,' but other people's details still make me antsy. Debbie has to snap her fingers several times to remind me to smile; my expression is leaning more toward something between a flinch and an eye roll.

Once my turn is mercifully over, I retire to the makeup table in the corner of the room to remove the dangling beaded earrings that have been driving me batshit ever since I put them on. The mercy is short-lived, though, because Stan *follows me to the table* to finish telling me about his ex-wife and the pineapple farm. I nod absently as I unclip the earrings, unclasp the beaded necklace, wrest the dozens of too-small gold dime-store bangles from my arms. Nadine flits nervously behind me, peering over my shoulder into the makeup mirror, smudging her kohl-smudged eyes still further with a twitching fingertip. And Stan keeps on talking.

'You know,' he says, and his voice somehow sounds even creepier than it already sounded, 'I know this probably isn't the traditional way, you know, the way it's done, over in Egypt or wherever, but I think some shots without the top would look very exotic.'

Nadine about pokes her own eye out. I give Stan what I hope is a Miss Manners-style 'I *beg* your pardon' look in the makeup mirror, but he keeps on.

'I mean, they wouldn't be explicit or anything. You could kind of put your arm across in front of you, or your

133

hair or something, and it would be suggestive but not crude. It really would be very artistic, I think. You should consider it.'

'I don't think,' I say, measuring my words carefully, 'that I would be interested in posing for any pictures of that type.' Then, politely, if not a wee bit sarcastically, 'but thank you very much for the offer.' Nadine turns her head and snickers into the corner of her veil, but the tone is lost on Stan.

'Well, let me know if you change your mind. I'd love to do those shots.'

'Sure ya would,' Nadine mutters into her veil.

I roll my eyes and zip my jewelry into my makeup bag. Only when it's too late do I remember the retort I once heard offered as a comeback for the ill-informed 'do you strip' question – 'As much as I paid for this costume, and you want me to take it off?'

'Well, either you can tell Sheva or I can tell her.' In the Corner of the Room at Sheva's class on Monday, beneath the *doom tek tek* of Dr Mendez's *doumbek* and the wail of Sheva's scratchy old records, I am shocked at Susan's patently unblasé reaction to my snickering reportage of Stan's proposition. I had hoped for a wry comment, a commiseration along the lines of 'the nerve of him' – but what I didn't expect was a direct order to do something that I know is going to stir up no end of trouble.

'I'm sure he didn't mean anything by it,' I hedge, wishing I had kept my mouth shut. 'And he did ask politely. He wasn't pushy about it.'

'But the point is that he *asked*,' she insists, her green eyes flashing. 'He wouldn't ask a ballet dancer to take her tutu off. He wouldn't ask a flamenco dancer to show him her *maracas*. I'm just sick of it. Assholes like him need to get it through their fat heads that belly dancers aren't *strippers*.'

134

I lay my fat head on the table and wonder how I'm going to get myself out of this one. As annoyed as I was at Stan's proposition, I hardly think it warrants ratting him out to Sheva, which will almost certainly cost him his gig with her. So he's a little letchy. At least he was polite about it. Maybe if I put it off, Susan will forget about it.

'I'll talk to her,' I sigh. 'I'll talk to her next week.'

'You'll talk to her right now.' So much for that brilliant plan. Boy, do I *not* want to talk to Sheva about this right now. Boy, do I *not* want to talk to Sheva about this ever – but especially not right now, after Susan's reaction. I lift my head and look pleadingly at Susan.

'At least let me wait until I pick up my prints. I don't wanna have to go in there and face him after Sheva gets through with him!'

Susan narrows her eyes at me and shrugs. 'OK, fine. But if you haven't told her by Monday, I'm telling her.' She wiggles her fingers into the black elastic bands on her *zils* and stands up. As Sheva cranks up a crackly George Abdo *chiftetelli* number, Susan slams her *zils* rapid-fire about an inch from my left ear.

Tek a-tek-a-tek tek tek tek!

Raising her arms high above her head, she slides her head, first to the left, then the right, then left-right-left and glares at me one last time.

'And don't think I'm going to forget, because I'm *not*.'

Tek tek tek! She dances off to the far side of the room, shimmying her hips defiantly all the way. Just in case I didn't know I was screwed. I lay my head back down on the table and groan. *Doom* tek tek indeed.

'OK, remember. Don't say *anything* about the topless pictures.' I am already regretting my decision to bring Karen along to pick up my prints. Keeping her mouth shut is not her forte. But she promises anyway, and as we hurry through the mall toward the photo studio, my excitement about seeing my pictures grows.

I've always hated having my picture taken. From school portraits to candid shots snapped at parties and clubs, I always end up looking puffier than I want, my hair stringier, the circles under my eyes darker. Even the pictures we posed for after the show at the fair were a huge disappointment. Sure, I had a gorgeous costume on, my veil was pretty, my eyes heavily painted, but I winced when I saw them nonetheless. My stomach was too pale, my jawline too soft. Really the only thing I liked about them was the creepy painted sideshow banner that Nadine and I had trekked across the midway to pose underneath. 'Alive! Why?'

For all Stan's poor judgment, he had tried hard to get some good shots of me, and it looked like he did. When he let me check them out on the digital screen after he took them, they looked glamorous and professional. My hair was shiny and full, my skin glowed, my expression was sultry. I hardly recognized myself. My gratitude at his sincere and succesful effort at making me *look* like a glamorous belly dancer was the main reason I was hoping Susan would end up letting the topless incident slide. Besides, I might need more pictures someday. I didn't buy all that many prints, after all.

At the studio, Karen busies herself leafing through albums of wedding photos while the girl fetches my prints. Stan is, fortunately, out on a job. I look around at the photos on the walls, mostly brides, mostly younger than I, in blindingly white wedding gowns and flowing chiffon veils. I push down feelings of envy, of loneliness, of that-will-never-be-me. I was never the type of girly girl who planned elaborate wedding costumes in her head, but at the same time I had just assumed that one day Chris and I would be married. It felt inevitable. Now, though, I know that nothing is inevitable and that the unexpected can be counted on to happen when you least expect it. After all, look at me. I'm a belly dancer. *Besides*, I tell myself, *my veil is cooler*. The girl comes out of the back room and hands me a large manila envelope, which I eagerly tear into with Karen peering over my shoulder.

The pictures are just as gorgeous as they were on the digital screen. My hair shines a deep reddish brown, my sequins sparkle, my fringe glimmers. Against the pale backdrop, my skin has a golden glow, fair but not un-attractively so. I look self-assured and graceful. I also look . . . skinny.

I hold the pictures closer, examining them against my memory of the screen the night we took them, and my memory of the body I see in the mirror every morning before I get dressed. The pooch that I am so proud of, my tiny belly dancer dome that means I've been practicing my undulations, is gone. In its place is a concave nothing-ness, a lack where there was once a perfect belly dancer tummy. You can almost see where it used to be. There isn't even a navel; like a Barbie doll, I have nothing but smooth, flat nothingness from my bra to my belt. My chest, already impressive, looks obscene with nothing below to balance it. I look like I am about to topple forward. My mouth is hanging open as I drop the pictures on the desk. I feel like I've been robbed.

'What's the matter?' The girl behind the desk is baffled.

'These pictures. They've been retouched.' I'm stunned. Did he think he was doing me a favor? Propositions are one thing, but stealing a belly dancer's belly is another entirely. That *rat*.

'No, they haven't.' She speaks with conviction. Tapping the receipt, she shakes her head emphatically. 'There's no kind of note on here about retouching them. We only do that if you ask us to.'

'Well, I didn't ask you to, and you *did*.' It only adds to the insult that, other than my missing belly, the pictures are fantastic. My first good pictures ever, and someone – albeit an oily, lecherous someone – deemed me fat enough to warrant unauthorized retouching.

'Maybe it's the lighting,' she offers obtusely. 'Sometimes different lighting will make you look bigger or smaller.'

I have just about had it with this little mall bunny and her defense of these obviously retouched prints. I lean in close and glare in what I hope is a threatening manner. 'Do I need to *show* you my stomach right now so that you can see that this is *not* what it looks like?'

She steps back, looking nervously at me and Karen, obviously dangerous, unpredictable city girls who have come out to the suburbs to cause trouble in her safe little mall. 'Um, no, we do offer a *guarantee* on our work, and if, ah, if you feel the prints are not what you wanted, we can redo them.' She pulls a yellow Post-it note from a pad by the register and sticks it to the receipt. I watch carefully as she writes, in big loopy mall-bunny handwriting, sneaking looks at me nervously in between words:

> *Stan: Customer is v/upset that you removed her belly! Please reprint from original shots – do not retouch – OK!*

I feel like a bottle of Dr Bronner's – *Do not dilute! OK! OK!* – but I am relieved to know that the photos can be salvaged and I can get my belly back. I'm also glad she didn't call my belly bluff, because in my one-piece (and apparently threateningly unmall-like) black sack dress, I would have had to show her a lot more than just my belly. After exacting a promise that the redone unredone photos will be ready by Wednesday, Karen and I retire to the food court for Dairy Queen ice creams and fries – State Fair style, of course, with salt and vinegar. As we nibble the greasy fries one after the other, Karen poses a very important question: 'How in th'hell you s'posed to *belly* dance if you ain't got no *belly*?'

138

Susan wasn't kidding when she said she wouldn't forget about the pictures. I skip class for a week – in fact, I use the time to sneak by the studio at closing time to pick up my prints without fear of running into Stan. I'm hoping that the extra time will work in my favor, but Susan's got my number. She tells Sheva the whole story that night as they're loading out – and Sheva calls the studio the next morning.

The next Monday, Sheva asks to see me in the kitchen. Usually when she asks to see someone in the kitchen, it's because they haven't paid that month – and I know I have – or she's about to book them for a paying gig, dancing for someone who's looked her up in the yellow pages for a belly gram or a theme party. Since I know I'm not up to theme party snuff yet, I'm terrified. I know what this is about. I fidget with my coin belt while I wait for Sheva to finish handing the reins over to that traitor Susan. I imagine news of Stan being fired, Stan out on the street – first the pineapple lesbian and now this. I have enough of the Buddhist in me to feel bad about being a part of anyone's downfall, even inadvertently. I am leaning on the counter, feeling sorry for Stan, when Sheva sails into the kitchen.

'Susan told me that you had some *concerns* about something that was said at the photography studio,' she says in her customary vague way. 'So I called the studio and I spoke to Stan.' Here it comes. I picture Stan walking down Midlothian Turnpike with his head down, his photography equipment bundled in a bandanna on the end of a stick. Sheva pats me on the arm and looks sincerely into my eyes. 'He wanted me to tell you that he is *terribly* sorry that you misunderstood him. He has no idea how you got the idea that he was proposing anything – *indecent*. He was just as shocked as he could be. And he's very, *very* sorry that you misunderstood him.' There's that word again. Sheva smiles and clasps her hands; everything is all smoothed out. 'And, after I talked to him, I was sure that's all it was,' she adds, as if she is still trying to convince herself. 'It was just an unfortunate misunderstanding.' Maybe she thinks that misunderstanding is like a Muslim divorce and saying it three times will make it so. It seems to work for her, and she sails serenely back out to oversee the hip circles.

In the kitchen, my pity for Stan melts like a Dairy Queen cone in the Sahara. Where his proposition was merely annoying, his insistence that it didn't happen is infuriating. A *misunderstanding*? I wonder which part I misunderstood – 'without' or 'the top'? So now he's sitting pretty, still on the job, still probably able to count on the gig for next year's recital, and meanwhile Sheva thinks I'm a paranoid flake on some kind of Andrea Dworkin witchhunt! I am seething! I untie my hip sash and jam it into my dance bag. I'm in no mood for shimmies. I'm going home.

Susan and Nadine follow me out to the parking lot. I really don't feel like talking about it, but I stop to be polite. Nadine gets her feelings hurt so easily. She offers me a cigarette, and I graciously accept.

'I know Sheva can be kind of gullible sometimes,' Susan apologizes, 'but I didn't think she'd take that asshole's word over yours and mine.'

'I was there,' Nadine pipes up. 'I can tell her what he said! I'll tell her right now!' She starts to stub her cigarette out on the asphalt, but I stop her. I suppose, in a roundabout way, I got my wish. Stan is off the hook, the controversy is over, and the only casualty is my own credibility. I just know I don't want to drag it out any further. I thank them both for their concern and throw my bag in the trunk. I feel betrayed, by Susan for telling, by Stan for lying, and by Sheva for believing him. The only person who comes out clean is the fiercely loyal Nadine, and, as she's fond of reminding me, I *know* she ain't right. As much as I want to belong as a belly dancer, sometimes I feel that same hovering-on-the-outskirts feeling I've gotten so many other places – at St Anthony's, on the Sunset Strip, at the tattoo parlor. I feel let down, not 'a part of,' and a dozen other self-helpy buzzwords that basically translate into '*this sucks*.' I start to head home, but then I think better of it and cut a left and make for Karen's. It feels like another couch-lying, cat-holding, secondhand pot smoke kind of night. It's just like old times.

7

Dancing Sheik to Sheik

Dating Adventures in Arabia,
Part One

It's three in the morning and I should be asleep. I should be, but instead I am fooling around on my newer, faster computer that my brother assembled for me to replace the archaic Mac I had been using. On this computer, graphics materialize in seconds, searches take mere moments, and, Allah help me, for the first time since signing onto my first Internet account in 1995, I am actually curious and net-addicted enough to try out the chat feature. After suffering a huggy-bear overload in the twelve-step chat room and sating my morbid curiosity in 'HairyM4M,' 'MarriedButLooking,' and 'HouswifeHomeAlone,' I stumble on what looks like a net-addicted belly dancer's Valhalla: 'Arab Chat.' I quickly sign off, sign back on under my belly dancer handle, SamiraSafi, and click my way into the room.

You have just entered room 'Arab Chat.'

BedouinQ8i: any girl from skaka? lol
Super Hot Arab: bedwin lol
NOVAFORMOSA: super, don't u mean supa?
BedouinQ8i: enzain 3ar3ar?
Super Hot Arab: ama supaa not now. if there was a jaddwi
    girl or lebanese ama be supaa hot
Oo iillusion oO: Anytime :-)
Super Hot Arab: Do u have a bf?
VV ANANY VV: Bedoui loo kl wa7ed y7e65 fee profile
    MALE welaa FEMALE kan ert7t

I'm disappointed to find that, with the exception of a
few 'Yallas' and 'Mar3ebeks,' it's pretty much the same as
any other chat room – a meat market for lonely twenty-
year-old boys . . . and one lonely just-turned-thirty-one
belly dancer. I learn early on to keep that number to
myself; when I naively respond to one of the pop-up IM
(instant message) boxes on my screen with my *actual* age,
my disappointed suitor responds, '31? *Akh laaa, wallah*,
you are already expired!' Two mopey, whiny, Oh-my-
God-I'm-over-the-hill days later, though, I am back on
Arab Chat until the wee hours, filling my screen with IMs
from OneHotQ81, ArabPrince4U, and SaudiPlaya, and
my download file with jpegs sent by the contenders. The
over-there men, mostly middle-aged and desperate, send
studio photos with romantically fuzzed edges, their high
foreheads and big brown eyes pleading and lonely, like
Keane urchins all grown up. The Arab Americans are
younger, better looking, and less polite. They send IMs
full of innuendo, asking for phone numbers and visits, and
attach snapshots from nightclubs and parties, swathed in
gold chains, hair slicked back, their arms usually draped
over a Lycra-clad girl I'm told to ignore – 'she's my *cousin*,'
I'm told more than once.

Karen takes it all in with a grain of salt, my latest
obsession, my most recent quirk. 'What's with all them

threes and sevens?' she asks, sipping a Coke as we spend a rainy evening on-line.

'The numbers are for sounds we don't have letters for,' I explain vaguely. I'm not too sure about them, myself, but there are an awful lot of them flying around Arab Chat at any given moment. Karen nods.

'You mean like *kkkkkhhhhhhkkkhhhhh*,' she offers, the sound coming from deep in her throat.

'Yeah, like that.'

'Is that a three or a seven? Or maybe a five?'

'I dunno. It sounds kind of like a seven to me . . . don't you think?'

She shrugs and we return to the chat, trading jibes with IraqiPrins and 1Sheik2Lov. 'Put a seven in there,' Karen urges, but I demur. As we sit, waiting for their next innuendo, the omnipresent IM alert pops up in the corner of the screen. I click it, reminded of Dorothy Parker's response to the doorbell – 'What fresh hell is this?' I am greeted by a new handle, one I've seen in Arab Chat but only on the list of those logged on, never as an active chatter.

Fahed007: Marhaba
SamiraSafi: Marhaba
Fahed007: You are belly dancer? In Richmond?

Uh oh. Looks like I've been found out. My profile, while suitably vague, does list a city and includes mention of both teaching and belly dancing. OK, maybe it isn't vague enough. But the Internet is a big place, a global place, and the last thing I expected was to encounter a Richmond Fahed in Arab Chat.

I hesitate, trying to remember what the Faheds at St Anthony's look like. Are they cute? Are any of them my age? The only person I can picture is old Mister Fahed with the hairy back. I quickly click my way into Fahed007's profile.

Name: Fahed007 – the leopard from the land of oil!
DOB: 7-15-76
Location: Richmond, VA and Dubai
Occupation: part-time student, part time millionaire
Quote: In a world of reality, I am a dream – too good to be true!

Even without the giveaway quote, I would have cause to doubt the rest. I am quickly learning that I am one of the few people naive enough not to lie on my AOL profile – directly, anyway. While I don't lie outright, after the 'expired' comment I did remove my birth date from my profile. Whoever Fahed007 is, he almost certainly *isn't* a millionaire. But he also almost certainly isn't Lebanese – the fierce nationalism that is the hallmark of the Middle Eastern man would preclude any Lebanese from posing as an Emerati, no matter how wealthy.

Fahed007: You are still there wallah?

'Well, answer him, Annie,' Karen urges. Easy for her to say. But in the past week I have made the acquaintance of less promising Arabs – witness poor Emad, the Egyptian transplant who could not come up with a more appealing photo attachment than himself in a tuxedo, serving meatballs on a hotel buffet line. Even a phony millionaire seems more appealing.

SamiraSafi: Yes, I am a belly dancer in Richmond. Where are you in school?
Fahed007: I am in engineering school at VCU to help my father in family business. Do you have picture?

'Well, he don't beat around the bush,' Karen exclaims. 'Make him send you one first.' She learns fast. I fire back a tit-for-tat request and am almost immediately greeted with the chime of an e-mail appearing in my inbox. Part-time millionaire or no, at the very least he's wealthy enough to afford a fast computer. I click open his e-mail and there, in all his *thobe*-wearing, headdressed glory, is the very un-Lebanese, clearly *Khaleegy* Fahed. In the photo, he is seated at a dining room table in front of a china cabinet filled with unassuming knickknacks. I don't pay much attention to the room; it fades behind the stark whiteness of Fahed's *thobe*, the exotic allure of his red-and-white checked *kaffiyeh*, the deep brown of his eyes . . . and then, of course, that nose. It's Prince Ali in the flesh. I am smitten.

'Huh. Fahed. *Towel*-hed is more like it,' Karen snorts, obviously not as impressed as I am with my new pen pal's unibrowed charisma. But then, *she's* not the belly dancer he's chatting up.

'I dunno, I think he's kinda cute, don't you?'

Karen squints at the screen, tilting her head as she examines him. 'Oh, I guess so, Annie,' she says resignedly. 'He's kinda sexy, in a scary Not-Without-My-Daughter kinda way. Go 'haid and send him a picture.'

I quickly upload Stan's best shot and fire it off his way. Then we lean back and wait for the response.

Fahed007: Ah wallah you are so beautiful! So come over here and dance for me!

'OK, now what?' I ask Karen. She shrugs. We both sit, staring at the screen like a couple of idiots. This was all fun and games when they were random, average-looking Arab men from thousands of miles away. Now I've got one on the line who's handsome and local and I don't have a clue where to go with it. I mean, obviously I'm not going to rush over to wherever he is and dance for him . . . and where is he, anyway? I trot out my chat-room deception skills in order to learn more about my would-be Sheik.

SamiraSafi: I need to know where you are if I'm going to do that.

Fahed007: Do you know Midlothian Turnpike? Cloverleaf Mall?

'Oh, yeah,' Karen says, pulling a dumb-dumb face. 'He's one of those millionaires from over by Cloverleaf Mall. You know the ones.' I roll my eyes. The only thing I know about Cloverleaf Mall is that you're as likely to get knocked in the head as you are to get any shopping done, and, outside of boasting Richmond's only Frederick's of Hollywood and an impressive array of airbrushed T-shirt vendors, it has been something of a no-fly zone since the mid-1980s. Part-time millionaire, indeed.

SamiraSafi: Midlothian Turnpike is a long way from Dubai.

Fahed007: My apartment is nice. My father wanted to buy me a big house to stay while in college, but I didn't want so much trouble of a house.

A likely story. I begin to imagine he may be one of the swarthy guys who run the Philly Steak and Fries in the Cloverleaf Mall food court. He's cute, but a guy this young and this full of crap promises to be nothing but trouble. I make a couple of more polite comments regarding nothing much and then say I have to go.

Fahed007: So you will give me your number and I'll call you.

SamiraSafi: No need to do that – you'll see me on-line –

And before he can protest, I quickly click the screen shut and close the connection, vanishing like a desert oasis. For the rest of the night, his true identity is the subject of much speculation and amusement. By the time Karen heads back to Lakeside, he has been a shoe salesman, a Taco Bell burrito wrapper, a Hezbollah terrorist under an assumed identity, and a T-shirt airbrush artist. We even consider the possibility that the photo may not even be him, in which case he might also be a twelve-year-old Milwaukee girl, a retired Teamster, or an FBI agent keeping tabs on possible Muslim extremist sympathizers, in which case my name is now on one more list. As anonymous as the Internet is, in many ways it's a lot more public than I'd like to believe – something I became painfully aware of the first time I ran a Google search for my e-mail address. Who knew? Not me all those nights I was spilling my guts in the pseudo-anonymous glow of the alt.recovery Usenet groups.

But for all my joking around, there is a part of me that wants to believe that Fahed007 really is a part-time millionaire and that fate has him studying engineering in Richmond, Virginia, simply as a pretext for meeting me, the half-Lebanese belly dancer of his dreams. Ever since the breakup with Chris, Karen has been drumming it into my head that everything happens for a reason, and maybe all of this has just been part of a grand conspiracy to lead me to my true destiny in life – a palace in the desert and a nursery full of little brown babies. I allow myself the guilty pleasure of projecting my Princess Jasmine fantasy onto my ongoing e-mail correspondence with Fahed, imagining marble floors, first-class flights, a smooth – if not altogether wholehearted – conversion to Islam, and a life spent skulking around the *souks* in a long black veil. My obsessiveness swings into full force in light of this potential future.

Tolerant to a degree, Karen finally begins to worry when I tell her that after some serious thought I've decided I'd be willing to settle for third-favorite wife, but no lower. To me, favorite wife carries a few too many expectations and obligations when you're part of a field of many, but a second- or third-favorite position would afford you a hefty allowance, a lot of nice trips, and plenty of free time to pursue hobbies with no bossy husband breathing down your veil. Beyond third-favorite, though, would just be insulting, and the wifely duties and expectations might be less than pleasant. I have heard stories. Karen asks me repeatedly to assure her that I am only kidding. I am . . . mostly.

While I know the empowered woman in me ought to bristle at the idea of life as a married *Muslima*, swathed in black and forbidden the freedom to which I know I am just as entitled as any man, the fantasy has a disturbing appeal. I think that it's partly due to my lingering bitterness over being dumped so hard by the erstwhile love of my life. As much as I want to believe in the Western ideal of the life partnership based on mutual love, respect, and devotion, I can't. I did once, and I got punched in the teeth. I know that, were I ever to meet another man who promised me I was the one, the only, his match made in heaven for all eternity, my gut response would be *yeah, right. Tell me another one. On second thought, don't go any further, because I've seen this movie before and I don't like how it ends.*

With a guy like Fahed, though, everything would be on the table. I'd know what was expected of me and what I could expect from him. Without any messy emotional entanglement or pie-in-the-sky promises of everlasting fidelity, I'd be free to live my life without that feeling that I was forever waiting for the inevitable punch in the teeth. I could pick back up where I left off on my schedule – marriage, children, home ownership (heck, I could upgrade to *palace* ownership without missing a beat) – and have the added cachet of finally being *more* Arab than the St Anthony's kids. Self-haters! Where are their veils?

Unfortunately, before I can sign my life away to the *fatwa*, I am probably going to have to eventually meet Fahed in person. Why do things always have to be so complicated? I have gotten comfortable flirting with him on-line, and now I have to go and complicate things by having to *leave* my *apartment*? The idea! So far, having a cyber-boyfriend has been nothing if not ideal – there are mash notes waiting for me every time I log onto AOL, I've got a handsome photo I can show my friends, and I never even have to shave my legs. And, as an added bonus, he can be every bit the controlling Arab man and *I don't have to do anything he says*! He tells me I have to stop belly dancing – 'I will not discuss the idea of you dancing before other men!' I agree, then log off and head to Sheva's. I log on at three a.m. after hitting a late-night AA meeting and dropping in on a GWAR rock show at Twister's; he asks where I've been and of course I've been in bed asleep like a good girl, hidden away from the evils of the big bad world! Who's to know? One day, after I post a casual picture of myself on my cheesy AOL do-it-yourself Web page, he fires off a curt e-mail: 'You will not wear those glasses again. This is the way it must be now.'

'Tell him if you can't wear the glasses, he can't wear the towel,' Karen suggests when I inform her of this, Fahed's latest order. I don't dare take her advice, but I don't take off my glasses, either. Sure, I take the picture off the Web site; no need to be rash about things. Being obedient is easy on-line. Everybody's happy. In this text-only relationship, we can be everything we want each other to be. But it can't last forever.

I decide that, if only for my own sake, I'll need to start off slow. I give him my phone number one night when we've been IMing back and forth for a while and I'm tired of typing. Ten long minutes after I log off, the phone rings. Feeling stupid and giddy like an eighth-grade girl, I pick it up and try to sound casual, like good-looking transplanted oil sheiks call me all the time.

'Hello?'

'*Marhaba* . . . It is me!'

'Oh . . . (pause) . . . *hi*.' I am out of my element on the phone. The instant message has been a courtship boon for writerly nerds like myself, and responses like 'Oh, hi' are just the reason why. 'Oh, hi' indeed, first impressions being what they are.

'So you'll tell me your address.'

'No, that wasn't part of the deal.'

'You'll tell me your address and I will come over and we will go for a drive in my car.'

I know from our e-mail correspondence that he has, or at least claims to have, a red Ford Thunderbird (license plates reading 'DIE4UAE,' for those of you keeping score at home). The T-Bird is a point of great pride for him, as he and the group of Gulf guys he runs around with are quite fond of American sports cars. To hear him talk, they purchase sports cars with the same aplomb that my friends and I purchase CDs. They go out for the afternoon, hopping from car lot to car lot, eventually settling on one particularly ostentatious American-made car with turbo this and chrome that. Then one of them purchases it and they spend the rest of the day tearing around town in it, eventually growing bored with it and heading out to find another.

Were I a gearhead, or even someone for whom the amount of money one can spend in a day acts as an aphrodisiac, I would right now be giving Fahed detailed directions from Midlothian Turnpike to my front door. But I am a more complicated wannabe Arab nerd belly dancer than that. Money and sports cars do little for me. Hook noses and *thobes* are another story entirely, and *oy*, that *kaffiyeh* – but as tempted as I am, I know that allowing him to come to my apartment at this hour and at this point would mean certain death for my dreams of little unibrowed babies. So, after about a half hour of verbal eyelash batting, I excuse myself and end the call.

If dating was bad, and sober dating was worse, Muslim

dating is the absolute pits. Every reply has to be carefully weighed before I open my mouth; every one of his deceptively casual questions is a land mine that could blow me clear out of the running for third-favorite wife or beyond. I am walking a delicate line – I have to keep the conversation interesting enough to keep him coming back for more, but at the same time I have to keep it chaste enough to keep him coming back for more. I see now why so many Muslims depend on arranged marriages. Courtship is almost impossible. For me, anyway. Maybe, if you were not a far-from-virginal tattooed Catholic recovering alcoholic belly dancer with a smart mouth, it would be easier. Too bad I didn't meet him when I was twelve.

Somehow, I do OK. He calls again the next day, and the next, and on through the week, and I am actually able to keep from running him off with honest replies or anything rash like that. I am mollified; this telephone dating is even better than the on-line dating. I look forward to his nightly phone calls – his deep voice, exotic accent, and repeated half-English, half-Arabic descriptions of how pretty I am. I am starting to wonder how I am going to fit 'Anne Soffee bin Saif bin Nasser bin Saif' on my luggage tags for all of those jet-setting vacations when he throws yet another monkey wrench into my Queen Noor fantasies.

Fahed007: If you are not going to let me visit your house, you will meet me at Cloverleaf Mall. I must meet you. I can wait no longer!

I knew it was bound to come to this. I have bought as much time as I possibly can, between coy phone calls and vague e-mails, and now I have to pony up. Negotiations are fast and furious; no, I won't meet you tonight, not any night, in fact – daytime only! OK, Saturday afternoon then. But we're not to leave the mall! I can't believe these demands are coming from *my* mouth – Miss Hop-on-a-Harley-on-Hollywood-Boulevard. I am queen of the hypocrites. But, I tell myself, the ends justify the means. I have the nagging feeling that the mere fact that I am agreeing to meet him at all is labeling me a hopeless *sharmouta* in his upper-class Muslim world view; however, I am also starting to feel like the phone-and-e-mail setup is wearing a bit thin with Fahed. I am torn. Do I go ahead and meet him and risk being labeled a decadent westerner, or do I refuse and risk him losing interest in me completely?

Fahed007: OK, 4 p.m. Saturday at Cloverleaf Mall it is.
SamiraSafi: Where would you like to meet?
Fahed 007: Don't worry, *wallah*, I will HAUNT for you!!!

To my mother's credit, she has taken all of my boyfriends with a Gibraltar-sized grain of salt. From my high school first love, Andy, who lived in an unheated squat and did laundry half a dozen times during the two years we dated, to renowned punk auteur Legs McNeil, with whom I had a brief Pygmalion-like relationship during my attempted music journalism days, she has usually kept her counsel save for the odd biting comment. About Legs, she casually mentioned during a coast-to-coast phone call, 'I went in your room and found his picture in *SPIN* magazine, and your father was glad to see that he could easily break him in two.' When I finally, mercifully, broke up with Paul Bearer after he blithely informed me he would be spending Christmas in New York shooting heroin with his *other* girlfriend, she instructed my father to take me out shopping 'and let her buy anything she wants, because she just broke up with that little *Yehud* we didn't like anyway.'

So it is not without precedent that I expect her to be

equally blasé about Fahed. When I call to fill her in on the latest developments, I am actually expecting her to be *happy* that I have a date with such a stellar catch. I am especially pleased that I am going to be able to recount all of the safety and propriety rules upon which I have insisted. Besides, he has so much to recommend about him! British boarding school education, college student – practically unheard-of among my suitors – devoutly religious, handsome, and did I mention filthy rich? What mother wouldn't be thrilled? Try mine – although the last thing I am expecting is that she will forbid me to go.

'You can't tell me what to do! I'm thirty-one years old!' The catch in my steadily rising voice makes me sound thirteen. She is adamant and I'm hysterical. There's something about arguing with my parents that instantly turns me into an insolent teenage girl every time. It's even worse with my father, but this is pretty bad. I have to listen to a recounting of every Dear Abby column that has ever rehashed an urban legend about the dangers of meeting people on-line.

'But that's why,' I protest, trying not to whimper, 'that's why I'm meeting him in the *daytime*! In *public*! That's what they tell you to do!'

'Oh, so now *Cloverleaf Mall* is your idea of a safe haven?' Like me, my mother gets sarcastic when she's angry. Once the sarcasm comes out, there's no reprieve. I go off the deep end and throw a few ugly accusations at her – you don't want me to be happy, you hope I'll die an old maid, fine. I'll just go back to Paul Bearer, nothing I do ever satisfies you. Blah blah blah. I stop short of recounting the Hollywood Boulevard story, though I do allude to it – 'Just so you know, I've been on much more dangerous first dates' – which has the opposite effect of what I want. I get the verbal equivalent of a sneer and a 'And that's somehow supposed to give me more faith in your judgment?'

There is no meeting with Fahed at Cloverleaf Mall. He is left to haunt for me unsuccessfully, while I snivel and sulk at home in my bed with a migraine and a pack of spiteful cigarettes. Even with a Muslim Prince and third-favorite wifehood at stake, I am still just a little too Catholic to outright disobey my mother. Sins of omission are another thing entirely; had I never mentioned the meeting, Fahed would have snuck through under the radar with the rehab biker, Paul Bearer, and any number of minor Sunset Strip Hair Gods I dated in L.A. Me and my parental approval-seeking mouth.

Unbeknownst to my mother, my no-show at Cloverleaf Mall puts me in the position of having to make it up to the now insulted Fahed by agreeing to meet on his conditions if I am to meet him at all. When he calls the next afternoon, he is adamant. He is leaving for Washington that night for a luncheon tomorrow with the Crown Prince of Abu Dhabi – 'I hate these things, but my father says 'If you do not go, you are no son of mine' – and he wants to stop by my apartment on his way up I-95. It is made resoundingly clear to me that he is not used to being stood up, and that if I expect to hear from him again, the answer had better be yes.

What's a would-be third-favorite wife to do? This is the way it must be now. With no aces left up my sleeve, I hang up the phone and start cleaning my apartment. When the doorbell rings, I brace myself against the arm of the couch and take several deep breaths before heading downstairs. I have never felt like there was this much at stake for a first meeting. I have swept and dusted, fluffed sofa cushions, and hidden Bettie Page photos. I have stashed my laundry in the closet, my erotica in the desk drawer, and my self-help books under the sink. For my first face-to-face with Fahed I have chosen the article of clothing I have that is most like a *hijab* – a black, ankle-length Ann Taylor linen dress, suitably baglike and, save for the bare arms, concealing. At the last minute, I decide against the gold Allah necklace my uncle gave me for Christmas; I don't want to look like I'm trying *too* hard. With my knees knocking under my demure disguise, I descend the stairs to let him in.

About halfway down the dark stairwell, I catch an overpowering whiff of Drakkar Noir. I wonder for a minute if I somehow left the front door open, but no, his cologne has actually permeated the front door. Somehow I'm not surprised. I open the door and look up – thankfully; I had a fleeting moment of panic earlier when I realized I had no idea how tall he was – and there, in all of his hook-nosed, unibrowed glory, wearing a Ralph Lauren sweatshirt and a black baseball cap, is Fahed bin Saif bin Nasser bin Saif.

'*Mmmmmmmarhaba!*'

'Um, *Marhaba*. Come in.' I lead him awkwardly up the stairs to my apartment and steer him into the newly presentable living room. He plops down on the couch, peering around at my thrift-shop decor – framed Elvis paintings, mismatched end tables, an array of Mexican Jesus candles lined up on the mantle. I take the opportunity to check him out. He is definitely hot. He catches me. Minus 500 potential third-favorite wife points for me.

'So – how do I look? The same as you assume or different?' he turns proudly to one side, and then the other, holding his chin up to be observed.

'Except for the clothes, the same.'

'Yes, because in America, I wear western clothes only, except at home. Also – ' he takes off his baseball cap to reveal closely shorn locks. 'I went for haircut, and *stewpid* woman cut it too short. So, I am wearing *cap* for the first time in my life!' He puts the cap back on and pats the sofa next to him. 'You are so far away! Come sit.'

'I'm fine, thanks.' Sitting on the same couch would, I'm sure, be a huge no-no. I perch primly on the edge of my chair, trying to look ladylike.

The living room banter is stilted and uncomfortable, at least on my end. Fahed seems quite content to talk about himself, occasionally interjecting yet another request for me to join him on the couch. Conversely, I am preoccupied with saying the right things, not saying the wrong things, and resisting my very un-*Muslima* urge to join him on the couch and take his cap off again, for starters. After about a half-hour of fidgety back-and-forth, I'm relieved when he suggests we go for a ride in his car.

I grab my new Diana Haddad CD to play in the car and follow him outside. It occurs to me that my mother might be right and these may be my last moments on earth – but the lingering insolence from our phone conversation causes me to think nothing more of this than *it serves her right*. At least Karen will know how to track Fahed down when the time comes to extradite him. My disappearance will be the catalyst for an international incident – or the very least, a suspense-filled article in the back pages of *Cosmo*.

His car is exactly as he described. As we tear through the darkened streets of Richmond, with Diana Haddad blaring – 'Lebanese accents are sexy on women only; on men they are too *gayish*' – I sink into the leather bucket seat, breathe in the smell of Drakkar Noir, and sneak peeks at Fahed's profile as he steers us through downtown. I play with the array of electronic buttons on the handle of my door and I think *I could get used to this*. Adding to my nagging feelings of hypocrisy, I am suddenly reminded of the 'I'd never' game I used to play with my college roommate Janet as we were falling asleep in our dorm room, trading ultimatums in the dark. One of the ones on which we agreed was that we would never date a man with a red sports car.

Some things override giddy girlish promises. I don't know what they are for Janet, but for me a unibrow and a Gulf accent would be two of those deal breakers. I would be content to cruise around all night, but Fahed says he has to head for Washington; I have never been to lunch with a crown prince but I assume it is something for which one wants to be well rested. When we pull up to my front door, Fahed turns off the ignition and looks at me expectantly.

'You'll invite me up for just a little while?'

I know better than to even begin to entertain this idea. I laugh in what I hope is a ladylike way and shake my head no. Surely he doesn't think I would agree.

'Come on, *wallah*, just for a minute?'

'I think,' I say, hypocritical to my fingertips, 'that it's a little late to be inviting you up. Don't you have to get to Washington?'

'Wallah, *pleeeeeease*?'

I don't like where this is heading. I recognize this scenario from way too many disastrous dates in my past. If a guy is this insistent on trying to get some on the first date, he usually isn't planning on a second. It's never fun to be the kind of girl they want to bang once and forget about, but when so many fantasies are at stake, it takes on a whole new punch-in-the-gut effect. With each of his repeated pleas, I feel my chances at third-favorite wifedom blowing into the distance like so much desert sand.

'Good night, Fahed,' I say in my best Miss Manners voice, trying to salvage something from the experience, if only the image of Lebanese American belly dancers in the eyes of this Emerati cad. Opening the door, I slide my feet out, ankles together, in my best Princess Di exit. 'Tell the Crown Prince I said hey.'

Before I can get the rest of my chastely clad body out of the car, Fahed makes a last desperate lunge across the armrest and grabs himself a fistful of belly dancer boob. I smack my head on the door frame in my haste to free myself, and he is halfway down Floyd Avenue before I recognize the sound of Diana Haddad still blaring from his expensive American speakers. Standing in the gutter in my black linen *hijab*, rubbing the nascent lump on my scalp, I know I will never see Fahed or my Diana Haddad CD again.

I go about the rest of my week in a dejected haze, mourning my future as a third-favorite wife, my little brown babies that never were, my hook-nosed Prince Ali who turned out to be little more than a pushy frat boy – in a red sports car, no less. I avoid Arab Chat, delete his pictures from my hard drive, and spend night after night wondering what I could have done differently. Never mind that from the very beginning I was destined to be nothing more than a conquest in his scrapbook of America, a wild belly dancing oat that was sown before he settled down with a suitable girl – or girls – back home in the UAE. In my mind, I could have been a contender.

Friday morning in the staff lounge, I'm sipping my coffee and perusing the *Richmond Times-Dispatch* for suitable news stories to cover in current events class, when something blips on my Arab detector. It's a tiny blurb on the third page, and when I read it, I unconsciously let out a loud '*Huh!*'

UAE TO BUY 80 F-16 FIGHTERS FROM LOCKHEED MARTIN

Abu Dhabi Crown Prince and Deputy Supreme Commander of the UAE Armed Forces HH Sheikh Khalifa bin Zayed al Nahyan yesterday informed U.S. President Bill Clinton at a meeting in the White House of the UAE's intention to purchase 80 F-16 fighter-bomber jets from

Lockheed Martin. The contract for the total program, expected to be signed later this year, is valued at $7.0 billion, including weapons and support, according to Lockheed Martin.

'Huh what?' Kenny, one of the youth counselors on duty, peers over my shoulder at the newspaper.

'Huh this.' I point at the article and he reads it over my shoulder.

'Seven *billion* dollars. That's a lot of money.'

'Yeah,' I say, sipping my coffee. Then, with just a touch of self-importance, I add, 'I knew the Crown Prince was in town and all, but I didn't know that was what he was here for.'

Eyebrow raised, Kenny steps back and looks me up and down. I can almost see what he's thinking – *Allah necklace, Arabic music playing in the classroom during her planning period, and now this. It all makes sense to me now.*

It probably won't make a difference if I explain to him that the Emeratis are just going to zip around the sky in our F-16s like so many American sports cars, and I sure don't want to explain the source of my information. So, under Kenny's suspicious gaze, I clip out the article and slip it into my purse as a memento of the time I was almost in the loop on a seven-billion-dollar arms deal. He shakes his head and backs out of the staff lounge. I can't wait to hear what this gets turned into among the youth counselors. I'm already a mad scientist, a library nerd, a communist, and a stripper, depending on whom you ask. One nervous older counselor once asked to see me in private so that he could ask, too scared to meet my gaze, 'Do you worship the devil? I mean, are you in *Santana*?'

Considering that I wasn't completely innocent in fueling at least some of those rumors, I know that my prospects with Fahed were always doubtful at best. Keeping my mouth shut is not my forte; it was hard for one night – how on earth was I planning to do it for the rest of my life? Little details like that are conveniently overlooked when one has a vivid imagination. My tenure as the future Mrs bin Saif bin Nasser bin Saif may have been brief, but I have memories to last a lifetime – and a few of them are even real.

Well, OK. Maybe a couple.

8

Moose Lodge Redux

The Desert Jewels

'And these are from the SPCA benefit in North Carolina, which is always our *biggest* show of the year.'

I shift the paper plateful of potato salad and Cheese Doodles I have perched on my lap so that I can look at the pictures. I'm attending a picnic luncheon hosted by the Desert Jewels, a local dance troupe I've been invited to join. The invitation was extended to all of Sheva's students, but aside from Rosie, who stands regally beside the stereo nibbling a pretzel stick, I was the only taker. The troupe invite is the belly dancer equivalent of sorority rush. Depending on the caliber of the troupe, an invitation might be extended with no caveats, or you might receive an 'invitation to audition,' which means you'll have to present a short routine to the troupe demonstrating your proficiency before being voted in officially. The Desert Jewels are in the former camp. Most of their shows are Saturday afternoon nursing home performances, and they hold none of the stringent further study requirements that the more established troupes insist upon – the Women of

Selket, for example, require their members to take work-shops with at least two major dancers per year. The Jewels are strictly a 'show up and suit up' kind of troupe. In fact, several of the principal members of the Jewels don't dance at all outside of the troupe – not as teachers, students, or workshop participants. I'm meeting dancers at this picnic that I've never seen before at any dance event.

'This is the one where I play the queen,' Mary says, handing me a photograph of herself, seated on a throne, a tiara plunked haphazardly atop her white curls. 'We did a cute little number here, but I wasn't in it, I just sat on a throne and they were s'posed to be *worshippin'* me, and bringin' me *offerins*. And look – ' She pulls another photo out from behind it – 'that mean ol' Joyce brought me a *banana*!'

Joyce lets out her trademark cackle and claps her hands at the recollection. In the photo she is dressed in a chiffon harem outfit, replete with veil, and she is holding a splotchy brown banana out to the horrified queen.

'I guess she thought I looked like a *chimpanzee*,' Mary complained, setting the pictures down and reaching for her punch, 'but I don't let her get to me; she's always pickin' on me. We do have fun, though, and you know we're only jokin' with each other,' she adds, as if she is afraid I might not want to join a troupe where someone might offer me a banana.

'Yes, North Carolina is always fun,' says Becky, a high school Spanish teacher who looks like she might be more at home at a craft fair. Her short grayish-brown hair, thick glasses, and plump figure belie the fact that she is a veteran belly dancer and one of the troupe's founding members. 'We have two or three big shows like that a year; let's see, there's the Williamsburg Campgrounds, the Tredegar Old Time Faire—'

'And the Bicycle Association,' Janet interjects. 'They just called us for September.'

The Bicycle Association? It's not exactly the Cairo Hilton, but I've been looking for a venue in which to hone my solo dancing skills. Sheva's group numbers are all well and good, but there is still that little issue of 'doing what I feel' – and I am still not sure what I feel. I figure if I make myself feel it more often, I'll be able to recognize it more easily. Fortunately, the Chesterfield County Fair provided an opportunity for me to bond with Sheva's assistant, Janiece, over a shared love of Tilt-a-Whirls and elephant ears, and now that I'm not expecting her to smack me in the head anymore, I can run solo questions and performance problems past her. I'm still unsure of myself; I feel my transitions are not so smooth, my hips not too crisp, my hands still often stupid. But since the fair I have decided that group numbers are not enough. I have tasted the fruit that belly dancing has to offer, and I am hungry for more. I am scared, and nervous, and more than a little self-conscious, but I am hungry nonetheless. Hungry for a solo at the Bon View Convalescent Center.

I nibble a Cheese Doodle and study the photos in the stack. I do see a few familiar faces – there are Mary and Joyce, of course, and Vicki from Lucy's class, and another Mary, tall and toothy, who I have seen at the Selket shows. I have heard she's some kind of big-time Ph.D. chemist at the Medical College of Virginia; all I know is she's got a Madame Abla costume and she always plays her *zils* in perfect sync when she dances. I'm still intimidated by *zils*. There's a sort of patting-your-head-and-rubbing-your-stomach thing going on with simultaneous *zil*ling and dancing that I haven't quite gotten the hang of yet.

Most of the other Jewels are unknown quantities. There is a tall, intense woman on the couch with enormous swoopy-framed glasses and a white streak in her long black hair. On the floor sits Janet, pretty, dark-haired, and apparently deaf. She's reading lips, and she doesn't have any trouble holding her own in the conversation, but the deaf belly dancer angle is something else I just can't wrap my head around. I assume you could choreograph everything, but then what if you lose your place? How do you know where you are? It's awfully hard to lip-read a *taqsim*. Behind Janet, perched precariously on a folding chair, is a scowly-faced woman with her hair pulled in two barrettes pinned so tightly that the corners of her mouth are showing the stress. An older woman in a Jewels T-shirt, who I'm told is Shirley Shropshire, the mother of Marsha, the scowly-faced woman, hovers in the background, clearing plates and arranging stacks of photos with grim determination. I am fascinated. I didn't know belly dancers had stage mothers; especially not forty-year-old belly dancers who perform at nursing homes and Bicycle Association parties. The idea.

Just as we all head into Mary's family room to watch some videos, a forest green SUV pulls into the drive, dispensing Jennifer and yet another Mary. I quickly surmise that this particular Mary is known among the Jewels as 'Too-Tall Mary' (as opposed to white-haired Mary, our hostess, who is called 'Mary Mary,' and Ph.D. Mary, who somehow earns the esquire title of just 'Mary'). Too-Tall Mary is a willowy five-foot-eleven. She has long brown hair and a sweet doll-like face with enormous brown eyes that make her look like an overgrown first-grader, though she's probably almost thirty. I know her from Lucy's class, where I stand behind her. She rarely speaks to anyone, but she doesn't seem the least bit snobbish, just shy and sometimes a little sad.

Jennifer is another semi-unknown quantity, though she has sprung up dancing at the rarefied Selket *haflas* lately, full-blown out of nowhere like a belly dancing Athena. The Girls in the Corner have intimated that, as the daughter of a founding Woman of Selket, Jennifer seems to be exempt from the dues-paying slow climb that would be mandatory for less pedigreed dancers. Then, as if the Selket *haflas* weren't enough, Jennifer somehow lucked into a bit part belly dancing in a Dave Matthews video, forever cementing her label as Rival Belly Dancing Interloper from Parts Unknown. Still too gee-whiz new to be bitter about another dancer's relative success, my only niggling resentment toward Jennifer crops up when I learn she is an alumnus of Saint Catherine's school, a tony girls' boarding establishment favored by the debutante set. This tidbit of information scratches at old wounds left from the years I spent running with a crowd of boys from Saint Catherine's 'brother school,' Saint Christopher's. I found out too late that 'city girls' are to Saint Christopher's boys as Lebanese American belly dancers are to Emerati zillionaires.

It's largely based on the Saint Catherine's factoid that I am shocked to see Jennifer and Too-Tall Mary at the Jewels picnic. There is something decidedly Moose Lodge about the Jewels, and it's not just the fact that they hold their weekly practices there. On the whole, their hair is a little poofier, their makeup thicker, their fabrics more synthetic. If the Women of Selket are the Kappa Kappa Gammas of the Richmond Dance Scene, the Jewels are the Alpha Phi Omega – well-meaning, hard-working, and earnest, but not exactly exclusive. As with APO, one assumes that most of the members of the Jewels are there because, well, nobody else asked them to join.

Personally, I am pleased to be invited to be a part of *any* dance troupe, and I am not so delusional to think that I belong with any other troupe than the Jewels. Most of the other members seem to feel the same way. Becky, Mary Mary, and Joyce are having entirely too much fun waltzing from nursing homes to RV conventions. And I am sure Mary's medical career does not afford her the time to fulfill the Women of Selket's myriad obligations and engagements. Groucho Marx may not have wanted to join any club that would have him as a member, but the Jewels seem content to leave the entrance requirements and prestige to somebody else. Indeed, watching video after video of the Jewels's performances, I may not see a lot of ethnically correct folk numbers or stunning displays of technical acumen, but I *do* see a lot of performances, a lot of audiences, and what looks like a lot of fun being had by all.

What the hell. I figure I'll give it a go. What's the worst that can happen?

'*Goooooo hooooooome!*'

I'm about a minute into '*Waghalawtak Andena*' when the heckling starts. Granted, for heckling, it's fairly mild – a single cranky ninety-something woman in a wheelchair – but since here at the Virginia Masonic Home she is perfectly representative of the audience demographic, I grow concerned. I wag a finger at her playfully, giving her what I hope is an endearing smile. I shimmy toward her, then back, shaking my beautiful rainbow fringe for all it's worth. And I keep smiling.

Janiece and I came up with this number in the middle of 18th Street at one A.M. after a show by my uncle's band, the Scariens. I had cranked up a cassette of Hanan in my Tercel and rolled down the windows. Janiece showed me where to put the chest lifts, when to figure eight, and when to travel. She even added some cute over-the-shoulder glances that I could imagine Aegela doing, if Aegela were dancing to a tinny Tercel sound system in the middle of a downtown Richmond street after midnight. I have been practicing my heart out in my living room for weeks, and now, here in the day room of the Masonic Home, I am being told to go back there.

'*We've seen enoooooooooouuuuuugh,*' the woman drones, unimpressed. An attendant makes some clucking

167

noises at her and tucks her yellow afghan into the sides of her wheelchair. '*Goooooo hooooooooome,*' she calls again, trailing off at the end and nodding into an unsteady doze.

It's enough to throw me completely off my game. I can feel my hands getting stupider as I repeat the same lame traveling step for forty-eight counts. I can't unpurse my lips or they'll quiver, and I cringe as the first beads of 'flop sweat' form under my bangs. I forget to lift my chest and leave out my saucy twirl. I try the cute glance over the shoulder, but I think it just comes off looking paranoid. Three minutes eleven never seemed so long. When I hear the merciful fadeout, I lean down and snatch up my veil like a handful of weeds, butt to the audience – one of Lucy's big no-nos – and make a break for the dressing room.

'I can't believe I just got *heckled,*' I mutter, tearing my sequined wristlets off and cramming them into my costume bag. 'That old lady told me to go home!'

'Is that all?' Vicki pulls her brass saber out of its hilt and inspects the blade. I am beginning to think that the blasé voice thing is a belly dancer character trait. Like Susan, Vicki always sounds like she's heard it all before. Of course, with Vicki, it may have less to do with belly dancing and more to do with being Laura's big sister. She flicks some dust off the hilt of her sword and wipes it on her harem pants. 'You should have been here when Ellen danced with us for the first time.' She perches the saber on top of her head, adjusts it for balance, and slowly lets go with both hands. 'The whole time she was dancing, this lady was screaming '*Devil Child! Demon Baby!*' at her.' She takes a few small steps forward, then back, then shimmies her hips. 'Ellen almost quit the troupe after that.'

'Really?' I think about this as I unpin my bra. I would probably pay someone to scream 'Demon Baby' at me while I'm dancing. It kind of *adds* something. 'Demon

168

Baby' has flair and intrigue – not like 'go home' at all. It's daunting to think that maybe I am such a rotten belly dancer that I need to be sent home. Am I really that much worse than the rest of the troupe? I know my moves aren't very polished and my transitions are a little rough, but not nursing home worthy? That smarts. I fold up my sequined bra and lay it on top of the wristlets. Perhaps I should lay off the performances until I've had more practice. I wonder if Susan could give me some private coaching? That is, if I'm not beyond hope.

'Well, *that* was encouraging.' Too-Tall Mary, looking sadder than usual, jingles into the dressing room, absolutely adorable in a sparkly blue *beledi* dress and beaded headband. She slumps into a chair and sighs heavily, her brown eyes looking huge and moist.

'She tell you to go home, too?' Vicki grins wryly beneath her saber. Mary slips off her *zils* and looks surprised.

'Oh – so it wasn't just me?'

My sentiments exactly. I feel better. Anyone who would send Too-Tall Mary home is obviously in the late stages of something serious.

Saturday after Saturday I hone my solo skills dancing with the Jewels. From Beth Shalom to the Ginter Hall, I dutifully trot out my shimmies, hip circles, undulations, and snake arms under the watchful eye of Shirley, the troupe mother. I learn early on not to look directly at Shirley when I am performing. From her post behind the boom box, arms crossed and jaw set, she always looks as if she is barely able to tolerate what she is seeing. Sometimes she even shakes her head – just barely, but enough to really make me paranoid. Is my nose dirty? Did my boob pop out? Am I somehow disgracing my ancestors and the Moose Lodge all at once? I casually mention this to some of the other Jewels and am relieved to find out that it's not me, it's Shirley. That's just her normal resting face. I'm reminded of my friend Mariane, sent out in the hall by offended nuns year after year in Catholic school with the admonition 'don't you look at me with *that face*!' Poor Mariane . . . it was the only face she had.

I learn to avert my eyes from Shirley while I'm performing, but unfortunately the problem doesn't stop with her face. Before the show, collecting the tapes for each dancer's solo, she asks casually, 'are you going to be doing that same old number?' Later, after the show, she doesn't fail to mention that the second row was asleep through my number – 'but Janet woke 'em up with her fan number; that's always a crowd pleaser.' Her negativity permeates every nursing home appearance – and most of the homes we visit are plenty negative without her help. I wonder what her motive is in continuing to run the Jewels, since it is so obviously not making her happy. Even Marsha isn't immune to the Shirley treatment – in full earshot of the entire troupe, Shirley points out a photo in a dance catalog and notes, 'Marsha used to have a cute figure like that, before she put on weight.' Her contagious gloom is particularly frustrating in that it squelches the whole thing that makes me love belly dancing so much in the first place – the cartoonish glee of the dancer onstage; the wink, the grin, the look-how-much-fun-I'm-having gleam that invites the audience to join in and smile along. I've been working hard to get my dancing to that level, and it's near impossible to pull off with Shirley gritting on me in the corner.

I resort to desperate measures in order to maintain my onstage smile. I show up as late as possible, already in costume, ready to slap my tape in her hand and go hide until it's time to go on. I listen to upbeat Arabic pop in the car on the way there, slather my body with Cotton Candy teenybopper perfume and glitter spray, flirt shamelessly with any octogenarian who dares to meet my gaze. But my one ace in the hole in defeating the Shirley Shropshire Bad Attitude Mind Ray is my reliance on a higher power to deliver me to a state of serenity and peace that is so invincible that not even the stoniest glare of disapproval can begin to penetrate my joyous aura.

Two higher powers, actually. Chip and Dale.

Yes, Chip and Dale, the cartoon chipmunks of Disney fame – 'Apple Core!' 'Baltimore!' 'Who's your friend?' 'Me!' Yes, that Chip and Dale. After much reflection, I've determined that the attitude that I find most endearing in other dancers, the smile that draws me in and the glance that keeps me watching, is not the least bit come-hither, sultry, or exotic. The real draw, at least in my eyes, is the dancer who looks as if she knows a really funny joke and that she might be willing to share it with you if you play your cards right. The smile I look for is the smile that says 'I'm up to something, and don't you wish you knew what it was!' And that's a smile I remember well from two old friends – Chip and Dale.

There is also another, more utilitarian benefit to assuming the mental persona of Chip and Dale before taking the stage. Especially for a career wallflower, the possibility of audience rejection can lead to some pretty mighty stage fright. Shirley's glare and audience heckling notwithstanding, I know that I have been historically proven to be not pretty enough, not sexy enough, and not Lebanese enough more times than I care to recount. The very idea of presenting myself as a sexy and exotic belly dancer in front of an audience is, to me, an invitation to a potentially ugly scene of ego-smashing proportions. To say nothing of dancing, to say even less of 'doing what I feel.'

Chip and Dale do not fear rejection. Chip and Dale are not trying to be sexy. Chip and Dale just want to have a good time and maybe get away with something in the process, and anyone in the vicinity is welcome to be an accomplice to the merriment. Chip and Dale are always smiling, always joking, always there to entertain and amuse – my goals. When I step in front of an audience, I become the belly dancing embodiment of Chip and Dale. I consider making a beaded rainbow bracelet to match my costume, with the letters WWCDD in black-and-white baby beads – 'What Would Chip and Dale Do?' They would dance, and smile, and cajole, and frolic, and have a grand time doing it whether anyone clapped or not. And if nobody clapped, Chip and Dale wouldn't care. They couldn't, because in the end, they are only anthropomorphized cartoon chipmunks, and anthropomorphized cartoon chipmunks don't get their feelings hurt. WWCDD becomes my credo, and it carries me through Saturday after Saturday with the Jewels.

I begin to get a sense of why the Girls in the Corner reacted so skeptically when I announced my intention to join the Jewels. I had originally chalked their lukewarm reaction up to a loyalty to Vera, an adjunct member of the Corner who had been unceremoniously ousted from the Jewels roster after an unprecedented and somewhat sketchy vote among the other members of the troupe. I know Vera mainly from her friendship with Janiece, Doris, and Tammy. She's been banned from most of the dance classes in town for various reasons, none of them any clearer than her removal from the Jewels. I hear second- and thirdhand stories of dance class insubordination, of strong-arm choreography, even one almost unbelievable incident where she supposedly shoved white-haired Mary Mary.

'Vera says what she means,' Janiece explains when I ask, as diplomatically as she can manage, 'and what she

172

means isn't always that nice.' Be that as it may, it hardly seems enough to get one blacklisted from every class in town. The few times I've been in Vera's company at dance events, I've found her abrasive, to be sure, but no more so than Shirley Shropshire, and, for better or worse, no one is asking *her* to leave. The most disconcerting unanswered Vera question is the fact that she makes Nadine absolutely batshit. Nadine can't even bring herself to attend *haflas* that she thinks Vera might also attend. Something about Nadine makes me trust her instincts, much in the same way one would trust a trick knee or an inconsolably howling hound. I make a note to keep a cordial distance from Vera, which isn't difficult given that she is so widely banned.

Much harder to avoid are my new troupe mates, the Jewels, whose rigorously enforced rehearsal schedules and mandatory group numbers are taking up more and more of my dwindling free time. I am pressed into learning a gypsy number, a cabaret number, and a mechanical, graceless *zil* number performed in two stiff lines that Vicki archly refers to as the Hamster Dance. I draw the line at *Insh'Allah*, a horrendous line-dance number choreographed to a grating adaptation of a traditional Muslim folk song. I plead offense at the desecration of the religious, but in truth I am simply appalled at the entire thing – the hop-skip-and-jump choreography, the inane lyrics that have been crammed over the top of the melody, and, most of all, the annoyingly perky woman's voice at the beginning of the tape that encourages you to 'grab a partner or dance by yourself!' Vicki later tells me that the song was lifted from an exercise tape entitled 'Bellyrobics' – as if I needed one more reason to hate it. I vow never to perform the number. Shirley can grit on me all she wants. A girl's got to have her scruples.

If the Jewels have scruples, to borrow from Tatum O'Neal, they probably belong to someone else. The more

I learn, the more I regret my eagerness to join the troupe. The Hamster Dance, it turns out, was choreographed by Chelydra, aka Lucy Lee, of Newport News – not that I've ever heard her name announced when we perform it (to her credit, it is actually a solo, and as such involves more moving around and less marching up and back). The cabaret number turns out to be a Sheva recital chestnut that was adapted from an Amaya routine, and I spot the gypsy number, which I had been clinging to as my last bastion of faith in the Jewels' originality, being performed years ago by an out-of-town troupe on a video from Beach Blanket *Beledi*, Lucy Lee's big yearly dance festival held on the Outer Banks of North Carolina. It's cold comfort to learn that *Insh'Allah*, the one number so unpalatable I cannot even dance it, is the closest thing the Jewels have to a truly original choreography – and even that is nothing more than bastardized aerobics.

Unfortunately, knowing when to quit has never been my forte. I continue to suit up and show up, rolling my eyes through rehearsal after rehearsal of filched numbers and secondhand suites. I tell myself that it's not that bad, that I'm getting valuable experience, that I'm doing community service, that I'll quit when it gets *really* bad. I feel like the Jewels are my new loser boyfriend, and I'm just waiting for them to *really* fuck things up before I walk out.

And wait I do, like the faithful enabling girlfriend I am, plugging away at nursing homes and convalescent centers for a summer's worth of Saturdays. As summer fades into fall, we begin diligently rehearsing for the Olde Time Faire, one of the Jewels' highest profile shows of the year – and that, as it always seems to happen in small-time local belly dancing troupes, is where things begin to unravel.

When I arrive at the Moose Lodge for practice on Thursday night, the distinct lack of jingling is my first signal that something isn't right. I am usually – no, always – late for practice, and the rest of the troupe is generally halfway through the first walk-through of whatever number we're borrowing at the time when I arrive. This month it's been a veil number by Laurel Victoria Grey, a D.C.-area diva who threw a major monkey wrench in the Nadia Hamdi show by refusing to allow her performance to be taped for fear of other dancers stealing her precious choreography. Each week, as we bumble through our rendition of one of her closely guarded group numbers, I contemplate sending her an anonymous tip from a 'friend' just so I won't have to suffer through this number any more. As taught by Laurel Victoria, I'm sure it's lovely. As taught by Marsha, who for the past two weeks has been rendered even loopier than usual by the Percocet she's been taking after some minor surgery, it changes from week to week, follows no perceptible count, and is accompanied by facial gestures that probably feel intense and meaningful but look comically grotesque.

Tonight, though, no veils are in evidence. The assembled troupe members – Joyce, Mary Mary, Too-Tall Mary, Janet, Vicki, Aileen, Marsha, and Sara – Jen had announced last week that she would be off on yet another Club Med trip – are seated at one of the long dining tables along the back wall of the lodge. Shirley is standing above them, scowling and holding a sheaf of papers. She hands me one off the top and I read it with a sinking feeling that my dysfunctional relationship with the Jewels is about to get even more unpleasant.

1. Do you believe that Jennifer should automatically get a solo at the Olde Time Faire? (Yes or No)
2. Do you think it should be decided diplomatically, as with names from a hat? (Yes or No)

3. Do you trust Shirley as your Troupe Director? (Yes or No)
4. Do you want the names to be drawn again, in front of everyone? (Yes or No)
5. Do you want Shirley to resign, effective immediately? (Yes or No)

'I suppose I should explain again why we're doing this, since you missed it,' Shirley says with characteristic pointedness. 'A member of this troupe seems to think that I did something dishonest to keep Jennifer's name from being drawn for a solo. She questioned my honesty. She questioned it more than once.' Shirley glances imperiously around the room at this last bit, as if to turn the offending Jewel into salt. 'I am an honest person; I've always been an honest person. I had an impartial third party draw the names; I carried it across the street and let my neighbor pick the name.' This last bit of information leads to several logistical questions and simple solutions, but Shirley presses on. 'Anyhow, this person seems to think that Jennifer is a better dancer than the rest of you, and that it would be good for the troupe if Jennifer did a solo at the Olde Time Faire. Now, we've always been diplomatic in this troupe and we don't feel any one of you deserves a solo any more than anybody else, but that's where it is. So I made up this ballot and we're going to settle this right now.'

I look at the ballot and wonder if it is too late for me to turn around and walk out. Even attempting to answer the questions, worded such as they are, would make it look like I was cosigning a level of bullshit that I absolutely refuse to be a party to. I wonder briefly if they deliberately waited until Jen was out of the country to vote, then realize how silly I am being. *Of course* they waited. It is patently obvious.

176

'I would like to say something before you all vote.' I look up, shocked. Too-Tall Mary is standing solemnly at the end of the table and speaking in an uncharacter-istically forceful, if still sad, voice.

'I am the troupe member Shirley was speaking of, and I would like to say a few words about what took place.'

'I wasn't going to name names,' Shirley says defensively.

'Well, you named Jennifer, and she didn't even know about it.' Whoa. I didn't know Too-Tall had it in her. She hesitates a minute and continues. 'I suggested to Shirley that maybe we should get together as a troupe and decide who would dance for the Olde Time Faire, because it is a high-profile show and we want to be asked back. I know that they really enjoyed Mary's performance last year,' this being Ph.D. Mary, who has since moved away, 'and they are probably expecting an equally experienced dancer.' I am impressed with her diplomatic wording. It belies the fact that Jennifer has less experience than most of us, but stating the *real* issue – 'an equally *talented* dancer' – would ruffle some feathers that are already ruffled enough. I nod in silent support, sending strength waves her way. 'But Shirley said that it had to be by random drawing, and that's fine. When she told me who was picked, I just said it was too bad that Jen didn't get a solo. I just said it because that's how I felt.'

'You said it twice,' Shirley interjects, a bit too loudly.

'I might have,' Mary says, unwavering. 'I might have repeated myself. But the fact is, you have really turned it around with this ballot, and this meeting or whatever it is—' and she lays her ballot on the table and picks up her dance bag – 'and I don't think it's fair to Jen to drag her into this. Now if you'll excuse me, I'm going to leave.' She pushes her chair under the table and walks briskly through the swinging doors, with Mary Mary scurrying in her wake. I look at Shirley. If I didn't know better I'd think she was smirking. I'm aghast. I can't

177

believe we're all over thirty. I feel like I'm in middle school. Bring on the Slam Book.

'Well,' says Marsha, slapping her thighs with exaggerated purpose and nodding at her mother, 'I think we're all in agreement here.' We are? She nods sagely as she adds her own editorial comment, obviously sure she speaks for us all. 'The Jewels have always been democratic. There are no divas in this troupe.'

No divas. I think the problem is there are too many divas – and Jen and Too-Tall Mary aren't among them. In fact, it's anyone's guess if Too-Tall Mary is ever coming back – and poor Jen is oblivious, somewhere, drinking an umbrella drink and slathering on coconut oil. I think I feel more sorry for Too-Tall Mary.

'Well, I hope you're happy.' Mary Mary returns and plops angrily in her chair, shaking her head at Shirley. 'You made that poor child cry.'

'I didn't mean to upset her,' Shirley says unconvincingly. 'I just felt like we needed to address this now.'

Of course, I think, *because Jen will be back by next practice*.

'Well, I tried to get her to come back, but she's gone on home,' Mary says, waving her hands. 'Gone home cryin', and that sweet little girl doesn't have a mean bone in her body. I declare she's just the sweetest—'

'We all like Mary,' Marsha snarls.

'Sounds like it,' Vicki mutters under her breath, rolling her eyes at a Thursday night at the Moose Lodge gone horribly wrong.

'Well, we could sit here all night and talk about whose fault this is,' Shirley goes back into martyr drive, her default setting – 'but we need to practice that *zil* number. We've only got three more practices before the show.'

'Well, how am I supposed to practice the *zil*?' Mary Mary throws her hands in the air. 'My partner went home cryin'!'

178

Vicki puts her head on the table, defeated. Aileen is inspecting the whole scene open-mouthed, speechless for once. Joyce looks pissed, Mary Mary is completely flabbergasted, and the Triumvirate – Shirley, Marsha, and Sara – are exchanging imperious glances, just disgusted that the rest of us could make such a big deal out of something as simple as a troupe vote. And me? I'm wondering how it came to this. How did I, the tattoo guy's old lady, trudging the path of hipness, end up in the middle of a Moose Lodge Jihad with the Olde Time Faire at stake?

Jihad or no Jihad, our performance at the Olde Time Faire is, I think, our best ever. The Hamster Dance goes off without a hitch, Vicki does her riveting sword number, Mary Mary steals the show (as usual) with a bawdy rendition of 'Little Egypt,' and the cabaret is glitzy, glamorous, and fault free. Unfortunately, Jen decides to decline the solo that is eventually and grudgingly offered. I know she is hoping that this will help things blow over, but it disappoints me anyway. I don't want the Triumvirate to claim this as a victory. I'm still angry at them for making Too-Tall Mary cry. Still, the Faire itself is a success from my viewpoint. It helps that the stage is set up like a sideshow, complete with a portly barker and a canvas banner depicting a dog doing arithmetic, captioned 'the Amazing Thalia, Learned Dog of Wonder!' Truly, I have arrived.

A month after the Olde Time Faire, my hairdresser Julie asks if the Jewels would be interested in performing at a charity fashion show the salon is organizing. It sounds lovely – we'd be onstage at a downtown dance club, have our own dressing room, and the possibility of local press coverage to boot. I check with the troupe and extend our acceptance. We'd be glad to.

The night of the show, I arrive last, as usual. I pull up to Cafine's and schlep my dance bag and costume hanger inside – only to be hit immediately with the Shirley Shropshire Bad Attitude Mind Ray.

'We're not going on until nine.'

'Nine? That's two hours from now.' We had been told eight o'clock by the promoter.

'They're saying it might even be nine-thirty. The girls don't want to wait around that long.' She's switching over to the Blame Ray, but I'm impervious. 'Besides,' she adds, leaning over conspiratorially, 'some of the girls are uncomfortable because there are so many *gays* around.'

I try to give her the Anne Soffee Homophobe Shame Ray, but her powers dwarf mine. I consider asking her several questions – Didn't she know Cafine's was a gay bar? Did she not expect to find any gay people at a fashion show? Where did she think haute couture came from? I realize before I even open my mouth that these questions are futile; she wouldn't know haute couture from Fashion Bug. Shirley's idea of dressing for a gig is pulling a powder blue Jewels T-shirt on over a long-sleeved blouse. I actually feel a little sorry for her, so out of place does she look under the disco ball here at Cafine's.

'Well, let me talk to the girls,' I sigh. 'I'll see if I can work something out.' I navigate down the basement stairs, past clusters of primping models and harried designers. I see my counter girl from World Cup, her hair coiled up into Princess Leia muffs. She calls out to me and I wave to her, only a little disturbed to have my worlds collide on the back stairs at Cafine's. I find the other Jewels sitting sullenly on a stack of pallets in the basement, awaiting permission to leave in a huff.

'So, I hear you guys want to leave,' I start hesitantly.

'No, I'll stay,' Jen offers, and Too-Tall Mary nods in agreement. I should have known better than to think this was unanimous. It's that good old Jewels democracy again.

'I'm not waiting two hours,' Marsha growls and shakes her head. 'I don't know what we're doing here with all these skinny little models, anyway.'

I'm baffled. What were they thinking when I said fashion show? Frumpy hausfraus in Butterick patterns? To me, fashion show means two things: skinny girls and gay men. Whose warped reality scheme are they operating under?

'Well, I think whoever wants to leave should go ahead and say so now, so the rest of us can try and work out a lineup.' Jen earns a glare from three-eighths present for this obviously outrageous suggestion. I guess she figures she has nothing to lose. Mary Mary is the first to speak up, gathering her makeup case and costume bag and standing to go.

'I would like to stay,' she says, sounding truly earnest, 'but I have a date, and I'm already keepin' him waitin'.' This is what happens when you belly dance – you still have hot Saturday night dates in your seventies.

'I'm going,' Marsha says, offering no hot date or anything else as a reason. She hasn't stopped scowling since I laid eyes on her, so I figure that's for the best. Hardly a crowd pleaser, that scowl.

'Me too,' and Janet is added to the deserters. Next are Becky and Sara, leaving only me, Too-Tall Mary, and Jen to carry the show by ourselves.

We quickly decide on an assortment of numbers – a Nubian duet by Mary and Jen, Sheva's cabaret, and the godawful *zil* number. Mary and I nominate Jen for a solo and she graciously accepts; thank God one of us is fearless. We still have an hour and a half to wait after all is said and done, giving me a new appreciation for the late arrival theory of performing. Nothing heightens stage fright more than ninety minutes of staring at the stage you'll soon be on, imagining all the things that could go wrong.

When the moment of truth finally arrives, everything fades into a blurred mess of strobes, disco balls, and blackness. I wish for once I'd left my glasses on to dance; hardly haute couture, but better than the broken neck I'm risking to appear that much more fashionable. The main culprit is the black egg-crate cushioning that covers the narrow runway we're using for a stage – without my glasses, the black of the runway is barely discernible from the black of the two-foot drop to the floor, to say nothing of the effect the cushioning is having on our spins. I wonder if the models will be wearing heels, and, if so, how they're going to walk on this stuff? I don't plan to stick around and find out. I'm praying for the exit music, and I'm not going to stop exiting until I get home.

It's a mixed blessing that, due to the intense stage lights and blaring sound system, I can't see or hear whether there is really an audience at all. They could be booing or cheering, and there could be three people or three thousand. All I can see are huge balls of light directly in front of me, and blackness below. I know I spin the wrong way on the Cabaret, and I notice Mary forgetting a shimmy on the *zil* – but everything else fades into oblivion with the audience, our *zils*, and the black egg crate stage. By the time Jen wraps up her solo, which is smashing – as usual, damn her – I've got my bag in my hand and I'm waiting by the door. Chalk one up to 'at least it's over.'

Monday night at Sheva's, I am sitting out the shoulder shimmies in my tentative new spot in the Corner. My friendship with Janiece and obsessive attendance at all things dance-related has earned me enough belly dancer brownie points to be *sort of* in the Corner. I say *sort of* because I am still just this much in awe of Doris, just this scared of Tammy, just barely impressed with myself when Janiece asks my opinion about a costume or a new hank of fringe. I still can't figure out how I, small-time poser nerd that I am, can rate being invited out on the town with *real live belly dancers*, cool ones like Susan and Tammy and Janiece and Doris. But it is happening with more and more frequency, and sometimes I just have to Chip and Dale at myself in the mirror when it does. Being a belly dancer, to me, is *cool*.

So I sit on the edge of the Corner, and I listen to the gossip, and I add my two cents when I think it's OK, and I make mental notes of who's getting the paying jobs, who's getting the high-profile solos, who's dropping out, and who's coming back. And each week I just can't believe I'm included in this rarified circle of smart-assed glamorous belly dancers who seem to set the standard in these parts for what flies and what doesn't in the world of veils and *bedlah* . . . for the Sheva circuit, anyway.

That's another thing that's becoming clearer to me as I learn about local belly dancing; the folky-ethnic types and the cabaret-glitzy types tend to polarize in places where 'the scene' is large enough. There are always those brave few who have one foot in each camp – witness the Women of Selket's Yasmina, who has just enough time between numbers to change out of her ethnically exact Georgian robes and into the most painted-on custom Egyptian *bedlah* you ever saw as she shimmies effortlessly between folkloric and cabaret. And Susan, Sheva's right-hand woman, who was a fixture at the Phoenicia during the heyday of the cabaret circuit, is now as at home in a tribal-style turban and tassel belt as she is in beaded fringe. But for the most part you'll find Sheva's dancers in *bedlah* and the Selket set in full-on ethnic regalia.

Tonight's Corner discussion is particularly feline, regarding two of the babealicious babes who were sent out on some kind of nightclub gig for Sheva and how ladylike they did or didn't act. There is talk of excessive body tipping, of coverups not being donned, of inappropriate schmoozing with the audience. We know all of this because one of Sheva's better dancers was also sent on this gig and she was shocked, *shocked*, at such goings-on! So of course she came back and told Janiece all about it. And Janiece tells us, and much gossiping is done.

'I wonder if anybody's gonna have the nerve to tell Sheva?' Doris asks pointedly, looking right at Susan.

'Somebody's got to,' Susan agrees, 'because otherwise she's going to send them out again, and that doesn't look good on us.'

'It might be too late,' Janiece adds with the air of someone who's about to drop another juicy tidbit. We all lean in close. 'Now, Sheva didn't say anything to me, but one of the guys at work said *he* saw three belly dancers down at Cafine's Saturday night. And,' she adds conspiratorially, 'He said only one of them was any good.'

The Corner Girls all nod knowingly. Obviously the babealicious babes. Obviously some sub-par belly dancing being done. Shame on them. Shame indeed.

Shame on me, but I keep my mouth shut. I'd be the first to admit that I did some seriously sub-par belly dancing on Saturday night, but there's a time and a place for true confessions, and this ain't it. It's bad of me, but I let the babes take the rap. It's just one more offense; they can write it off. There is too much at stake for me.

Back at the Moose on Thursday, the Triumvirate couldn't be more thrilled at our lackluster report on the show. Never mind the fact that our complaints had everything to do with our own missteps and screw-ups and nothing whatsoever to do with homosexuals or skinny girls; to their minds, we got our just desserts for agreeing to perform in that den of iniquity in the first place.

'I don't mind homosexuals,' Marsha says unconvincingly, 'but I really don't think I need to see them crawling all over each other.' I wonder where she saw such a display; I have a strong suspicion the incident to which she refers was probably nothing more than a fashionista air-kiss or an encouraging pat on the shoulder.

'Well, I think that's their business,' Mary Mary chides. I'm glad she had a date, but I do wish she'd have stayed – I get the feeling she would have been a massive hit with the Cafine's crowd. 'I mean, I don't want some ol' pair of tits rubbin' up against me, but that's what some people like.' They would have *loved* her.

The conversation continues in this vein until anyone listening would think we had been hired to dance at a Fire Island bathhouse instead of a charity gala. By the time Shirley calls us to attention, the visual picture that has been painted is something akin to a scene from *Caligula*. Any illusions I ever had about belly dancers being cosmopolitan and worldly wise is out the window with a vengeance. I feel like I'm at a Moral Majority Meeting.

As I lockstep mechanically through yet another rehearsal for the *zil* number, I think back to the discussion that Jen, Mary, and I had over baba ghanouj and falafel at Aladdin Express the night before. Our reward to ourselves for sticking it out at the fashion show, dinner quickly disintegrated into a major league bitch session about what we wanted and didn't want from a dance troupe. Hysterical homophobic rationalizations fell squarely in the latter camp. We agreed that we wanted a troupe that was structured enough to avoid incidents like Shirley's ballot debacle, but loose enough to allow us to inject our own style – some tribal, some North African, and even fusion if we dared. We wanted rehearsals to be places for members to bounce ideas for new choreographies off one another. We wanted to dance somewhere other than nursing homes once in a while – children's hospitals, art galleries, charity events.

What it boiled down to was that we didn't want the Jewels. Jen had already effectively quit, telling Shirley that she wouldn't be available on Thursday nights any more after that month. Mary was hanging in, but less actively than before; much as in Lucy's class, she showed up, said little, and left early. But what about me? Was I going to have the balls to follow through on my 'if it stops being fun, I'll quit' decree that I had made to the Girls in the Corner when I joined?

Apparently not. As I suffer through another *one-two-three-four turn five-six-seven-eight shimmy*, I grit my teeth and clap my *zils* along with the music like I'm supposed to. The Jewels are the thorn in my proverbial side, a drain on my time and energy and a source of nothing but hassle. So why don't I quit? What am I gaining? To be honest, I don't know. I think it's the fear of having to put my money where my mouth is and actually try to organize the kind of troupe we talked about over dinner. Not only would it take tons of time and effort, but I could only imagine the combined chorus of the Girls in the Corner and the Triumvirate together – '*Who do they think they are?*!'

I guess what it boils down to is knowing my place. As a small-time belly dancer with a year of experience, my place is not starting and running a troupe. My place is on the back line, second from the right, with the Desert Jewels, giving it away for free at nursing homes and bicycle associations. I've still got dues to pay, time to serve. And that feels like exactly what I'm doing with the Jewels. *Shimmy six seven eight.*

9

They Don't Serve Hummus in
the Faculty Lounge

Dating Adventures in Arabia,
Part Two

So when are you gonna outgrow all this, anyway?' I am
leafing through a stack of photos from local nightclubs,
sweaty musicians and lanky singers, more than a few of
whom I can count among my past mistakes. I'm visiting
my friend Mariane, she of *that face*, who produces the
Richmond Music Journal almost singlehandedly in her
dining room. I pull a black-and-white photo of the Useless
Playboys out of the pile and squint at it. 'Did I take this
one?'

'I think you might have,' she says, barely looking up
from her light table. For a time, some five years ago, I
used to drag Mariane out to every one of the Playboys'
shows so I could ogle their six-foot-seven bald-headed
singer. Such taste I have. Mariane is more than twice as
old as most of the musicians she interviews for her
magazine. She started the *Journal* six years ago in a failed
attempt to to win the heart of a cheesy keyboard player
who wasn't worthy of her anyway. He played Eagles

covers in a Holiday Inn lounge and didn't think Mariane was hip enough to keep up with him. We bonded over loser boyfriends in the back booth of the Moondance Saloon.

'So what's gonna be in this issue?'

'Same old stuff. Some GWAR pictures, an Ultra Bait interview. About the only breaking news I've got is a turf war in the letters column between Dickie Disgusting and Mack Sinatra.'

This intrigues me. Dickie Disgusting I remember from my middle school days; in the late 1970s he was one of Richmond's original punks. He sang for a band called the Blind Boys, and their name was spray-painted on buildings all over town. Years later he made something of a comeback with a series of nightclub shows where he mud-wrestled a four-hundred-pound transvestite named Dirt Woman. The flyers said, 'You can wash the Dirt off Dickie, but you can't keep Dickie off the Dirt!' On Halloween night in 1981, Dickie taught me to play 'Peter Gunn' on the bass. It was my consolation prize for not having a fake I.D. to get into the Iggy Pop show with Melissa that night. Mack Sinatra, though, is a name I've only seen in the music journal as a byline. I'd always figured it was a pseudonym for some musician who didn't want to seem biased. Odds are I've probably dated Mack Sinatra, whoever he is.

'Who is Mack Sinatra, anyhow?'

'He's actually a history professor. His name is Hal Rashid. You probably know him. He's about your age and he used to play guitar in some bands.'

Stop the presses – literally! I reach over and click off Mariane's light table in mid-layout.

'*Mariane*! Is he Arab?'

'Yeah, I think he's Iraqi or something. His first name's Halim. I've never seen him in person. He mails everything in.'

'*Mari-ane*! He's an educated Arab guy, he's my age, and he plays in bands – and you've never mentioned him to me? What were you thinking? Is he married?'

'No, he's single. In fact, he's something of a ladies' man. I've heard rumors.' Well, that's good – at least we know he's not dateable.

'Hook me up!'

'Hook yourself up. I thought I was still in the doghouse with you over the last one.' This about a manic-depressive Methodist lay preacher with a Buddy Holly cover band – the less said about him, the better.

'Uh, Mariane, if you recall the details of that episode, you sent me an e-mail asking if you could give him my phone number, and I responded, and I quote, "under no circumstances whatsoever may you give him my phone number." And he called me, like, an hour later.'

'Well, I didn't think you were serious.' She switches the light table back on and resumes pasting up a photo of a topless woman squashing her breasts against the back of a lucite guitar. 'If you want to introduce yourself to Hal, why not send him an e-mail?'

'What, just out of the blue like that?' I'm not sure how that's going to fly with an Iraqi, even a guitar-playing Americanized one.

'Sure. Tell him his name came up. Ask if you've met him. Honestly, I don't see how you two never came across each other. You know everybody else in town.'

Unfortunately, she's right. It's the blessing and the curse of living in the same town in which you were born and raised. It's part of the reason Mariane and I became friends; she was always calling me to get the history of this band or the lineage of that musician. I am a walking Rolodex of Richmond guitarists. But Hal Rashid I've never heard of. I can't imagine how I missed him. In all my phases – new wave teenybopper, proto-punk wannabe, half-assed Deadhead, art-rock nerd girl – I never once met a guitar-playing Iraqi. I do know one Pakistani cowboy singer in town, but that's about as close as it gets.

Mariane is kind enough to print me off a couple of reams of Mack Sinatra's articles to aid in my burgeoning stalking career. She even includes the Dickie Disgusting letters, so I can reminisce about the good old days at the same time as I'm embarking on yet another conquest. I can say with confidence that I was never romantically linked with Dickie Disgusting – but that's about all I can say. She tries to stick a photo of faux Buddy Holly in the pile, but I flick it out and leave it on her dining room floor. She really does owe me for that. This Rashid thing might be her best chance at a reprieve.

Back at my apartment, I dash off what I hope is a cool and casual sounding e-mail to the address Mariane scribbled on the margin of a Death Piggy review. I note that she conveniently forgot to tell me that he was a professor at the University of *Tennessee* – hardly local, but not as far away as some of the cybersheiks I was considering mere weeks ago. I word and reword my e-mail several times, trying to find a happy medium between desperate and disinterested.

From: SamiraSafi@aol.com
To: hrashid@utk.edu
Subject: Hello Hal . . . .

Pardon me if I'm being presumptuous, but I'm just trying to figure out if I know you. I was over at Mariane Matera's tonight, and your name came up (in connection with the Dickie Disgusting mail bombing that seems to be ongoing). Apparently we were around the same scene at the same time for God knows how many years, are both currently novelists, and educators, both writing for Mariane occasionally, and both Arab-American, if Mariane's got your genealogy straight. So, you tell me –

do I know you? Search your memory – see if I come up (and maybe don't tell me if you dig up something mortifying)!

Best,
Anne Thomas Soffee

The reply comes almost immediately – heartening in that I figure he must be almost as much of an Internet nerd as I am.

From: hrashid@utk.edu
To: SamiraSafi@aol.com

Dear Anne,

Well, maybe we did cross paths once, many moons ago. I wish I could say I remembered for sure. I finished High School in '84, then went to college and grad school. I'm teaching adjunct here while I work on my Ph.D. Here's a link to a web page with my picture if it'll jog your memory. As for being Arab-American, yeah – my Dad is from Iraq. How do you know Mariane? Sincerely, Hal Rashid (aka 'Mack Sinatra')

I quickly jet over to his Web page and check out his picture. The nose is definitely Iraqi, but other than that, he looks like your standard white boy. That part is disappointing, but who am I to begrudge a lack of melanin in my fellow half-breed? Besides, a *Ph.D. candidate*! And a *guitarist*! Truly this is providence at work – or Kismet, or karma, or another one of those esoteric things I try so hard to believe in. I read over his resume; heavy on the European history, but the NPR commentaries are a nice touch. Clicking further, I'm able to view his song lyrics but not hear the actual songs; probably just as well, as I can't imagine rocking out over a tune that includes the word exigency. But these are details! Mere trifles! I file his e-mail in my 'Arabs' folder, bookmark his Web page, and go to sleep, content in the knowledge that I have a new potential sheik over whom to obsess.

Over the days that follow, I rack up sheaves of e-mail correspondence from Hal, and he from me. Mostly light banter, a lot of flirting and look-how-clever-we-are word-play and literary references. I feel good; I'm honing my verbal skills, which had been getting rusty during my tenure at 'Arab Chat' – 'LOL! What r u wearing?' I play my cards close; I mention my M.F.A., my teaching job, and my favorite bands, but say nothing of my belly dancing or my twelve-step membership. Some things are best left for later. At least, I think I am leaving them for later, until I get an e-mail from Hal that reads like this:

To: SamiraSafi@aol.com
From: hrashid@utk.edu

Mariane just e-mailed me, with an interesting picture of you . . . subtle, she ain't. But I'm not complaining. You have really gorgeous hair, Anne. I mean, staring-at-the-ceiling-searching-for-the-metaphor gorgeous hair. Chinese women would follow you through the streets of Beijing, offering to buy it. Chinese men would follow you through the streets of Beijing, offering other things. You'll have to stand in a separate line at Customs, paying luxury tax on it. If O. Henry were alive today, he'd dedicate 'Gift of the Magi' to you. If Poe were still alive . . . well, he'd be too stoned to notice, BUT I WOULD NOTICE. ('Oh, thanks Hal, that's sweet, but I cut it all off last week . . .') OK, OK. Right. Enough. Back to the utterly less interesting world of 18th-century German merchants. Thanks for the little electronic visit.

'MARIANE!!!' I'm screaming into the phone, but in her apartment two blocks away, she could probably hear me without it.

'What?'

'You sent him my belly dancing picture!'

'Yeah, so? He wanted to see what you looked like.'

'And that's what you sent him? I know you have at least a dozen regular pictures of me in your files!'

'Why are you complaining? That's a really good picture of you. What did you want me to send him, the one of you and Lewis Bucket? You don't want to run him off, do you?'

'Well, *no*, but I was waiting for the right time to tell him about the belly dancing.'

'I think this was the right time. You should see the e-mail he sent me back.'

'Was he talking about Poe and O. Henry and Chinese customs?'

'Yeah.'

'Then I've seen it. It was a bit much, I thought. I just have plain brown hair. It's not all that.'

'It photographs well.'

'Well, jeez, Mariane, I don't know what to do now!'

'Try saying "Thank you for the lovely e-mail, Hal."'

'OK.' Sigh. 'I gotta go. *And don't send him any more pictures*!'

'OK, OK.'

'Bye.'

The only thing bad about long-distance courtship with someone as nerdy as myself is that life quickly becomes a nonstop IM marathon, with each of us trying to impress the other with the quickness of our on-line wit. I find myself on the computer at the exclusion of grading papers, lesson planning, housework, and meetings – and when I'm not bantering with Hal, I'm e-mailing Mariane with obsessive questions about our pending face-to-face meeting, during Hal's upcoming visit to Richmond. He claims he was coming anyway for Father's Day, but I'm dubious. We've been discussing the visit for days and I have yet to see where he's going to fit dear old *Baba* Rashid into his proposed schedule of fine dining, belly dancer worship, and generalized woo pitching. His e-mails become more frequent, more poetic, more personal. And yet always with the casually inserted mention of his tenuous presence in my life, his free-and-easy view on life and relationships, and, most annoyingly, the running tally of how many undergraduate Tennessee co-eds came on to him that day. I am burning up the modem lines to Mariane yet again. He's a loser boyfriend already, and I've never even met him. Can't I pick them.

To: MusicJournal@aol.com
From: SamiraSafi@aol.com

So Hal and I had our usual two-hour talk tonight, and he did the whole 'I will be moving far, far away next year to teach' speech again, with the underlying message that he was on some kind of one-year Mission Impossible blow-up-in-your-face timer. More and more, I'm thinking that I must be nothing special to this guy. Just someone else that he might hang out with for a while before he moves on to the next one. And I don't want that. I'm too fucking old to be getting involved with someone who already has his suitcase packed when he picks me up for the first date! I can't even get geared up to clean this stupid apartment, because now I am convinced that it is, in fact, doomed, doomed, doomed, and why am I even bothering? I am setting myself up for a big fat heartbreak. That is what I get for trying to force things. I never should have e-mailed him in the first place. I dunno . . . he says this is different, but I think for him different still involves taking off without looking back sometime in the not too distant future. Do you think I even stand a chance here, or should I try and save some shred of dignity while I still can?

She replies.

To: SamiraSafi@aol.com
From: MusicJournal@aol.com

Hal was lurking on IM when I signed on at work today. The only one more negative about this than you is him. He thinks because you live so far apart, the whole thing is doomed. He doesn't know where he will be next year when he starts looking for a position. So it's all doomed, doomed, doomed. I don't think he wants it to be doomed, just like I think you don't want it to be doomed, but you both keep coming up with escape clauses. So far you're the perfect couple. Why don't you both stop thinking in terms of marriage and a relationship and just meet and be friends first? Or, when he comes to the door, just say 'We're doomed, we're doomed, we're doomed,' then lie on the floor and say, 'Step on me now and get it over with.' Have him kick you a few times, and then slam the door and then you cry. That sounds like a perfect first date. Cut to the chase. Either way, I withdraw from talking to either of you. You're driving me nuts!!!

Over the days leading up to Hal's arrival, we both do our best to throw spoilers into the mix, attempting to avert the no-doubt crushing disappointment that will be our first date. He announces that if I'm not willing to enjoy a glass of '86 Chateau St Emilion with him when he publishes his first novel, I'm not the woman for him. I fire back that if he can't understand that a glass of '86 Chateau St Emillion for me will likely lead to a trip to the ER for him and possibly the slammer somewhere down the road for me, after I bash him with a bottle and run off in his car with the first junkie loser I see, then he's not the man for me. He gets his feelings hurt when I'm forced to admit I can't get through reading the manuscript he sent me. (I honestly try, but it's a sci-fi thriller and, like Beavis and Butthead reading a warning label, I see 'words, words, words, words . . .') I get my feelings hurt when he, after reading *my* manuscript, a breezy chick-lit novel about (you guessed it) a nerd girl and her loser rock 'n' roll boyfriend, sends an unsolicited two-page critique. And Mariane, after swearing off corresponding with either of us until after the meeting, almost blows the whole thing when she responds to Hal's 'thanks for introducing us' e-mail by writing back, 'Aw, shucks, don't mention it. I hand her out to guitarists all the time. She's the *Journal* Door Prize.'

I trot the black linen dress out again for my first date with Contestant Number Two. I refluff the pillows, rehide the recovery books, and change the sheets. There's no false modesty to hide behind this time, as he'll be staying at my apartment for the weekend. The morning of his arrival, I check my e-mail and find the following brief note, penned just before Hal's scheduled departure time:

To: SamiraSafi@aol.com
From: killer@utk.edu

You're such a mystical presence in my life right now; a flicker-promise at the edge of the horizon, suggesting all kinds of possibility. Today I set out for that horizon, come what may.

A normal girl would be flattered. A normal girl would be impressed. A normal girl would get all misty at such florid prose and flattery. But normal was never my forte. Somehow the poetic imagery makes me cringe, wondering what I've gotten myself into. But, like with so many other things in my life, I'm in too deep now to turn back. Somewhere between Knoxville and here, maybe even in a red sports car, is an Iraqi singer-songwriter Ph.D. candidate, and he is expecting the weekend of his life with a Lebanese American belly dancer.

Sweet Allah. What have I done?

It is a good sign when I can't smell Hal's cologne through the door when he arrives. At least he has that much on Fahed – and his sports car is white, not red. Unfortunately, he looks even more Caucasian in person than he does on his Web site, and I have to remind myself that I don't exactly resemble Samia Gamal, myself. I lead him in and let him set up in the living room, which doubles as the guest room. He politely compliments my Jesus candles, my Elvis paintings, and my impressive assortment of leftover weighty tomes from my grad school days – though I suspect he is only sincere about the last part. In person, he strikes me as much more buttoned-down than he came across in his e-mails. Maybe it's the Gap wardrobe, or the tennis-player physique – tall, thin, and straight-backed, as if slouching might wrinkle his whites. I am rationalizing my little heart out about how first impressions aren't always correct and he's sure to relax any minute now when he produces the biggest spoiler of them all – so far.

'I figured we might need a little ice breaker, so I stopped at my favorite gourmet shop and picked us up a *magnificent* Cabernet.'

Unfortunately, Emily Post hasn't gotten around to the

edition yet when she addresses proper etiquette regarding offering wine to people who have already informed you that they are members of AA. Suffice to say that it's a major faux pas. I try not to sound too stony when I gather enough of my wits to respond civilly.

'I hope you enjoy it. Unfortunately, you'll have to enjoy it alone, since I don't drink.'

'You don't drink at all?' Jeez Louise! Didn't we already have this argument?

'No; I thought I made that pretty clear.'

He stuffs the bottle back in his overnight bag, looking offended.

'Well, I didn't realize you were a zealot about it. I mean, I don't know *anybody* who won't have a glass of wine once in a while.'

Right! Now that the weekend is off to an absolutely smashing start, I figure I might as well be myself. When we set out for a walk around the neighborhood (a nostalgic request by former Richmonder Hal), I don't hesitate to suggest that we stop off at World Cup, where we quickly encounter faux Buddy Holly, the little gay lawyer, *and* a friendly schizophrenic I know from AA meetings ('Hey Annie! They're sellin' dolls of you up at the KB Toys! They got your face on 'em! I'm gonna buy you one when my DSS check comes!') Not to be outdone, Hal graciously points out the church where he was married ('Uhhhh . . . you were *married*?') and the apartments of several former girlfriends (one of whom, a waitress named Heidi, he sniggeringly refers to as 'Heidi Heidi Ho'). Determined not to turn our first date into a pissing contest, I keep my comments to myself when he points to a corner bar popular with the frat-boy set and brags, 'In my wilder days, I danced on the table in that bar one night.' Wild man! I wonder what he'd say if I told him some of the things I've done on barroom tables in *my* wilder days. Discretion is truly the better part of valor. I have to spend the weekend with this man.

We wind up at Bogart's, a jazzy-yuppie-trendy-ferny eatery that Hal waxes nostalgic about as we wait for our sandwiches. Hal has a gimlet; I have coffee. We settle into a friendly if impersonal conversation about teaching, writing, and books we've read. I get the distinct feeling that he's trying to guide the conversation toward more intellectual topics, but I'm not interested. In high school, my friends and I spent a lot of time sitting around bars in the Fan, engaging in mutual intellectual ego-stroking, but seven years of college later, it's lost its appeal. I know I'm smart, thanks. I don't need to prove it – not to myself, not to the patrons in this bar, and not to an Iraqi history professor, no matter how many hours he drove to meet me.

'Ho-*lee*! Will you look at that!'

I look over my shoulder, toward the door of the restaurant, and am not at all prepared for what I see. It's the brunette from Sheva's class, the one with the stupid hands. She's wearing a skin-tight chartreuse bell-bottomed pantsuit, with her boobs spilling over the plunging neckline. Following closely behind her, peering unsubtly down her front, is a white-haired, stoop-shouldered gentleman who's gotta be pushing eighty, at least. The brunette reaches back and grabs his hand, pulling him into a booth where they quickly disappear from view.

'Whaddaya think?' Hal asks, leaning across his plate conspiratorially. 'Is she a call girl or a trophy wife?'

I think of responding with 'none of the above, she's a belly dancer,' but I realize that this would reflect badly on me and my *bedlah*-wearing sisters, so I stop myself. 'Maybe,' I say weakly, 'she's his daughter or his niece or something.'

'Well, if she is, he should be arrested for looking at her like that,' Hal responds, peering around the booth to try and get another look at her. 'I think she's a call girl.'

I don't say so, but I think he may be right. I feel almost

as let down as I did when I saw the blonde with the silver costume at Dot's Back Inn. It's not as big a disappointment, because as belly dancers go, this one was a little on the seedy side to begin with, but still. The Fahed experience is still a little too much of a fresh wound for me to be able to handle the occasional reality of belly dancers as hookers in harem pants.

Back at my apartment, sleeping arrangements are a foregone conclusion. This is the drawback of the long-distance relationship – if you don't hit it off that well in person, you still feel obliged to put out because a) they've come a long way to see you, and b) you've already done 'everything but' in writing. In the days prior to Hal's visits, our e-mails had grown steamier, the descriptions of what we would do this weekend more lurid, until so little was left to the imagination that he might as well have shown up naked. So, though the rest of the visit is pretty much a wash, the sex is, at least by my estimation, worth the trip. After the Fahed episode, being able to play *sharmouta* for a night is actually a relief. Besides, it's been a while. I am actually disappointed when morning comes and we have to come up with more 'date things' to do to fill the time until nightfall, where we can once again get down to the real business at hand and go at it like the desert-dwelling savages that the Crusaders made us out to be.

I hide my disappointment when, after breakfast, Hal suggests a trip to Belle Island. The site of a confinement depot for Yankee POWs during the Civil War, Belle Island is one of those Confederate historical sites that I have avoided visiting for my entire life. Few things interest me less than Confederate history; I am a lousy Richmonder in that respect. I have always heartily agreed with Mariane's description of Monument Avenue as 'the world's largest collection of second-place trophies.' I'm all for preserving history, but after spending one's entire life in Richmond, the Civil War starts to wear a little thin. Just a little.

But I'm a trouper, and Hal's an Arab, so I humor him. We spend a sweltering afternoon tramping through the mud on the trails of Belle Island, and Hal accompanies our tour with what sounds like his canned lecture notes for U.S. History 102: The War Between the States. 'The guard encampment was on that hill, and from there they could see the Yankee encampment. Captain Norris Montgomery was the head of the guard. He and his men made camp in a schoolhouse not too far from the Yankee settlement.' He goes on about Captain Montgomery, pointing out some vantage points along the James, a few historic markers, and spots where various skirmishes and defeats ostensibly took place. When he pauses dramatically after describing the Confederate battle plan, then adds 'but it was not to be,' I look around for the PBS cameras hiding in the trees. Is this a date or a field trip? I'm beginning to have my doubts.

Thank merciful Allah it begins to drizzle, so we head back to the car and then to the apartment. Hal has dinner plans with some old buddies from his table-dancing days, leaving me the remainder of the afternoon to drink coffee, review e-mails, and wonder why I thought this was such a good idea in the first place. Granted, the night before had been fun, and I'm looking forward to a replay this evening when he returns – but Confederate history and fern bars are far from my idea of a great way to spend a weekend. I think back to first dates I've enjoyed – a revival house showing of *Faster Pussycat! Kill! Kill!* A secret unannounced Guns 'N' Roses appearance on Hollywood Boulevard I lucked into with a coke dealer beau. And then, of course, there was the Harley ride that concluded with a tattoo in the kitchen from my musclebound rehab biker. Now *that* was a first date to remember.

Maybe I'm just not cut out for this Arab dating stuff. I change out of my demure Indonesian print pantsuit (I had picked it thinking it made me look academic, very faculty receptionish) and pull on a ragged pair of Levi's and a Misfits T-shirt. Pouring another cup of coffee, I shake my butt wistfully to Dick Dale's surf guitar and wonder if there is an Arab man out there somewhere who can appreciate a sober, nerdy, rock 'n' rolling, coffee-drinking, school-teaching, erotica-reading, kitsch-loving, Lebanese American belly dancer?

My second night with Hal proves even more rewarding than the first; since getting sober, I had almost forgotten how much fun there was to be had falling into bed with someone who you know you're likely never going to see again. I wonder how anyone this much fun with the lights out can be so incredibly bland in the light of day? I suppose it's the converse of the phenomenon I've experienced time and again with musicians – the bigger the name and the wilder the stage act, the more pedestrian in the sack. I guess in the same way a heavy metal drummer uses up all of his originality and stamina onstage and has nothing left by the time he hits the hotel sheets, a history professor is just saving it up, saving it up, waiting to cut loose when the lecture is over. In any case, I forgive him for the Belle Island episode entirely. He makes up for it in spades.

When he leaves the next morning, our good-bye is friendly but hardly bittersweet. I walk him to the car and thank him for dinner. He says he'll e-mail me and let me know he made it back to Tennessee safely. Mrs Longbottom, the nosy old lady downstairs, watches the whole exchange from her porch, then asks me if Hal is my cousin. Yes, I say, he's my Iraqi cousin from Tennessee, but I know she can't hear me because she's deaf as a post. I wonder if she thought Fahed was my cousin too? I take a tiny bit of pride in thinking that, if I can pass for Hal's cousin, maybe we both look a little more Arab than I thought? Or maybe she's just blind, too.

'Maybe you can just keep datin' him from a distance.' Karen and I are doing some early evening balcony sitting and going over the play-by-play from Hal's visit the previous weekend. When his car pulled off from the curb, I had been secure in the knowledge that we were a bad match and that things would fizzle out naturally now that we had both seen this firsthand. What I hadn't counted on was the fact that somehow our on-line chemistry was as strong as ever. Hal might be a boring date in person, but he gives really good e-mail. Chalk up another one for nerds with strong verbal skills.

'Yeah, but how am I supposed to sleep with him when he's there and I'm here?' I wonder how long technology will be in coming out with those virtual reality cybersex goggle helmets that everyone on HBO is always talking about.

'Well, Annie, what you do is just keep sendin' letters back and forth, and then every couple weeks, y'all meet at a mo-tel halfway between here and there. No restaurants, no movies – just hair-pullin', ass-slappin' sex. Then y'all can go your separate ways, and you can do your belly dancin' and he can drink his vintage '89 *fooly fooly foo* and everybody's happy.'

I giggle at the prospect of torrid weekends at the Wytheville Motel 6, but I wonder if maybe I'm not being too picky. An Arab man with whom I can be myself? Are there any who aren't already related to me? I know that life is all about compromises, but how much am I really willing to compromise to fulfill my Princess Jasmine fantasies? Indeed, how much would I be *able* to compromise? The concessions I would have had to make to be Fahed's third-favorite wife would have been easier than the ones Hal would demand. I'd rather take my chances with the *muttawa* than spend the rest of my life listening to history lectures and sipping *fooly fooly foo* at cheese-and-cracker receptions for visiting lecturers.

'So is he still writin' to you?'

'He had been. I haven't heard from him today, though.'

'Well, maybe God's doin' for you what you cain't do for yourself.' I love Karen's pragmatic view of God's involvement. To hear her tell it, God micromanages my love life with the zeal of a *yenta*. It makes me wonder why I don't have better luck, but anyway. It's reassuring to think, even if I can't really get behind it all the way.

'Yeah, maybe so. I'm going in to get some more coffee, and I'm gonna check my e-mail while I'm in there.'

'Way to let go and let God.' She looks at me sideways as the screen door shuts between us. I think about replying that faith without works is dead, but I'm already logging in by the time I think about it – and when I read the message therein, I am immediately sorry.

To: SamiraSafi@aol.com
From: hrashid@utk.edu

Have you noticed any . . . ill effects since our weekend? Problems of a personal nature? Perhaps there's something you neglected to tell me?
 – Hal

'*Karen!!!*' I'm frozen to the spot in mortification and shock. I can't believe a) that he's making the accusation, and b) that he's doing it by e-mail. I am stunned.

'Oh, Lord have mercy, what now?' Karen comes

running in from the porch, slamming the screen door behind her.

'He's accusing me of giving him VD!'

'Do *what*?'

'He thinks I gave him something!'

Karen scans his e-mail, pursing her lips in disgust. 'An' that low-down li'l wimp ain't even got the balls to tell you what he thinks he's got.' She shakes her head. 'If I was you, I'd get checked out. If he really has got somethin', he mighta given it to *you*.'

My concern for my health is running a distant second behind my concern for my good name. I have never, in all my days of catting around, been accused of giving someone a social disease. I'm usually on the cleaner side of the equation, should the truth be known. I'm used to being the questioner, not the questionee. I guess this is what it feels like to be rough trade for a day. I don't think I like it.

'Well, find out what he's got, so at least you'll know what you're dealing with.'

I send Karen back out to the balcony and make the call. Hal is curt and businesslike. It seems he has a rash of sorts, a burning one, and it's *interfering with his tennis game* (and no, I am not making the last part up). I proclaim my assumed innocence repeatedly, but I don't feel he's buying it. I swear up and down that I don't have anything, have never had anything, am not showing any symptoms at all of having anything. 'Maybe you just, kind of . . . *strained* it,' I suggest weakly.

'A strain and a rash are two distinct injuries,' he responds primly.

'Well, then, maybe you *chafed* it.'

'Look,' he says, with condescension oozing through the lines, 'I have a lecture to write and a play to attend. I would appreciate it if you would let me know as soon as you get everything checked out and we'll take it from there.' *Click.*

Take *what* from there? Obviously not the relationship. The lawsuit? The public flagellation? I'm numb. Karen returns from the kitchen and I tell her what he said.

'Oh, so he thinks *you're* the one who should get checked out? Ain't he the one with the dick rash?' She hands me a cup of coffee and sits down. 'I think he's tryin' to get out of payin' the doctor bill by makin' you go instead.'

'But I don't even *have* anything!'

'Well, you best make sure; you did sleep with him, and he's got something.' She reaches up to the windowsill and takes down one of my Jesus candles. This one is a novelty, purchased after I broke up with Lewis Bucket. It shows a skeleton wearing a Mr Weiner Boy uniform selling hot dogs from a cart, and the prayer beneath begs, 'Dear Lord, please help. This life sucks.' Pulling her lighter out of her pocket, Karen lights the candle and eyes me sternly. 'You go 'haid and go to the doctor, and when she tells you you're all clear, you send that gimlet-drinkin' son-of-a-bitch your test results registered mail. And you put a note on the bottom and let Dick Rash know that we lit a weenie candle – ' and she sets the candle on the coffee table with a *thunk* – 'in his *memory.*'

I wipe away a tear of humiliation and thank Allah for friends like Karen. Cybersheiks may come and go, but cool girls stick around.

When faced with Iraqi yuppies bearing rashes and allegations, cool girls and a good German gynecologist are the first line of defense. 'Zere is *nossink,*' declares Dr Beuttner, snapping her rubber gloves off and declaring me one hundred percent disease free. I press for details – maybes, laters, and what ifs. Is there any chance I gave him something, or got something from him, that I have no symptoms of myself? She shakes her head.

'I sink maybe his is *nossink*, too.' She smiles sympathetically, choosing her words carefully. 'Maybe your friend does not use it all that often; now it is sore.' She scribbles her name at the bottom of her report and hands it to me. 'And he sounds not too nice either, so maybe you want to look for another friend.'

Ja. Maybe I do. I clasp the report gratefully in hand and race home to scan it and send it off to Hal.

'So basically, he couldn't handle the high-test Lebanese coochie,' Karen surmises, reading over Dr Beuttner's report.

'No, and he was really miffed when I sent him the paperwork. Had the nerve to get indignant, after he basically accused me of being a disease-ridden *sharmouta*. Besides, it didn't help. He's still convinced he's got something.' I pull up his most recent indictment on the screen and show it to her:

To: SamiraSafi@aol.com
From: hrashid@utkux.utcc.utk.edu

I, for one, would be thrilled if this turns out to be 'nothing.' So far, though, it is still very much 'something.'
 – Hal

'Yeah, I'll bet it's something,' Karen snorts. 'Maybe it'll fall off.'

'Well, in any case, I guess that's the end of that,' I say, and I really mean it this time. If history lectures and gimlets weren't a big enough clue for me, a persistent genital rash and repeated accusations certainly are. Maybe Karen is right about God doing for me what I can't do for myself. He certainly disposed of Hal pretty handily.

'So what's on the agenda for this weekend?'

'I dunno. Do you know a place where can we meet some nice white boys who haven't been to college?'

An hour later, we're happily ensconced in a booth at the Village, eyeing anyone who comes in with blond hair and blue eyes. There's not a unibrow in the house, but there's not a Ph.D. or a gimlet, either, and if I am learning anything it is that life really is about compromises – and cool girls and buff boys, no matter how Aryan they might be. My Princess Jasmine fantasies can go on the shelf for a night. Besides, I don't think Prince Ali would ever be so ungallant as to accuse Jasmine of giving him a rash. I don't think he'd order a gimlet or use the word *exigency* in a song, either, but here in the back booth of the Village, I'm preaching to the choir. The good thing about girlfriends is they usually hate your exes before you do, so there's no need to try and win them over. I buy Karen another beer. She really is the best date I've had in ages. And she's not even vaguely Middle Eastern.

10

Tassel Twirling 101 and
Loving the Beast

Debkeing Around the Clock in Norfolk

'I feel like I'm forgettin' somethin'.' Nadine's arms are loaded down with luggage – a bag of dance outfits, an overnight bag, a *ghawazee* cane, a balanced sword for dancing, and a foot-high South American fetish doll whose wooden head pulls off to reveal a dagger. It's not exactly what I would pack for a weekend at the beach, but then again I'm not Nadine. I myself have brought all of the same items, save for the doll and plus one laptop computer – geek that I am, I can't go two days without Internet access. I guess Nadine feels the same way about evil wooden dolls with daggers in their necks.

Nadine and I are off to Norfolk for a weekend-long belly dancing festival, which promises the likes of Morocco, Tasha Banat, Niran Al-Ubaidi, Dunia, Cheri Berens, Laurel Gray, and Shakira – names that may not be common to the guy on the street but that drive belly dancers into a frenzy of anticipation – Nadine and me included. In the three years that I have now been belly dancing, there has not been an event in Virginia that has come close to this for sheer belly dancing star power. Along with most of the Desert Jewels and no doubt most of the belly dancers between here and New York, we rush to get our reservations in the mail for this once-in-a-lifetime opportunity. The chance to see one of these dancers, much less take a workshop from them, much less have the opportunity to *see and take workshops* from all of them in one weekend – well! It is an event we surely would not miss.

The occasion is a benefit for the Palestine Children's Relief Fund, or, as my mother insists on calling it, 'Some of the Palestine Children's Relief Fund.' It's an old reference left over from the mid-1970s, in the early days of the Lebanese War. She had spent all weekend working on posters for a benefit our church was having for Lebanese war orphans. When she presented them to Father Salwan after church on Sunday, he insisted that she change all of them to read 'to benefit *some of the* Lebanese war orphans,' adding by way of explanation, 'there are so many of them, you know, and we cannot help them all.'

This weekend's benefit for some of the Palestinian Children has been organized by *Zaghareet* magazine, a glossy belly dancing publication out of Virginia Beach that is the pampered baby of a dancer named Taaj. Taaj is young and gorgeous and apparently independently wealthy, able to devote herself fully to her dancing, her magazine, and her frequent trips to Egypt – which, as I am seeing proven true time and again, is no way to win friends among belly dancers. It doesn't surprise me when a few of the seasoned dancers at Sheva's give me the pinchy face when I ask if they'll be attending the workshop. It makes me a) happy that I am not cuter and more talented, as I don't need any help making enemies, thank you, and b) happy also that I am not so petty as to let my own jealousy keep me from attending such a star-studded event. Sheer selfishness would override my jealousy of

Taaj if I had any. This is a big deal. It's the Lollapallooza of belly dancing, and I can't afford to miss it.

What I can afford is a hotel room where I don't have to cram in bed with a half-dozen belly dancers, and I take advantage of my good fortune by booking a room with Nadine at a hotel across from the dance studio. The ever-frugal Jewels are staying across the river at a Red Roof Inn – 'the rooms are twenty dollars cheaper' – and are bunking four to a room. As much as I want to attend this festival, if it came part and parcel with sharing a bed with Marsha, I would probably have to pass. I imagine those beady, nervous eyes staring fixedly at me in the dark. 'You're hogging the sheets!' No thanks. There are some kinds of weird I'm not willing to jump into bed with.

Nadine's weird doesn't faze me a bit, though, and her mysterious Visa Gold ensures that she won't insist on a Red Roof Inn across the river, so she is my obvious choice for a roommate. Besides, we can get a smoking room *and* listen to Middle Eastern music on the trip up, which I have a feeling would not be on the agenda with the Jewels. As Nadine gathers a few last-minute tapes from her collection and crams them into her bulging shoulder bag, I take a look around her cluttered townhouse, checking for new additions to the decor.

Since Nadine and I have been classmates, I have alter-nated with Rosie as her designated cat feeder when she goes on her frequent trips to exotic locales. She was relieved when I agreed to do it, she'd said, because so many people were scared of her apartment that it was hard to find a fearless cat feeder she could depend on. I understand, but I don't find her home frightening in the least. It is more cluttered than my own, which is im-pressive, and the decor is exotic/spooky, a mix of *Dios de los Muertos* figurines, animal skulls, swatches of foreign fabrics and bits of jewelry tacked to the wall, and a liberal sprinkling of Halloween novelty items – stuffed vampires, plastic skeletons, cardboard Frankenstein door hangers. If she were ten years younger she'd be goth, but this is no fashion statement – it's who she is. 'I got so excited when I first went to VCU and I saw people dressed like me,' she once told me on the topic of goths. 'There wasn't anybody in Southwest Virginia anything like that! But when I tried to talk to them,' and she shook her head wistfully, 'they weren't like me at all. They were just *dressing up*.'

If there is anything Nadine is not, it is 'just dressing up.' This is who she is. Nadine is Nadine twenty-four hours a day, with no slips, no snacks, no breaks in between. I think this is why I feel so comfortable around her. If she's going to be herself, I feel like I can sure as hell be myself. There really isn't a lot I can say or do to shock her, and, after hiding so much of my 'weirder side' around the rest of the belly dancers for so long, it's refreshing to be able to cut loose. Around Nadine, I feel downright boring.

'Should I bring my guns?' Nadine is standing at the top of the stairs, a leather cowboy-style holster belt buckled overtop of a typically Nadine black diaphanous bare-midriffed ensemble. On either hip, a pistol butt sticks out of her holsters, jutting out like a pair of blue steel hip scarves.

'I don't know. Do you think we need them?' I often find myself answering Nadine's questions with more questions.

'We might.' She clatters down the steps in her strappy black stilettos past a goat skull, a severed hoof, and a painting of the devil. 'People just ain't right, ya know.'

'That's true,' I agree sincerely, rearranging a dried snakeskin around a small animal's skull on Nadine's bookshelf. 'Maybe you should bring them.'

She looks down at her holsters, considers, and shakes her head.

'Naw,' she says, taking off the belt and clomping back up the stairs. 'Maybe we shouldn't have 'em in the hotel room. I don't wanna bring *bad energy* with me.'

I wonder which thing in her apartment has the best energy – would it be the four-foot-high pentagram, the mobile made of tiny bones, or one of the many daggers and swords? I love Nadine but sometimes her logic eludes me. No matter. She trots back down the stairs sans handguns and we are off for a fabulous star-studded belly dancing weekend – and a hotel room, which always sweetens the pot for me.

The trip down is uneventful. I introduce Nadine to Tom Waits, which is a moderate success – she seems to like his later, more experimental dissonant stuff more than his boozy-growly-yet-tuneful piano bar stuff, which I could have predicted. She has brought along a new tribal drum tape, which I enjoy even though I am more of a cabaret girl at heart. We make one stop for gas and snacks – 'one of these days I still want you to show me how to pump my own gas' – and one for directions. As we browse the souvenirs at the Stuckey's on 64, Nadine picks up some stickers for the neighborhood children in her townhouse complex.

This week, she's teaching the kids how to make tissue paper flowers and stained glass. She pulls a card table out into the front yard so their parents won't get nervous, and any kid who wants can stop by and make a flower. Nadine has a tendency to attract small children and the mentally ill. Often when I call, she is either making crafts with kids on the back patio or she's explaining to Gordon, the local schizophrenic, why he has to keep his pants on when he goes to visit other people. She is patient and sympathetic when he explains why he keeps taking them off, and she agrees that it's hard to remember how to act in public. And Gordon seems relieved, because he knows she really understands.

Sometimes I think that Nadine's spooky outfits and eerie home decor serve the same purpose as a porcupine's quills. Nadine is unquestionably one of the sweetest, most kindhearted people I've ever met. She's sensitive to a fault, deeply sympathetic to others, and wouldn't lift a finger to hurt another living thing . . . but you wouldn't know it to look at her, which I think is exactly the plan, if maybe just subconsciously. Black eyeliner and skulls are scary. Spiky Bedouin jewelry and stiletto heels are off-putting. Paintings of the devil and severed animal parts are a red flag. In the real world, people who are sweet and kind-hearted and giving get chewed up and spit out – unless they're wearing armor. Nadine's armor works for her.

Unfortunately, it also is enough to send the average suburban belly dancer screaming for the hills. Nadine laments that she feels like other dancers are 'looking at her,' or that she gets a 'weird vibe' from them – and I have heard other dancers say exactly the same thing about her. Thank heavens for Rosie and Susan – and Lucy, who once again could give a crap. I think that Mephistopheles himself could sign up with parks and rec to take Lucy's class and, as long as he didn't lift his heels off the floor to do snake hips, she'd be glad to have him.

Nadine doesn't fare quite as well in Sheva's class, but only because Sheva's is as much a *kaffeeklatsch* as it is a dance class. The Girls in the Corner may stare and whisper, but Sheva, bless her soul, is completely oblivious to Nadine's idiosyncrasies. Sheva is oblivious to most things, which works to her benefit in situations that would otherwise baffle her. For instance, when a six-foot-tall pre-op transsexual signs up for belly dancing classes in preparation for the talent portion of a drag queen beauty contest, Sheva gives her the same *blink blink* that she gives every new student, hands her a sign-up sheet, and welcomes her to class. Later, when she decides she wants some additional lessons on top of weekly classes, Sheva clutches her by the beefy arm and leads her over to Janiece.

'Janiece, this is Raquel. He would like to get some private lessons.'

'Sheva, I prefer to be called *she*.'

'Right. Now, he's going to keep taking classes —'

'*She*.'

'Uh huh. But he feels like he needs just a little extra—'

'*Sheva*.' Raquel bends down until she is on the level with Sheva and looks her squarely in the eye. 'I am a pre-operative transsexual. I live as a woman. I would really prefer it if you would refer to me as *she*.'

Sheva does the half-smile thing and pats the back of Raquel's hand.

'Of *course*. Now, do you think you could give him some lessons?'

It doesn't take long for Raquel to find her way to Lucy's class – where, giving Sheva a run for her oblivious money, Becky welcomes her by marveling, 'Aren't you lucky! Not many girls have the good fortune to grow as tall as you!' No, not many at all. I am sorry when her pageant arrives and she leaves class before Nadine returns from a trip to India. I was so sure they'd hit it off.

We check into the hotel about an hour before the Friday night show is scheduled to take place. It occurs to us only after we are fully dressed and ready to go that the address of the venue is not printed on any of the registration literature we received in the mail. After calling the other hotel where participants are staying (no clue), all of the names listed on the contact sheet (answering machines), and hooking up the laptop and scanning the *Zaghareet* Web site (no luck), we begin to panic. This is the show we've been waiting for. Most of the big-name dancers will be dancing tonight – tomorrow's show is open floor and then Morocco – who will be fantastic, no doubt, but we didn't sign on to see just Morocco. We want Shakira and Dunia and Cheri Berens! We want to be dazzled and over-whelmed! We don't want to spend our Friday night in the

215

hotel room drinking soda machine drinks and watching cable.

We grow industrious. We try and think of all of the Virginia Beach belly dancers we know of and get their numbers from information. We call them. They don't answer. No doubt some of them are already en route. We finally hit the jackpot when the infamous Salina Asmin, the diva who opened the Nadia Hamdi show, picks up on the fourth ring. And it's her – I'd know that baby voice anywhere.

'Helloooooo?'

'Uh, hi. You don't know me, but I'm a belly dancer from Richmond, and I'm at the beach now . . . I drove down for the *Zaghareet* show, but I just realized I don't know where the show is. Do you know where they're having it?'

'No.' The baby voice is gone, replaced by a curt tone that makes 'no' sound like an expletive and an insult rolled into one two-letter word. And she hangs up the phone, just like that.

Well, damn. I knew that there were some hard feelings between some of the other belly dancers and Taaj, but I had no idea that she was public enemy number one. This nonsense is going to make it damn near impossible to find the show. I flop on the bed, stumped. Nadine is pacing and smoking by the window that overlooks the parking lot; the mere inconvenience of the whole situation has doubled her nervous energy level. She's flitting around like a mosquito on crystal meth.

I figure we might as well get in the car and drive over to the dance studio where the workshops will be held tomorrow. If the show isn't taking place there, maybe by now they've realized they left it off the flyer and will have posted directions. I aim Nadine in the direction of the elevators and let her go like a bottle rocket, and I follow her down to the parking deck and hope for the best.

Once we get within a couple of blocks of the dance studio, I begin to see signs that we must be in the right place. The first sign is a proliferation of cars with suspiciously exotic personalized plates – ZARIA, SCHEHERA, ISHTARA. The second sign, on the block where the dance studio is located, is small groups of women in dramatic outfits walking together in twos and threes. Several of them are redheads.

I don't know what it is with belly dancers and red hair, but there is definitely no shortage of redheads in the belly dancing community – and most of them didn't come by the hue honestly. You would think that if a belly dancer was thinking of coloring her hair she would go with, oh, I don't know, a lovely Persian black, or a deep Egyptian chestnut brown. I myself would want hair like the girls at Saint Anthony's – glossy, thick, and the color of ripe black olives. But *red*? I see red hair, I think Riverdance and Celtic folk songs, not snake hips and *Habibi ya Eini*. But I think I am alone.

Nadine and I park the car and hustle our nonredheaded selves toward the dance studio, where the line of women assures us that the show is indeed being held here. Before long I spot Taaj herself, giving orders and scratching things off on a clipboard as she directs dancers to the dressing rooms and workers to their posts. She doesn't look bothered in the least at the absence of Salina Asmin or any of the other holdouts – in fact, she looks self-assured, in charge, and absolutely stunning. No wonder they hate her. We pay our fifteen dollars and take our seats on folding chairs assembled in front of an auditorium-style stage. I see the Jewels contingent in the second row, and a few other Richmonders from Sheva's class. Lucy and her seven-year-old daughter, Katherine, wave to us from the vending area. I pick out Taaj's troupe mates, whom I recognize from pictures in her magazine. The house is about half full.

More noticeable than the dancers who are present are the dancers who aren't. I don't see anyone from the Newport News contingent except Lucy Lee, and Newport News has a pretty good-sized dance community – much bigger than you'd think if you were at all familiar with Newport News. Lucy is the only Woman of Selket I can spot, and I don't see any of the D.C./Maryland crew who usually drive down for the Selket workshops. I wonder if attendance will pick up tomorrow for the workshops? I can't imagine passing up the opportunity to take workshops with all these great teachers – but then again, I can't imagine missing a show with all these great dancers, either, and so many people aren't here. It's all about priorities, I guess – would you rather accept the fact that someone is younger, prettier, and richer than you and see a great show, or would you rather sit at home and stew?

I know what I'd rather do, and in minutes I'm doing it – enjoying top-notch belly dancing, marred only by some second-rate production values and a few star tantrums. I suppose I might throw a tantrum too, if I'd traveled halfway across the country to do a show, only to have the novice sound engineer turn off my tape in the middle of the dramatic pause I'd deliberately inserted between my *taqsim* and my drum – but no matter. From folkloric *Saidi* cane dancing to flashy veil numbers, we are mesmerized by the dancers.

One number has us both looking at each other with raised eyebrows before it even starts – Niran's flamenco-belly fusion piece performed to a Christian technopop song. 'Niran's dance ministry is an important and personal form of devotion,' notes the program. *Dance ministry?* Nadine looks like she might bolt; in her blue-collar neighborhood someone is always trying to save her, since her taste in both clothing and home decor simply scream 'witch!' I try and swallow my own preconceptions; since I've been working in youth corrections, 'ministry'

218

has become synonymous in my mind with 'we're here to tell your gay students they're going to hell' and 'don't turn your back on us or we'll smuggle your VCR out in our Bible box.' Both are regular occurrences – in fact, there's still a church on Hull Street being vacuumed with our vacuum cleaner. It's been positively IDed, but no one wants to accuse the good Reverend of taking it, even though it has 'Property of Youth Services' etched down the neck.

Even if it weren't for the ministry part, I would probably still be waiting to hate this number due to the use of the F-word. Before I started belly dancing, I didn't feel one way or the other about flamenco. Now, though, I feel the same way about flamenco as I do about hula. Not only does it seem like flamenco and hula are hotter, trendier, and more visible these days, but every day it seems like more belly dancers are defecting to Latin dance – then, if they even deign to keep belly dancing, they try to sneak flamenco moves in as if we're not going to notice. It's like having a sister who gets all the attention even though you know you're just as cute. 'All I ever hear is flamenco, flamenco, flamenco!' What's so great about flamenco? Look at us! We can *belly dance*!

Try as I might, though, I can't hate Niran's number, and I don't think Nadine can, either. First of all, it's a lot more belly than it is flamenco, and second, she's out-chipping Chip and Dale. Never have I seen a dancer look like she's having this great a time onstage. Maybe it's the glory of God, I don't know, but Niran is having an absolute blast bringing us her dance ministry, and her enthusiasm, if not her Christianity, is contagious. I find myself applauding wildly before she finishes twirling at the end.

The rest of the show is almost as spectacular, but only almost. I'm so glad I signed up for Niran's workshop tomorrow. She seems like she would be a fun teacher. I'm signed up for Niran's hip workshop, Dunia's floorwork, and Azur Aja's snake dance (with ropes, not real snakes, thank merciful Allah). I agonized over whether or not to take Morocco's workshop, and in the end I decided not to. Well, it wasn't exactly a decision per se. In a word, I chickened out. Morocco is the grande dame of American belly dancing, the final authority on all things undulating, and the Commander-in-Chief of the Ethnic Police. As Aunty Rocky, she rules the belly dance listserv with an iron mouse. I have seen list members shredded – *shredded*, I tell you – by Aunty Rocky's rapier tongue and inexhaustible knowledge of Oriental dance (she detests the B-word). If I am intimidated by the Girls in the Corner, Morocco makes my blood run cold with terror. I can't imagine subjecting my stupid hands and sloppy hips to her critique.

At the end of the show, Taaj comes on and announces that we have a very special finale in store – we will be seeing a dancer from over there. The audience oohs appropriately. In the world of American belly dance, anything from *over there* immediately carries a cachet that dancers from over here can only dream about. Whether it's the latest steps from Cairo, the newest costumes from Mohammed Ali Street, or a dancer who may at some point have broken into a hip circle somewhere in the vicinity of the fertile crescent, *from over there* is the holy grail, deservedly or not. One memorable 'not' was when, fresh from a trip to Cairo, Jen took to wearing black bicycle pants under her purple *bedlah*, because that's what the dancers in Egypt were wearing. Never mind that they were wearing them to escape the wrath of the *muttawa* should they show too much leg. No one in the audience in Richmond knew that. In fact, they didn't even know that anyone in Cairo was wearing bicycle pants. They just thought Jen had lost her mind.

The dancer we're seeing tonight from over there is Samraa al Nil. She is listed in the program as 'our only truly Egyptian dancer tonight,' which seems just a little gratuitous. She looks young, in her twenties maybe. A lot of the dancers we've seen tonight are forty and above and have been working their *zils* off for the past twenty years learning to interpret and portray Middle Eastern dance as best they can – only to be told, in essence, 'sorry, *habibi*, you just ain't got what she got!' I am too scared of Morocco to even insinuate her age, but suffice to say she has been belly dancing a *looong* time, and I have a feeling she could eat Samraa al Nil for lunch with baba ghanouj. The program goes on to gush that Samraa has performed in 'Cairo, Luxor, Aswan, and Alexandria' and has danced for 'a number of royal and presidential families.' Indeed! I do enjoy watching her dance; she is confident, capable, and extremely well turned out in a jewel-encrusted *bedlah* that sets off her olive skin and glimmering black hair. But give me the opportunity and I'll take Niran over Samraa al Nil any day – and the only *over there* Niran's got going on is Cincinnati.

When the show is over, Nadine and I beat a hasty retreat to the hotel to rest up for our workshops tomorrow. In the room, I crack open my laptop and Nadine resumes pacing and smoking by the window. With both of us in our elements, the room is silent except for the *clack clack* of my keyboard and the *clink clink* of Nadine's Berber jewelry.

I start composing an e-mail to Karen, telling her about the show. I keep the details minimal, focusing instead on the snafu finding it and quickly changing the subject to our hotel room and its amenities. As I always tell my students, you write to your audience. I am describing the contents of the minibar when Nadine throws her hands up in dismay.

'I love the beast!'

I stop in mid-keystroke and raise one eyebrow. I'm used to stream-of-consciousness ramblings from Nadine, but this is a stream we haven't waded into yet. I lift my head and look at her.

'I love the beast – you know, Satan. I can't help it. I think he's cute.' She worries with one of the Beanie bats that she keeps clipped to her cape. 'I just think it's so sad that he can't go to heaven. You know, Christians are always sayin' that everybody can repent and be forgiven. Well, why can't Satan repent so he can go to heaven, too?' She looks genuinely concerned, and I'm sure that she is. It's breaking her heart to think of poor Satan, unable to partake in the bounty of heaven. I choose my words carefully.

'I don't think,' I say, with all the sincerity I can muster, 'that Satan *wants* to go to heaven.'

'Well, maybe not.' She considers this, then looks thoughtful. 'But do you think if he wanted to, he could? I mean, if he repented and he really meant it?'

'I don't see why not.' This seems to cheer her up, and she lights another cigarette and stops pacing, plopping cross-legged on the other bed and dumping the contents of her purse in front of her in search of some unknown item. I return to my typing. Suddenly the contents of the mini-bar seem so dull and unworthy – nothing to write home about, literally. I highlight the whole letter and delete it, then start over.

From: SamiraSafi@aol.com
To: KarenRec@hotmail.com

Dear Karen,
You are not going to believe the conversation I just had . . .

The next morning, Nadine and I drag ourselves out of bed at the ungodly hour of ten A.M. and head back to the dance studio. It is another benefit of rooming with Nadine that she is even less of a morning person than I am. There's no forced cheeriness or good-natured ribbing to contend with when I snarl at Nadine in the morning. She snarls right back.

Arriving at the studio, we help ourselves to coffee and claim our spots in the room where Niran will be holding her workshop. Vicki and Mary Mary are there, too, and Aileen. Vicki and Aileen tell us they went out for dinner and drinks the night before and came back to the hotel near midnight, after Janet had already gone to sleep. They bumbled around the darkened room, whispering back and forth between themselves for twenty minutes before Aileen spoke up. 'I don't know what we're whispering for,' she declared in her flat New York accent. 'You know she's *deaf*!'

Niran flits into class just before the eleven A.M. post time, looking just as Chip and Dale as she did onstage. She introduces herself, apologizes in advance for not being at the top of her game – 'I have the *worst* cramps' – and leads us into the warm-up. She informs us that she has recently gotten into Pilates and that she will be drawing on a lot of Pilates technique in today's workshop.

'This is supposed to be a hip workshop,' a stout, middle-aged woman with long gray hair says accusingly from directly behind me.

'It is!' Niran nods cheerfully and continues leading us through our stretches, still talking animatedly about the wonders of Pilates.

'I didn't sign up for Pilates.' The woman is getting agitated. 'Nowhere on the registration form did it say anything about Pilates!'

'Well, I think you'll find it helpful as you begin to do the hip movements.' Niran is unflustered. 'Just wait and see.'

'I do not want a Pilates workshop!' The woman is practically bellowing now. 'I already *know* Pilates! I did not pay thirty dollars for a Pilates workshop!'

I have had enough bellowing and not enough coffee. I whip my head around and give her an icy stare. 'Taaj is out there at the registration table right now. Maybe if you go explain to her that you are displeased with the content of this workshop, she will let you switch to another one.' I use my best, most even teacherly tone. She looks annoyed, but she simmers down a notch.

'I don't want to switch workshops,' she mutters. 'I just don't want *Pilates*.' And fortunately, that's the last we hear out of her. Later that day, I am alarmed to hear her preface something with 'The technique I use with *my* students . . . ' Ye gads! This woman is a dance teacher? I can't imagine. At first I think that maybe she is so far out in Bumfuck Egypt (nowhere near Cairo, mind you) that her students don't have any other choice, but then I remember that some of the best dancers I've seen have been from the most obscure locations. The gorgeous and talented Miramar is from Cross Junction, Virginia, not far from where Patsy Cline lived. Aegela, the redheaded fireball who impressed me so much at my first *hafla*, lists Stone Mountain, Georgia, as her home town. And, while surfing through local dance directories, I am always intrigued by Samra, not the *Samraa* from over there, but the one from Fancy Gap, Virginia, a name that conjures up all sorts of interesting visions and seems as good a place to be a belly dancer as any.

It reminds me of a story I heard one time when I was getting one of my way-too-infrequent massages. Rachel Steele, my masseuse, is a redheaded, square-jawed Oregon Hill girl who grew up in Turbow, West Virginia. When I told her I was taking belly dancing lessons, she started off on a story about her childhood that, backed by the ethereal new age music she played in her massage room and the circular motion of her hands on my back, transported me back to the Appalachian town where she grew up. Seems that about the time she was ten years old, a Lebanese family moved in down the street. They had a lot of kids, five or six at least, but Fatima was Rachel's age and she could belly dance like nobody's business. She would stand out in the middle of the one big street that ran down between their houses and she would dance and dance, and the other kids would clap and cheer . . . in the dream world created by the music, the candles, the sandalwood oil, and Rachel's expert hands, I could see ten-year-old Fatima, undulating, undulating, *aiwa*. . . .

'And oh, she was hydrocephalic, so she had a really huge head and she had to wear this yellow plastic helmet all the time . . . '

Niran's hip workshop is thoroughly enjoyable and well worth thirty dollars, Pilates or no. We learn an array of sassy hip articulations and get a workout that will leave me aching until well after I return to Richmond. I wish that Niran were offering more than one workshop this weekend – there is so much more I want to learn from her. I'd even sit through a sermon if only she'd teach me some more of those 'butt bounces' when she was done.

The snake dance with Azur Aja does not go so well. It isn't what I expected; it's sort of a comedy number and Azur Aja reminds me a little bit of Aunt Clara on *Bewitched*. She keeps forgetting her place in the chore-ography and giggling nervously when the tasseled rope 'snakes' don't agree with her commands. It's all fun and I learn some interesting rope tricks, but it's not the exotic and sensual snake dance I had envisioned when I signed up for the session. Still, it's an enjoyable way to spend an afternoon, twirling my tassels around in a roomful of saucy ladies. I end the day thinking that I got plenty for my money and still pitying the dancers who boycotted the event.

Nadine and I opt to have dinner at the Middle Eastern deli that has set up shop in the studio for the weekend. We purchase aluminum containers of hummus, baba ghanouj, and grape leaves and a stack of pita loaves and set up at one of the long wooden tables along the edge of the main floor. I overhear some departing dancers inquiring if there is a TGI Friday's or Applebee's nearby. I am aghast. I can't imagine wanting to eat bland chain-restaurant munchies with this bounty available right here. I bite into a grape leaf and thank my parents for raising me to know what good food tastes like.

We still have more workshops to look forward to in the morning, but the real anticipation is reserved for tonight's club show. The Waves band is going to play live for any of us who care to dance in the hotel's banquet room, and at ten P.M., Morocco will dance. That's it. Everyone else, Friday night show; Morocco, Saturday night show. She's that big a deal. Nadine has seen her before, but I haven't. I only know her as this mythic figure, Aunty Rocky, dancing since the Mesozoic era, keeper of all records of *danse orientale*. I am eager for ten o'clock to come.

With less than an hour to spare, we head over to the hotel and claim seats at the edge of the dance floor. The place is filling up fast with dancers in what I am coming to recognize as the belly-dancer-on-holiday uniform – anything with rhinestones and sequins and a whole lot of makeup. Pretty much the same as the average costume, only more coverage. As usual, Nadine and I are woefully out of place in our all-black ensembles, but we don't care because we're about to see *Morocco*. Niran comes in wearing a lime green formfitting cocktail dress. Bless her heart. If Cincinnati weren't so far away, I'd be signing up for her classes posthaste. She sits at a table opposite us with Tasha Banat, the Palestinian dancer who did two numbers in the Friday show. For one of them, she dragged up as a guy and looked just like Kevin Zeheb from Saint

Anthony's when he danced with the Maroniteens. The Jewels are assembled on the far wall, and at the best table in the house there is an assortment of middle-aged Arab women and small black-haired children who seem to be with the band. I wonder if seeing belly dancing is a treat for them, or if we are the Middle Eastern equivalent of a minstrel show? I make a mental note to watch for their reactions.

At just before ten, Taaj motions the band to stop, which they do, remaining in their seats with instruments at rest. Arabic music begins blaring from the house speakers; I am shocked when I recognize it as the opening cut off 'Hitlist Egypt,' my favorite pop CD. I can't believe that I have the same taste in music as the exalted Morocco. The people in the cheap seats begin making their way toward the edges of the floor, now cleared of dancers. The houselights dim. The spotlights come on, and then, from the hallway, the sound of *zils* announce her arrival . . . Morocco!

She is siphoned into a red costume, her makeup subdued, hair tucked into a crocheted snood. Like most of the big-name dancers I've seen perform, she resembles her publicity photos only vaguely – as appears to be standard practice, it's been many years and several pounds since they were taken. I remember someone in Lucy's class doing some quick math and estimating that Morocco is over sixty; her black-and-white publicity photos show a fresh-faced, pigtailed girl of maybe twentysomething (though if she looks this good at sixty, she might well have been forty then). But added years and added pounds have done absolutely nothing to diminish Morocco's skill or stamina – or, if they have, she was some kind of marathon superdancer in the 1960s. Morocco plays her *zils* with astounding precision, never wavering from the beat. She travels the floor incessantly, from corner to corner, playing to all points equally. The song ends and *another* begins. That song ends and another begins – and Morocco

227

never stops moving. Literally. The most amazing thing about her dancing is her ability to hold a shimmy. She layers her other moves over an omnipresent shimmy, and not a little shimmy, either. That shimmy is the foundation on which she builds her show, and it's strong, steady, and sharp. Not to mention that it would have dancers half her age, myself included, panting for water after a minute and a half. Not Aunty Rocky, though. It's all in a day's work for her.

She shimmies right up to the end, and we call her back for an encore and she shimmies some more. I can't imagine. She definitely earns her reputation. Even if she didn't know squat about *danse orientale* you'd have to tip your fez to her. I regret not signing up for her workshop; maybe she would be giving out stamina tips along with the choreography. She'd better; otherwise I don't know of anyone present who would be able to keep up with her in the workshop tomorrow. I'm tired just from watching her.

As the band fires up their instruments and starts playing again, off-duty belly dancers make their way to the floor. Some of them are hesitant, sticking with shoulder shimmies and subdued traveling steps. Some look like they're ready for their close-up, pairing extravagant hands with expressions of deeply sensual import and everything short of floorwork. And some of the dancers just look like they're having a hell of a good time. Tasha Banat and Niran are among the first on the floor, and within minutes they have the matriarch of the Waves table up *debkeing* with them, to the delight of the band and their families. Before long the entire Waves table is involved in a rollicking *debke* line with Niran at one end and Tasha at the other, whooping and waving a napkin and stomping as hard as her sensible black pumps will allow.

I sneak along the back wall, by the bar, and down the hall to the ladies' room. Every once in a while I am struck by a little twinge of insecurity, and this is one of those times. Usually I feel comfortable and happy around groups of belly dancers. Usually I feel I've found a place where I belong, where I can be myself. But every now and then I get that old familiar feeling like that guy is going to show up with the badge and the clipboard and tell me that I'm going to have to leave, and this time I know exactly what he's going to say:

'Excuse me – Miss Soffee? Anne Soffee?'

'Yes?'

'You are Anne Soffee, correct?'

'Yes, I am.'

'And you are fully fifty percent Lebanese, are you not?'

'Yes.'

'Raised in the Maronite Church, were you?'

'Yes.'

'Belonged to the Maroniteens as well?'

'Yes, sir.'

'I just need to know why you are not out there on the dance floor with those people doing the *debke*.'

At that point I would have to break down and confess that I was no more able to do the *debke* than I was to do a Hopi rain dance, and I would be drummed out of the belly dancing community, the Lebanese American community, and any other community of people who had the least little bit of pride in their heritage. Thirty-odd years of being half Lebanese, three years of Middle Eastern dance training, and I, Anne Thomas Soffee, Lebanese American belly dancer, would be revealed as the non-*debke*-doing poseur that I am.

Fear of exposure as being devoid of *debke* keeps me in the ladies' room long enough for Nadine to come looking for me. I don't explain why I'm there, but I swear she understands. We smoke a reassuring cigarette together on the sink, and presently Tasha Banat and Niran come in together, giggling, panting, and dripping head to toe in sweat. They dry off with paper towels, splash their faces with water, and head out to do it some more. We both stare after them, waiting a few minutes before we head back to the banquet room. I check my pale complexion in the mirror as Nadine adds still more kohl around her eyes. As usual, she seems to know what I'm thinking.

'I know you sometimes wish you were darker, but I wish I was light like you.' Nadine's skin is an olive brown, its origin as mysterious as Nadine herself. She holds her arm up against mine; the difference is startling. I look ghostlike under the fluorescent bathroom lights.

'I'll trade you,' I say, and she giggles, throwing her black fringed shawl back over her brown arm. I am joking, but at the same time, I'm not. I am jealous of Nadine's skin, and Samraa al Nil's, and Tasha Banat's, and every other Arab, part-Arab, and wannabe Arab in this hotel who is darker than I am. Three years of belly dancing may have made me more comfortable in my skin, but why couldn't that skin be just a little darker?

11

This is Planet Earth

*Pink Floyd and Potato Skins
in the Strip Mall*

Some six months after the Cafine's debacle, I can hardly believe I'm still plugging away with the Desert Jewels. Of those who survived Cafine's, I am the last bastion of small-timeism. Our *zils* weren't even cold before Too-Tall Mary and Jen both were invited to audition for, and were accepted by, the Women of Selket. They auditioned with the hamster dance; it wouldn't have been my choice, but it did the trick – and the rumor quickly circulated that Marsha threw a screeching hissy fit when she found out, wailing, 'I can't believe they used *my zil* number!'

'We made sure to give due credit,' Too-Tall Mary tells me later, diplomatic to her fingertips. 'We announced before we auditioned that it was choreographed by Lucy Lee.' Ouch. Choreography credits aside, Too-Tall continues to lead the field in the competition for Nicest Girl in the World, sticking it out with the Jewels on top of the daunting schedule demanded by the Women of Selket. She practices group numbers without flinching and shows up for nursing home after nursing home, kissing countless

Saturday afternoons good-bye in the name of politeness. Jen resigns from the Jewels, and I can't say that I blame her – besides, it's a foregone conclusion; she all but vanished after the infamous vote.

I have to admit that I feel a twinge of envy when I see Too-Tall Mary and Jen performing the plebe duties at the Selket workshops – putting out plates of butter cookies, manning the card table where registration is held, refilling the ice buckets when they get low. I see them in the kitchen of the West End Community Center, chatting in low tones with my teachers and the dancers I only know from restaurant shows, sharing inside jokes with the blonde from Dot's Back Inn and Lucy. It reminds me a little of when I was living in L.A. and I went to a GWAR show at the Palladium with my friend Linnea, who was working for Arista at the time. We were milling in the crowded VIP section and she was casually talking about old times with the guy on her left. I assumed she knew him from work, but when I peered around her big hair I saw it was Henry Rollins – and there I was, with my small hair and my cloth after-show-only pass, not quite in the loop once again. Mary, Jen, and I used to be troupe mates, we used to be equals – and now they are Women of Selket and I'm still a crappy little Jewel.

Every once in a while, I'm able to convince myself that I'm having fun with the Jewels, that somehow it's still worth it. When Shirley calls and offers me a fifty-dollar bellygram job, stating that she knows I'm ready for bellygrams and everybody gets a fair turn at the paying gigs here in the Jewels, I am elated. It's my first-ever paying gig – a milestone. I do a cutesy Chip-and-Dale ten-minute routine in a split-level ranch house for someone's dad's sixtieth birthday. The family thanks me profusely, the birthday boy says it's the best present he's ever gotten. His four-year-old granddaughter follows me out to the car because I look like Princess Jasmine. That is worth more than fifty dollars to me. When Shirley calls to see how it went, I'm still flying. I gush about how great it was, how nice the people were, how they told me it was exactly what they were hoping for. On Thursday at practice, she announces that I have successfully delivered my first bellygram.

'It went well,' she says flatly. Then, just in case I was still feeling good about it, she added, 'At least that's what Anne says.'

BAM! Several of the Jewels come over to me after practice to ask about the bellygram . . . and to tell me why they had to turn it down. Apparently, 'everybody gets a fair turn' means 'everybody gets a fair turn if Janet, Marsha, and Sara can't do it.' I tell myself that it doesn't matter, that I know how much the family enjoyed it, that I have fifty dollars in my pocket now and they don't, that I don't have to let the Shirley Shropshire Bad Attitude Mind Ray drive me out of the Jewels, but it begins to ring hollow after a while. I am tired of having to brace myself before I get out of the car at the Moose Lodge. I am tired of having to bite my tongue through practice each week. I am tired of bastardized choreography and rule by dictatorship. I want to quit the Jewels, but I don't have the guts. Just like I didn't have the guts to speak up and say 'yeah, Jen is a better dancer than most of us,' or 'I won't learn that number because it's *stolen* and, besides that, it *sucks*' or even 'the bellygram didn't go *well*, it went *fucking great*, so put *that* in your boom box and play it.' As always, I am silent about what I really think because I am a piker, a beginner, and I am paying my dues like I am supposed to. With my *zils* on and my mouth shut.

Regardless of her apparent doubts about my bellygram, Shirley calls me for another gig a few weeks later. This one is a real peach – a 'rock 'n' roll band,' she calls them, who want two dancers to dance onstage with them at a 'sports bar.' She gives me a number to call and suggests that maybe Vicki or Aileen will do it with me. The translation that runs in my head is 'maybe some of you floozies will dance in a barroom, but not my Marsha.' Whatever. I go ahead and accept the gig. It sounds interesting, anyway: I'm getting just a little tired of wheelchairs and oxygen tanks. I call Vicki up to see what she thinks about it.

'I don't know,' she says pessimistically. 'I don't know if I want to put my four-hundred-dollar costume in some smoky bar.' I hadn't thought about it, but she has a point. She goes on to mention that she is planning to scope out the club, a Three Chopt Bar and Grill, later that weekend and she'll get back to me. We decide that since she has the bar covered, I should go ahead and check up on the band, billed as 'Another Pretty Face.' No problem. I still have my connections. I get on the horn to Mariane.

'Oh, so you're speaking to me again?'

'Well, only when I need something. What do you know about Another Pretty Face?'

'That's George Conradi.'

'And who else?'

'Nobody else. He's like a one-man show. He plays the keyboards and does old Duran Duran and David Bowie and stuff. Then he calls up here to the feedback line doing a lot of different voices, pretending to be big fans who saw the show and loved it and couldn't get enough of him. He thinks I don't know they're all him. Oh, and he wears clown makeup.'

'*Clown* makeup?'

'Well, yeah. I guess. White stuff. Maybe it's mime makeup. No, it can't be mime makeup, because he's singing and talking. It's clown makeup.'

Oy gevalt.

I call Vicki back and give her the bad news. Her news for me is equally discouraging. She checked up on the venue and deems it 'worse than Lakeside Tavern.' I know exactly what she means. It is evidence that we have both been in Richmond way too long. In any case, Vicki is not about to go through with this now that she has seen the bar. I wish I had such great news about the band that she would reconsider, but clown makeup and Duran Duran covers are hardly a winning sales pitch. I thank her for checking out the bar and hang up the phone.

After thumbing through my Rolodex, I decide to give the other Vicki a call. Vicki Goodman is a student at Sheva's and, besides me, one of the few 'city girls' who belly dances. She lives in Church Hill and ekes out a living modeling nude for life drawing classes at VCU. All of this works in her favor in that I know she will a) probably not be as freaked out as Vicki One at the idea of a seedy bar, and b) also probably really need the money. I pick up the phone and give Vicki Two a call.

I am right on both counts. She has to double-check her schedule, since she is going to be painted gold in order to portray a living statue at a black tie event at the Commonwealth Club – but as long as the two events don't conflict, she'll be glad to do it. I'll have to lend her a costume; she leans toward the earthy/tribal and a night-club gig is usually a high-glitz affair – even if it is at a seedy sports bar. I mean, David Bowie covers, *hello!* But that's no problem; it should fit her. The new arrangement has the added bonus of flying under the radar of the Shirley Shropshire Bad Attitude Mind Ray – since I already told her Vicki and I were taking the gig, I can continue to say that Vicki and I are now preparing for it without letting on that I have passed half of a paying gig on to a non-Jewel.

About a week before the show, I get the first of an unnerving number of phone calls from the Pretty Face himself. He wants to bring me a tape of his music so I can 'work something up,' though the original agreement was that we would dance to taped music between sets. He tells me that this will probably be 'a real powerhouse' and that he'd like to go ahead and book us for some more shows now, a comment I gracefully ignore as I attempt to steer him back toward the specifics of our one agreed-upon gig. He is pushy and self-aggrandizing, with a Sopranos accent and a smoker's hack. He has no day job, he tells me, because he needs to devote himself fully to promoting his musical career. Without prompting, he tells me the story of how he left New York for Richmond because Richmond was 'an untapped market' and 'prime' for what he was doing. I know from my research with Mariane that the venues he books are out of the way, even for Richmond – Three Chopt Bar and Grill and Ashland Coffee and Tea are hardly the Schwab's of the Richmond scene. Is he really expecting to rise to greatness from dank pubs in the 'burbs? I also decline to advise the hard-to-reach Mr Face that he may wish to wake up earlier than three P.M. if he wishes to do any promoting, and, failing that, he should not allow his school-aged daughter to screen his calls and inform the caller that 'daddy's still asleep and he said not to wake him up.'

Vicki One follows the saga like a bad reality show, cornering me at Jewels practice to hear the latest cringe-worthy developments in the Pretty Face saga. I begin to envy her foresight, but I realize, with what is becoming my mantra these days, It's Too Late Now. On the appointed evening, Vicki Two and I convene at my apartment and begin preparing for the show.

I have chosen to wear a simple gold-fringed *bedlah*; remembering Vicki One's rationale, I don't want to expose my precious rainbow costume to secondhand smoke and bar fumes. Vicki Two is borrowing a green-and-gold number that was handed down to me from Mary Mary, who is something of a costume philanthropist. It's nothing to be warming up for class and have Mary Mary sidle up and hand you a full bra, belt, skirt, and veil combo, replete with accessories. 'I don't have any use for this old thing,' she'll say, and wave you away when you try and thank her. There are girls all over town gratefully dancing in Mary Mary's castoffs – and they keep on coming.

We slather on the body glitter, figuring the bar will be pretty dark, and run through our routine a couple of times. We're going to do a scaled-back version of a Sheva group number that we both already know; it's called 'Star Dancer' and it's pretty glam, with a lot of spins and shimmies. It's ten minutes long, so that will make up half of our agreed-upon twenty-minute set. For the other half, we're going to use two numbers by Hanan, a female pop vocalist we both like. It's a happy coincidence that both of us have performed to these two numbers before, so we're familiar enough with them that we'll be comfortable using those for our improv part. That's where we'll go out and 'mingle,' dancing around tables and up and down aisles.

I've only been to one other belly dancing show at a bar. For some unknown reason, Sheva once scheduled a show at Piggy's Attaché on West Broad Street. I had never been to Piggy's – indeed, why would I want to, with a name like that – but the mere mention of it got the bug-eye response from my father, so I knew it was going to be choice. Sure enough, the dancers found themselves navigating around two pool tables and playing to a crowd of corn-fed good old boys in overalls and gimme caps, most of whom wouldn't have known an attaché if it bit them on the denim-clad ass. In an intriguing turn of events, Patricia, the only African American dancer that night, was the runaway show-stopper, ending her routine with so many tips stuffed in her costume that she looked like she had sprouted. One google-eyed three-hundred-pound Bubba must have tipped her a dozen times before he ran out of bills.

Based on this limited bar-dancing observation, I can only hope that tips will be involved. When Shirley booked the gig, she agreed to a price that was so low as to practically be two-for-one – and again, I find myself wondering why I agreed to do this in the first place. But maybe the tips will be lucrative enough to make it worthwhile. We can hope, anyway. If the place really is worse than Lakeside Tavern, the patrons should be good and drunk when we go on at ten, and it shouldn't take more than a little flirting and a well-placed shoulder shimmy or two to loosen a few of those well-lubricated bills from their wallets. I realize that even thinking along these lines would probably earn me a hearty smack across the face from the Dance Police, but hey. A girl's gotta eat.

We arrive at the bar at nine-thirty, plenty of time, we figure, to get our tape to the soundman, touch up our makeup, and confer with the 'band.' It is not a good sign that a heavy metal thrash band made up of high school kids is onstage when we arrive. Long greasy hair flies about in circles as the lead singer growls something vaguely sinister in that Linda Blair *Exorcist* voice that is so popular with thrash vocalists. We stand just outside the door, makeup cases in hand, dumbly surveying the scene. And it is not a pretty one.

Vicki One was dead on about it being worse than Lakeside Tavern. The bar is located in a strip mall off Three Chopt Road, deep in the suburbs of Richmond. It is bordered by a travel agency on one side and two large dumpsters on the other. It's one of those two-sided bars where the band plays on one side and, on the other side of a wall, there are pool tables, video games, and a television tuned to ESPN. The preferred watering hole layout of the hard-drinking meshback. It appears that most of the patrons on the band side are friends and family members of the opening band, whereas the prizes behind Door Number Two are of that elusive variety that are usually seen only in dank, seedy barrooms like this one – people who make you wonder where they go when the sun comes out. Pasty, bloated, rangy, scraggly – in a word, barflies.

We make our way to a back booth and seat ourselves.

So far I haven't seen anyone in clown makeup. I figure when our waitress shows up, I'll ask to see the soundman. That is, of course, assuming a waitress will show up. We sit for a good ten minutes and don't see anyone who resembles a waitress, much less one headed our way. I, for one, am parched and had assumed that free drinks were going to be a given. I remember that during more than one of George's interminable phone calls, he had offered as a selling point the fact that we would be entitled to a meal before or after our set. He seemed to think this was quite a coup and assured us that he *always* ate free at Three Chopt Bar and Grill when he played there, and this was one of the reasons that it was his favorite venue.

The free meal concept was flawed on so many levels that I didn't even attempt to argue with him about it. First of all, Women of Selket aside, I don't know of many belly dancers who want to undertake a twenty-minute set with a belly full of bar food. I envisioned greasy potato skins and nachos microwaved into a rubbery mess – not exactly my idea of shimmy fuel. Second, the fact that said bar food was worth maybe four bucks, eight for the both of us, did little to make up for the abbreviated paycheck we'd be getting for this gig. Third, and most important, staying for dinner would be in direct violation of the Belly Dancer's Code, Statute 23:64.

The Belly Dancer's Code, a long, complex, and often contradictory list of dos, don'ts, edicts, and bans, is handed down from dancer to dancer in the form of whispered warnings, stern lectures, and indignant stares. In every town there is a self-proclaimed Arbiter of the Code and more than a few dancers who flat out ignore the very existence of the Code. The Code Arbiters are not the same as the Ethnic Police, as the Code is less about authenticity and more about etiquette. As Sheva always says, we are ladies first and dancers second – and herein lies the basis of the Code.

According to the Belly Dancer's Code, we do not smoke or drink alcohol in public while in costume, nor do we curse, behave lasciviously, or canoodle with our sweeties (though the babealicious babes violate this one in spades at every recital). The Code is different for dance-world events and 'Joe Public' events. At the latter, the Code requires that we maintain the mystique associated with belly dancers in the eyes of civilians by staying in character for the duration of our presence at a job. That means no mingling, no revealing our real names or day jobs, no changing into jeans in the ladies' room and boogying the night away, and absolutely no chowing down on potato skins at the Three Chopt Bar and Grill. As Lucy would say, it's a sad story, but a true story. Love to stay, got to go.

After almost twenty minutes of booth sitting, a striking brunette in leather pants slithers over and introduces herself as the owner of the bar. I am immediately struck with an overwhelming feeling of sadness that this beautiful woman is saddled with the ownership of this portal of sleaze, but the more she talks to us, the more I realize she is probably fine with it. Beneath her good looks there is a hardness that tells me she probably knows her way around a seedy barroom. Give her a broken-off bottle and maybe a .22 and she'll hold her own just fine. She points out the Conradi family – a teenaged girl who appears to be with the opening band, a school-aged girl perched on a barstool nibbling a plate of fries, and a tough-looking woman jamming quarters into a Ms. Pac Man machine. And holding court in a corner over near the soundboard is George Conradi, Another Pretty Face himself. Clown makeup will only be an improvement, though it will probably do little for his obvious comb-over. I wonder if he will be wearing a clown wig, too? Leather Pants waves him over and he trots across the bar looking purposeful and in charge. He is truly in his element here on the video game side of the Three Chopt Bar and Grill.

'Hey, girls! You ready to knock 'em dead?'

We give him the Sheva blink, in stereo.

Blink.

Blink.

Finally Vicki speaks up.

'Can we please have some water . . . or *something*?'

After fetching us a pitcher of tap water, George proceeds to talk up the gig some more, telling us how much more the place is sure to fill up before we go on, which has now mysteriously been bumped back to ten-thirty. He points out the stage, a tiny makeshift affair covered with tangled wires and duct tape, and the dressing room, also known as the kitchen. Then he announces that he has to go put on his costume – 'I don't know how much you've heard about my show, but it's very much an event. People remember it.' He heads for the kitchen, stopping on the way to scold his daughter for not finishing her fries. I consider reporting him to Child Protective Services. Vicki and I look at each other and sigh. I didn't feel bad when the Jewels were unhappy with the Cafine's gig, but I do feel bad about dragging Vicki along on this one. And I feel bad about subjecting myself to it, as well. We may not be the Women of Selket, but we both deserve a hell of a lot better than this.

At ten-twenty, we gather up our veils and makeup and head for the dressing room. The only place large enough for us to set up is in front of the walk-in cooler, just to the left of the deep fryer. Vicki plops her makeup case down on a case of Icehouse and takes down her hair.

'I'm glad my mama taught me not to be too proud,' she says, looking skeptically at the giant inflatable Miller bottle perched precariously over the fryer's vent hood.

I maneuver my veil carefully around the fryer basket and drape it over a hand truck. *In half an hour*, I tell myself, *this will all be over*.

'Excuse me, ladies.' The stocky, tattooed bartender squeezes between us and into the cooler for another case of Budweiser. In the opposite corner of the tiny kitchen, not ten feet away, George Conradi is putting on his pretty face. Mariane failed to mention that, in addition to clown makeup, his stage attire also involves a top hat, a Paul Revere jacket with tails, and a white dress shirt with frilly Edwardian cuffs. I'm starting to feel like I am in a bad local production of *Spinal Tap*. He applies his clown makeup with exaggerated seriousness, stopping inter- mittently to drag on a Marlboro that he balances on the edge of his makeup case. I consider breaking the Belly Dancer Code and asking for a cigarette – God knows I could use one – but I decide against it. The Belly Dancer Code is one thing, but the health code is another. Are we really supposed to be smoking? In the kitchen? I look over at Vicki, who is picking out her voluminous black curls over the sideboard, and decide it probably wouldn't make much of a difference – but I decide against it anyway. Now that his makeup is mostly on, Conradi creeps me out even more. I can't wait until this is over.

After what seems like an eternity, Another Pretty Face takes the stage. He opens with Duran Duran's 'Planet Earth,' which I haven't heard since high school and haven't exactly missed. He does a pretty good version of it – but even a pretty good version of 'Planet Earth' isn't all that appealing in the grand scheme of things. As a con- cession to the ever-increasing lateness of our set, he agreed to let us go on two songs in, instead of halfway through the set as he had planned. He made noises like this was going to throw off the flow of his show, but frankly I couldn't care less at this point. I just want to see the Three Chopt Bar and Grill in my rear view mirror, and the sooner, the better.

Vicki and I position ourselves at the kitchen door, ready to parade out majestically when we hear the first strains of 'Star Dancer.' Conradi plays, and plays, and plays, and plays . . . .

'I think this is still the same damn song,' Vicki says disgustedly.

Eventually he does begin singing another song, a Pink Floyd cover, and we know we'll be up soon. We fluff our hair, adjust our veils, and wait. The Pink Floyd song goes on and on, finally beginning to wind down after the bridge. We refluff and wait.

'Coming through, ladies!' The bartender barrels through us again, and without missing a beat, grabs two fistfuls of frozen French fries out of a plastic tub on the sideboard and plunges them into the deep fryer.

HHHHHHSSSSSSSSSSSSHHHHHHHHHHHHHHHH! The kitchen is immediately filled with the sound of sizzling grease, drowning out the final – or at least what we think are the final – verses of the Pink Floyd song.

Vicki sticks her head out of the door. I stick my head out of the door. We stick our heads out together, like the Little Rascals spying on Miss Crabtree.

'Now?'

'Now?

'*Now?*'

Fuck it! We storm out of the kitchen, sequins sparkling, beads tinkling, veils smelling of day-old grease. It is only by coincidence that we are right on cue. Gingerly stepping up onstage through a thick cloud of dry ice smoke, we take our positions among the cords and the duct tape and break into a flawless rendition of 'Star Dancer.'

We can't see or hear the audience, but we are sure they love us. We look great, make no mistakes, and shimmy for all we're worth – and besides, Another Pretty Face is hardly a tough act to follow. When the number ends we stand expectantly, waiting for the applause that we so heartily deserve.

Nothing.

Obviously the acoustics in this bar aren't the best. No matter, though, because we're about to do the part they're really going to love, the mingling, where they will actually get to experience us up close and personal. I nod the go-ahead to Vicki and we scamper down the steps and into the audience.

To say the audience is unresponsive is like saying the Hezbollah is opinionated. Having to watch belly dancing is obviously the most terrible thing that has ever happened to this audience. They hate it – and they hate us. I paste on my best Chip and Dale smile and shimmy up to table after table of Three Chopt patrons. At table after table, I am greeted with scowls, snarls, and very strong, very unmistakable get-away-from-me vibes. In desperation, I employ a Turkish travel to take me all the way to the back of the bar and around into the video game room, which is now populated almost entirely by the opening band and their friends.

There is a code, not the Belly Dancer Code but a general performers' code, that you are attentive and appreciative to other acts with whom you share the bill. I learned this code during my years at the bottom of the groupie food chain, where I was inevitably keeping company with members of low-ranking opening bands such as this one. You clap heartily, dance where applicable, and, above all, you don't leave and take all of your girlfriends, room-mates, and beer receipts with you.

No, scratch that. Make that, above all, you don't glare at the other acts as if to say, 'you're as old as my mother and my girlfriend is better looking than you, and this music is weird and stupid, now get away from me, you freaky old broad.' That should be first and foremost. But apparently, no one has informed this opening act of the performers' code yet. They are, after all, quite young. I make a mental note of their scowling faces and tell myself that, upon their inevitable entry into the juvenile corrections system, I will make sure they are in my English class and I will make sure to fail them. It's only a matter of time.

I pass Vicki in the doorway and roll my eyes at her to signify 'Don't bother.' She doesn't see me, though, because she's rolling hers so hard that all she's got showing are whites. Zombie belly dancer! It's a good look for her.

Lamely tush-pushing back into the main room, I am faced with the same tables that have already hated me once before. I weigh my options, wondering if dancing out the front door and into the parking lot is one of them. I am about to backstep into the video game room to make the teenagers miserable some more when I spot what is sure to be my salvation in the far corner of the bar.

Lesbians.

Last New Years' Eve, I ditched the lame AA dance early in order to see the gorgeous Julijana dance at India K'Raja restaurant. Generic cola and 'Super Freak' are no competition for a plateful of *pappadom*, vegetable *biryani*, and Julijana in a breathtaking red *bedlah* dancing full routines on the hour all night long. From my seat on the aisle, I saw the restaurant door swing open at about eleven P.M. A half-dozen silver-haired dykes, dressed to the nines in tuxedo pants and festive sparkly vests, out on the town. Apparently they were lured by the curry, as it seems Julijana is news to them. The first woman through the door stopped in mid-sentence, frozen, eyes wide, arms stiff, when she saw Julijana undulating in the center of the room. She stood that way, not breathing, lips quivering, for thirty seconds. Then she spoke in a low, reverent growl.

'Sweet Mother of God! Somebody get me some *dollars*.'

The women here at the Three Chopt Bar and Grill are hardly as upscale as the women that night. There is not a pair of tuxedo pants among them. One sports cornrows, and several have greasy mullets that would look a little too butch on most professional wrestlers. I note more

245

than one gold tooth and several tattoos that look to be homemade. But I am desperate, and I can only hope that a love of belly dancing is something that is inherent in the Sapphic nature. I begin my descent.

I choose the woman with cornrows to be my focus, since she seems to be at the head of the table. As an added bonus, she is so large that her chair is by necessity facing out from the table – a perfect setup for belly dancing. I shimmy over, give her my best Chip and Dale, and do a quick snake hip level change down, down, down, keeping eye contact all the way.

What happens next is completely unprecedented. First, she rolls her eyes at me. Then she sucks her teeth scornfully. Then, grabbing the underside of her chair with both hands, she turns her seat until she has her back directly to me. Finally, without looking, she reaches around with one beefy arm and slides her pitcher of beer over to her new location. Her tablemates hoot and pump their fists in the air. I have been thoroughly and roundly rejected.

Vicki sweeps past me on her way back from the doom room. The second song is almost over; we have one more to go.

'*Fuck it*,' I mutter in her ear as she passes, my words hidden by her poufy hair. '*We're outta here*.'

'*Was that the last song?*'

'*As far as they know*.'

And without offering so much as a Sultan's bow, we dance straight into the kitchen.

It takes us another fifteen minutes of hounding the bartender and fifteen minutes of waiting in the parking lot to get our puny paycheck. Leather Pants gives us our money straight out of her pocket, then asks for our numbers so she can book us again. We stare at her in disbelief. I look at Vicki and see that her mouth is hanging open, which makes me notice that mine is, too. Was she there? Did she see how much they hated us? Or is that how this audience acts when they like something? I can't imagine ever setting foot in this den of iniquity again.

I mutter something unconvincing about not having a telephone. Vicki gives Leather Pants her number – easy for her to do since she's moving to Arizona in a month. We hardly talk on the way back into the city. I don't know what I could say to make it up to her. I'm sure she's biting her tongue to keep from cursing me out. This night has quickly risen to be one of my top ten least favorite evenings ever, right up there with The Night That Made Me Quit Drinking and The Night I Ate the Bad Crab Salad. It probably ranks at about number five. The Night I Belly Danced for Mean Drunks in the Strip Mall.

After Vicki heads home, I change into my raggedest jeans and my favorite flannel shirt, pour a cup of coffee, and curl up in front of the VCR. I put on my favorite video, *The Great Unknown* from the Stars of Egypt video series. It's a whole tape of nothing but clips of obscure belly dancing scenes from old black-and-white Egyptian movies. The best one is a Busby Berkley–style production number where a chorus of belly dancers undulate up out of gigantic coffee cups like so much human steam. I warm my hands around my own cup of coffee and watch the black-and-white girls shimmy and smile. I smile back at them. That's what I want it to be like. I want to rise up out of a cup of coffee, not duck under an inflatable beer bottle. I want to dance for a bedroom-eyed man in a fez, not a bloodshot-eyed woman in a mullet. And I want my ruby-painted toes to touch down on exquisite Moroccan tile, not microphone cords and duct tape.

I know my illusions about belly dancing are just that – illusions. But a girl's got to dream or it just gets depressing. I finish my coffee, hang up my costume, and turn out the lights. But I leave the video playing. They may be unknown, but they're my angels tonight.

12

From Oil Sheiks
to Jesus Freaks

Dating Adventures in Arabia,
Part Three

As with so many other things I've wanted out of in my life, I never do get up the balls for the dramatic exit I've been promising myself from the Jewels. Instead, I fade away quietly, fulfilling the last big workshop show like the dutiful codependent I am, then just not showing up for practice any more. When I run into the Triumvirate at dance events, I smile wistfully and tell them 'maybe later' when they ask if I'll be back. I plead a full schedule – papers to grade, lesson plans, housework – but the truth is, I am making the most of my blissfully empty Thursday nights. I'm hanging out with friends, eating dinner in the caf with my students, and hitting bookstores and coffee shops with a vengeance. Tonight it's World Cup, for a quick iced coffee and a crossword before I head home for some Internet and veggie wontons. The life of the single belly dancer – *quelle glamour*!

Scoping out the usual coterie of malcontents and malingers, I spot too many familiar faces and not enough

248

intriguing ones. On any given evening at World Cup, a disturbing number of four-dollar lattes are being paid for with my tax money. Apparently all of these folks who are too depressed to work aren't too depressed to flit around the coffee shop until closing time, talking about Buddhism and nibbling scones. I wonder if the government will give me a check when I become too resentful to work? I quickly pick out Faux Buddy Holly, a table full of AA zealots, a chain-smoking French astrologer I know, and some private school gothlings. 'Children of the night! *Shut up*!' my back-alley neighbor Lee has been known to snarl at them when they get too histrionic. And speaking of Lee, I can see him through the glass-paned back door, smoking and sipping coffee on the patio. I head back to join him.

'Don't you want to sit inside? I see your unibrowed friends up front.'

He is referring to three Turkish cousins who Karen has dubbed 'the Disco Ay-rabs.' Usually decked out in something shiny or formerly warm-blooded, the Disco *Ay*-rabs spend their days playing chess in the front booth at World Cup and their nights boogieing down at undisclosed locations in Shockoe Bottom. They are skinny, swarthy, and impressively unctuous. I have worked my way up to goo goo eyes, but no further. They are almost, maybe, a little too clichéd for me. If the Arab Chat Arabs are the SNL Roxbury guys, then the Disco *Ay*-rabs are the Czechoslovakian Brothers. They are three wild and crazy guys – and even their enormous noses and thick unibrows can't make up for the bell-bottoms and the butterfly collars.

I pull up a wrought iron patio chair and shrug. 'I dunno. I know they're Turkish and all, but – ' and I peer in the window at the three of them, chatting up St Catherine's girls and sipping espresso – 'they just don't do anything *for* me.' Truly, it is the rare Arab man about whom I can say this. Lately, in my single-minded zeal, even the guys at the falafel stand are starting to look good. Since my 'ethnic awakening,' I've been kicking myself for all the time I spent chasing Anglo rock 'n' roll wannabes. How many Arab Princes slipped through my fingers while I was looking the other way? Chris would never even-register on my radar now . . . not that I have to worry about that. Except for one tiny crowd shot in *Skin & Ink*, I've seen neither tattooed hide nor blond hair of him since the day I left North Carolina.

Be it the Rolling Stones, drinking, or belly dancing, or anything else I've had a yen for in my life, I am officially overboard. Moderation has never been my strong suit. Since I started belly dancing, ethnic pride has become the name of my game. I've filched my parents' *shisha* and mother-of-pearl inlay chairs and table for my apartment, where my seventy-odd Rolling Stones albums sit covered with dust because I play nothing but Arabic music now. The *m'joudra* I used to have to be bribed to finish is now my staple, along with hummus and anything else they will put on my tab at Aladdin Express. As far as dating goes, Fahed and Hal were harbingers of my changing taste. I am determined to find myself a sheik.

My steadfast refusal to give up my quest for Prince Ali has been particularly infuriating for the Creepy Huggers. Creepy Huggers are a breed of AA male who feel that twelve-step programs should serve not only as a place to get sober but also as a convenient free dating service with strings attached. It is their belief that, by virtue of having attended the same one-hour meeting as the object of their desire, they are now karmically bonded and said object has a spiritual obligation to welcome their advances, or at least go for coffee after the meeting lest she be accused of 'refusing to fellowship.' Creepy Huggers are also master eavesdroppers and conversation crashers, so all of the Creepy Huggers at my meeting know that I am a woman on a mission – and they don't like it.

'You know,' one of them groused one night as we scrubbed coffee cups after the meeting, 'I think you set your standards too high. You're holding out for Haagen-Dazs, and there just ain't that much of it around. You're gonna starve to death waiting for Haagen-Dazs! Just eat the Food Lion ice cream. There's lots of it, and it ain't that bad.'

Now, I like a good metaphor as much as the next girl, but this one did little more than piss me off. First of all, I don't think my standards are too high; in fact, they probably aren't high enough. Was he trying to imply I don't deserve Haagen-Dazs? I don't know what's more disheartening – his implication that I think too highly of myself, or his own self-identification as Food Lion Brand. That's some seriously low self-esteem. I couldn't even justify his argument with a real rebuttal.

'I don't like ice cream,' I shrugged, and put the last cup in the cabinet.

Lee nods his understanding, and we sip our coffee in the early evening breeze, with not much to talk about and even less to look at – that is, until an *extremely* well-developed, broad-shouldered, olive-skinned, chocolate-eyed specimen comes ambling into view through the coffee shop door.

'*Oooooooooh*,' I croon, fairly pressing my nose up against the glass.

'Danger, Will Robinson,' Lee chuckles, peering over his glasses at my newest target.

I stand up, zombielike, with an exaggerated casualness that looks more like catatonia. 'I'm going to get a refill,' I announce mechanically, never taking my eyes off my destination. 'Do you want anything?'

'Well, since I'm not betting on you coming out for a while, no, I don't,' Lee responds, looking dolefully into his near-empty cup. 'But I'll be in right behind you – as un-obtrusively as possible, of course.'

I get my refill, which baffles the countergirl since my cup is more than half full, and scan the shop. Sure enough, my target is seated at the computer, staring into the screen. A good sign – possible geek points! I saunter over and ease myself down onto the couch. He is glancing back and forth from the screen to the dictionary on his lap – another good sign. He looks back and forth, back and forth – screen, dictionary, screen, dictionary, screen, me.

'Hey.'

'*Hi.*' I wonder if my Allah necklace is showing? I hope it's showing.

'Do you know how to spell initiate?'

'Uh huh.' I proceed to give the breathiest spelling ever of the word initiate as he taps it out on the keyboard. 'I-N-I-T-I-A-T-E.' I stifle a Monroe-esque moan at the end.

'*Initiate.*' He points at the screen, gives a thumbs up, and turns and gives me a *dazzling* smile. 'Good thing you sat down here!' He closes the dictionary and slides it back onto the windowsill. 'I never would have found it. I was all up in the A's.'

I am willing to forgive the spelling *and* the high school slang, all on account of that smile. Oh, that smile! It's sexy, and open, and somehow very familiar. I'm used to feeling a sort of pseudo déjà vu sometimes when I meet other Lebanese Americans, just because there is something about the bone structure, the skin tone, the downward slant in the corner of the eye that is so instantly discernible. But this goes beyond that – this guy isn't just any Lebanese American. I feel I know him.

'Are you Lebanese?' I'm being horribly forward, but I'm so certain I already know him that I don't even care.

'Uh huh! Well, half. My dad is Lebanese.' He's unfazed. I keep digging.

'Yeah, mine too. Did you go to Saint Anthony's?'

He smacks his forehead and throws his hands in the air. '*Saint Anthony's*? Saint Anthony's! Climb up on the big green box and get the goodies!'

Rather than pegging him as a raving loon, this outburst confirms my suspicion beyond a doubt. During the summers when I was little, we, like all of the other Lebanese families in town, packed a cooler of sandwiches and headed out to the church rec center nearly every day. With three playgrounds, two pools, tennis courts, and shuffleboard, it was the Maronite version of a country club. Each morning as we disembarked from our wood-paneled station wagon, my brother, sister, and I were each given a quarter – our walking-around money for the day. We would hold out for as long as we could; then, when it finally started to burn a hole in the pockets of our cutoffs, we would run to the concession stand and climb up to the sliding glass window by way of a foot-high dark green painted wooden platform. There we could use our budget for either two different ice cream pops, a Coke and a candy bar, twenty-five jolly ranchers, or a small order of fries in a red-and-white cardboard boat. But before you could get any of these goodies, you had to climb up on the big green box – and Cute Boy knows that. Cute Boy is from Saint Anthony's.

If I were a Tex Avery cartoon, here is where my eyes would spin wildly before settling on three overflowing bags of gold. Here is where my tongue would reel out like a tape measure and my eyes would bug out of their sockets, then snap back. Here is where I would look at a Saint Anthony's Guy and see a big juicy pork chop where his head should be. But I am not a cartoon – not usually, anyway. I am a single Maronite Lebanese American belly dancer in Richmond, Virginia, who has just stumbled on what might well be the choicest specimen of potential partnership heretofore known to woman. I have found the Holy Grail, right here in the back of World Cup. This is my potential ticket to parental approval, St Anthony's acceptance, and little brown babies, all rolled into one.

And I thought *Muslim* dating was high pressure.

'I only went there for a couple of years, though. Then I moved to California with my mom.'

Blink. Blink blink.

'Are you Freddie Masmoud?'

'*Whoa*! Yeah! How'd you know?'

And here is where the world gets a little bit smaller. As a child, I always used to marvel at how many Lebanese people we knew, because looking at it on a map, the country of Lebanon seemed so impossibly tiny. How could there be so many of us – and in America, at that? Much less Richmond, Virginia? But truthfully, there are not as many of us as there may seem. And here is the proof.

'I *lived* with your *mother*.' When I moved to Los Angeles to make my heavy metal fortune, my parents tried everything they could think of to keep me from going. Failing that, they insisted that I stay with Freddie's mother until I found an apartment, instead of at a cheap motel as I had planned. I was graciously tolerated by his mother and stepfather and given a tour of Sunset Boulevard by his older sister Sheri, who spent her teenaged years in a Hollywood glam-rock haze but now runs a women's mission and has 'Jesus Saves' tattooed on her foot. I am quite sure that this information is going to blow Freddie's mind, or at least make him realize this is Kismet, at which point he will whisper 'come away with me,' but I have forgotten just how accommodating his mother was.

'Yeah, most people did at one time or another,' he nods, completely unfazed. I'm reminded of a discussion we had over dinner one night – me, Freddie's mom Barbara, two of his three sisters, and my mom. They were reminiscing about the original trip west, when Freddy was only two and his oldest brother was sixteen. Six kids in all, they were packed into the family van tightly enough before they added the hitchhiker.

'I don't know why Mom picked him up,' Maria recalled.

'If you remember, we took a vote,' Barbara reminded her. 'And besides, we needed somebody who could pay for gas.'

'Was that the night you made us all smoke pot so we'd shut up and go to sleep?'

'Not all of you, just the older ones,' Barbara corrected. My mom and I stared at each other, google-eyed. It amazed me that she lasted as long as she did married to a Lebanese man. I couldn't imagine any of the women who had stayed at Saint Anthony's pulling any of this. Organizing a whole food festival, sure. Raising five kids in a spotlessly clean house with a full course meal on the table every night, no problem. But letting their children democratically decide to pick up a hitchhiker or forcing marijuana smoking to make the kids behave? Hardly.

'I think you were already in Manteo by then,' I say, hoping still to somehow amaze him with how much I know about his life. I know that when he reached the inevitable rebellious teenager phase, he was shipped to the Outer Banks of North Carolina to live with his father and that he attended high school there, later joining the Marines and serving on the Presidential Honor Guard. Looking at him – and how can I help it? – I can see why they chose him. I imagine he'd look mightily impressive in dress blues.

'Yeah, I probably was. So, do you go to Saint Anthony's?'

'Uh huh,' I answer, rationalizing silently that I *do* – on Christmas and Easter, anyway. 'Are you living in Richmond now?'

'Pretty much. I'm staying with my brother Tony out in the West End.' Tony is the oldest of the Masmouds;

hearing his name I'm transported back to the last time I saw him, visiting home a couple of years after the move – he came chicken-walking into Saint Anthony's in a white John Travolta suit, his glossy black hair down to his shoulders. He was a virtual carbon copy of his father, who still, at sixty plus, has the most impressive head of hair this side of Samson. I inspect Freddie's closely cropped locks. Even as severely as he has them cut, they have the Masmoud trademark glossiness with just a touch of gray sprinkled about the top of his head. Not only is he handsome, but he's going to age well – both of his parents are still gorgeous. I move in for the kill.

'Have you been back to Saint Anthony's yet?' I am plotting and planning my triumphant return on the arm of Freddie Masmoud. '*What's! My! Name?!*' If I play my cards right, it could be Anne Masmoud someday. I can't believe my good luck, stumbling on such a find right here in Loser Central! Who'd have thunk that World Cup would be harboring a real live St Anthony's-born-and-baptized gorgeous Lebanese Man? Someone has no doubt been hearing my prayers.

'I went once,' he says thoughtfully, looking deep into my eyes. I am ready to commiserate, to share my tales of half-assed Catholicism, too, when he adds, with that same winning smile, 'Saint Anthony's doesn't really feed my soul since I got washed in the blood of the lamb.'

Continuing along my Tex Avery path, I feel like my heart has just walked off a steep cliff, looked down, and held up a sign that says 'Good-bye!' Washed in the blood of the lamb? As in born again? As in hallelujah? I start rationalizing a million miles a minute, having a heated debate with myself over whether this is the deal-breaker that I feel in my gut it must be. No, I argue, I'm sure he's a really *cool* born-again Christian. Probably very tolerant and open-minded and not the least bit cheesy! But won't that mean I have to be born again, too? Hey, I tell myself, you were willing to convert to Islam when Fahed was the Arab of the Week . . . surely you can deal with a little scripture. Do I have to mean it? No, of course not! It will be like school again! I can memorize passages and study Proverbs and all that without having to buy it hook, line, and Jesus Fish. But what about my past? Oh, like a *Masmoud* doesn't have a past! Was it Freddie who had to be exorcised back when he was a teenager? No, that must have been Tony – because it was back when *The Exorcist* was out and demonic possession was trendy again . . . but don't I remember stories about Freddie being wild, too? Or was that Georgie?

'So who are your folks?' Freddie interrupts my crisis of faith, bringing me back to my main objective – preserving the bloodline. I sit up a little straighter on the couch.

'The Soffees.' We may be half-white city folks, but Saint Anthony's started out in the living room of my great-grandfather, William Moses Soffee. The pedigree alone is enough to keep our name alive in the parish, even though we've been piss-poor breeders and the few Soffees who are left hardly ever show up for Mass.

'No way! I see your dad practically every day!' If God has been listening to my prayers, he has a wicked sense of irony. The only people who see my dad every day are the roofers who buy shingles from him. In high school, my brother was granted a sweet summer gig driving forklifts around the warehouse and loading pallets of roofing supplies onto trucks – but my sister and I have always been kept safely away from the family business. The unspoken reason was that my dad didn't want roofers anywhere near his daughters. My sister had the audacity to date one of the warehouse guys, and he had the audacity to mention it to my father. From her erstwhile suitor's description, he was treated to a rousing rendition of the Eyeball Thing that said, without words, leave my daughter alone or there may be a tragic forklift accident possibly ending in a trip to the canal. And that was just a warehouse guy.

Freddie finishes his e-mail and his soda, makes some nice-to-remeet-you small talk, then excuses himself to head home. I am disappointed that we can't continue our conversation, but eager to give Lee the play by play. It turns out Lee was holding out on me, as he has seen Freddie at – hold onto your turbans – *AA meetings* around the Fan with some of his born-again recovering brethren! I am not thrilled about the company, because the guys Lee mentions are cheesy and intolerant even for born-again Christians, but *AA meetings*! He *gets* it! I don't have to hide my past from him! He understands! I wish Lee had told me before I'd headed in to prey upon him. It would have been a whole different ball game. The disappointment of hearing he was born again is all but eradicated by the news that he's in recovery. I have a chance!

'Well, I'm sure he'll be here tomorrow,' Lee says as I begin to wail.

'He's here every night?'

'*Sure.*' Lee pauses dramatically. Like God, he is a master of irony. 'He's usually sitting on the stoop out front, singing guitar hymns.'

Gag me with a communion wafer. Nothing arouses the ire of a traditional Catholic, even a lapsed one, more than contemporary Christian guitar hymns. I roll my eyes so hard my head hurts. But I know I'll be back tomorrow.

'I want to know You
I want to hear Your voice
I want to know You more
I want to touch You
I want to see Your face . . . '

Sure enough, when I arrive Friday night, Freddie is

sitting cross-legged on the sidewalk next to Wyche, one of World Cup's resident evangelists, and his omnipresent acoustic guitar. Even without Lee's spoiler, the sound of salvation is unmistakable. The lyrics are vague enough that on paper they might read like a love song, but the bland chord strumming and Pentecostal gleam in Freddie's eyes ensure that everyone knows that's You with a capital Y. The Big Guy. And not the one I grew up with (or Freddie, either, for that matter), but a suburban white-washed guitar-massing savior who looks like Kenny Loggins and lets you come to church in your jeans, dude. Even singing wimpy guitar hymns, though, Freddie is still gorgeous, and his eyes light up with a purely secular gleam when he sees me. He stands up and greets me with a bear hug.

'I was hoping you'd come back!' He turns and points at his companions. 'Do you know Wyche and Kirby?'

'Yes, we've met.' I smile stiffly at them, showing all my teeth, and saying silently with that special Soffee eye-speak, 'So help me God, and not your wimpy contemporary one, if you say anything that blows this for me you will be pulling acoustic guitar strings out of your ass from now until judgment day.' Wyche and Kirby nod nervously and excuse themselves to go inside. Freddie sits down and pats the stoop beside him.

'So let me share the good news with you.'

'What good news?' I ask dumbly, immediately pegging myself as a heathen know-nothing who has obviously only been born one puny time. But Freddie just laughs, puts his hand on my knee, and says, '*The* good news, white chick! OK, never mind. Sometimes I just get so full of the spirit I want to share it. But,' and he looks me deeply in the eyes, 'I believe that God put us back in each other's lives for a reason. And that means there will be plenty of time for that later.'

Now *that's* the kind of good news I'm looking for. But I

have my own agenda tonight and my own kind of sharing in mind. I wind up for the pitch.

'Actually, I just stopped in for a quick coffee.' And . . . *fire*. 'I'm on my way to the late-night meeting.'

'What, like an AA meeting?'

'Uh-huh. Well, sort of.' I'm a switch hitter, to the dismay of separatists in both programs. 'An NA meeting.'

'Well, heck, I'm there! I used to be a coke addict.'

She shoots, she scores! I am starting to believe everything Karen ever told me to cheer me up during those long nights on the couch. Surely this is my higher power at work. Freddie goes in to bid good-bye to his friends, I grab a quick iced coffee and we're off, with Freddie's huge body barely making it into the shotgun seat of my little Tercel.

I scurry into the kitchen as soon as we arrive, hoping to catch Lee alone before Freddie gets there.

'He's here, Lee! And I've got hearts around my head!'

'Look out!' Lee mutters as Freddie bounds into the kitchen like a big Lebanese Labrador. 'Here comes contestant number three on The DNA Is Right.'

I turn to see Freddie introducing himself around, shaking hands and bear-hugging other meeting-goers before heading to the refreshment table to fix himself a hot chocolate. I'm relieved to see how at home he seems at the meeting. Not since Chris have I been able to assimilate my dating life and my meeting life, and it's such a strain to keep things compartmentalized. I make a mental note to suggest gratitude as the topic of the meeting. As overplayed as the topic might be, I'm really feeling it tonight.

Someone else beats me to the topic, suggesting the Third Step – 'Made a decision to turn our will and our lives over to the care of God as we understood him.' Even though it's not the topic, I've still got plenty of gratitude – mainly about the fact that this is a candlelight meeting so

Freddie can't see me cringing in the dark. Why did it have to be a God topic? Does he know he can't preach Christianity here? You can sometimes get away with it in AA, but not NA. People get *really* uptight about religion in meetings – present company one hundred percent not excepted. I pray to every god I can think of that Freddie won't start sharing the Good News.

'Hi. My name's Freddie and I'm an addict.'

'Hi, Freddie.' Everyone responds but me. I'm frozen in my seat.

'Before you introduced the topic, I was thinking that maybe gratitude would be a good topic. But this kind of ties in with gratitude anyway, because I'm so grateful for my higher power. I'm so grateful, and so full of hope and joy and light, that I want to share it with everybody. But what I don't get is how many people don't want it.' He frowns and looks into the candlelight. 'Sometimes I feel like I've got a vacuum cleaner that's the best vacuum cleaner in the whole wide world, and it works so great that I feel like I have to become a vacuum cleaner sales-man so I can turn the whole world on to this vacuum cleaner. And not only that, but I will give people the vac-uum cleaner absolutely free. And if they take this free vacuum cleaner, then their rugs will be spotless for the rest of their lives, guaranteed. Free! And they won't take it! They're like, "no thanks, my broom works just fine." It's free! And it's guaranteed. And it works so great! But I can't make anybody take it. I wish I could, but I can't.' He leans back in his chair, satisfied with his metaphor. 'I'm just really glad that I took the vacuum cleaner when some-body offered it to me. Thanks for letting me share.'

I breathe out, both relieved that he's done and impressed with his skill. A pretty damn good metaphor. I wonder if he came up with it himself? It is not lost on the midnight crowd. In fact, for the rest of the night, people bring it up again and again in their own sharing. Most

261

people seem to think he was using the vacuum cleaner to represent NA, which is plausible; however, a few definitely saw through to his real point.

'My sister's always pushing her fuckin' vacuum cleaner on me,' one heavily tattooed teenager shares, 'and she's got a really fucked-up vacuum cleaner! It doesn't suck – it *blows*!' No one laughs harder than Freddie at this bastardization of his analogy. Points for him – as if he needed more. After the meeting, we all caravan back to World Cup, where Freddie dives into the sing-along still in progress and I convene with Lee on the back patio.

'So do you still have hearts around your head?'

'Big time! But I don't think he likes me.'

'Oh, *pshaw*! Don't you see the way his face lights up every time you walk into a room?'

'I think he's just friendly. He does the same thing when he sees Wyche.'

'Hmmm.' Lee peers through the window. 'Maybe he's mentally ill.'

'Well, he probably is,' I shrug, figuring a) he's Lebanese, b) he's at World Cup, and c) I like him. Three sure signs right there. 'But I still hope he likes me. He hasn't even asked me for my number.'

'Give him some time. Guys are slow that way.' I consider this, then decide, after Fahed and Hal, slow is probably good. I have a cup of coffee and a consolation smoke on the patio with Lee, then head home to practice for Sheva's show. Nothing says civic togetherness more than sharing your *zils* with the neighbors at two A.M. If Mrs Longbottom wasn't deaf before, she is now. *Tek a tek a tek*.

I am jarred awake by the ringing phone mere hours after I finally hang up my *zils*. The only time the phone rings before ten A.M. on a weekend is when my father calls to invite me to breakfast. He has to make sure I don't starve to death before Sunday dinner or he would never forgive himself. I think maybe once in my adult life I have dragged myself out of bed and met him at Bob Evans for pancakes . . . and that was enough to keep him calling every week from then on. Everyone else knows better. Or so I thought.

'Huh-lo?' I mutter around a mouthful of pillow.

'*Good* morning! This is your nine A.M. Call to Prayer! *Ayooooyoooyooooyoo*!'

I sit bolt upright in bed, listening to Freddie do a very bad impression of a *muezzin*. I am suddenly wide awake. What the *fuck*? I never even gave him my number, which, coincidentally, is unlisted.

'Surprised?'

'Uh, yeah, how . . . who . . . I didn't think . . .'

'I called your father.'

'You *what*?' I can't believe what I'm hearing . . . but I know I'll hear about it, and soon.

'Yeah, I called your father. I said, "Hello Mr Soffee, this is Fred Masmoud and I would like permission to call your daughter." He sounded like I might have caught him off guard.'

'Yeah, I'll say.' I can't remember any of my suitors ever calling my father 'Mr Soffee,' much less asking for permission to call me. I feel like I'm living someone else's life all of a sudden. One of the girls from Saint Anthony's, maybe – except for the NA meetings, the biker tattoo, and the belly dancing. Except for that.

'Well, anyway, I'm calling to see if you want to hang out tonight.'

'Um, sure.' I know *The Rules* forbids last-minute dates, but he got my *father's permission* for God's sake, and that ought to count for something. We make plans to meet at five at World Cup. Not that I need any coffee now. I hang up the phone, fly out of bed, and begin obsessively preparing for my date with Freddie. The same books, pictures, and knickknacks that were hidden for Fahed's visit are hidden again for Freddie's. What's *haram* for the Muslim is *haram* for the gander. I get the apartment as clean as I can on such short notice, just in case things go well enough that I can invite him back for chaste chatter – even with Barbara for a mom, he still had Tony for a father – and pray to saints that I abandoned years ago to help me snag this perfect Lebanese man. Needless to say, the black linen *hijab* is trotted out again – here's hoping the third time's the charm – but this time the Allah necklace stays off. If I had a tasteful little cross, I'd put it on, but I'm not that kind of girl. I settle on a simple locket with no overt religious symbolism. Open it up, though, and there are two tiny pictures, one of Elvis Presley and one of Bettie Page.

What he doesn't know can't hurt me. I check the clasp and wait.

That afternoon, already having fielded the inevitable 'Why in the shit is Freddie Masmoud calling me for your number' call, I head out to my assigned meeting place for my first planned evening with Freddie. He is waiting at a table in the back, in mirrored sunglasses and a Tommy Hilfiger jacket. I feel like Molly Ringwald in *Sixteen Candles*. Girls like me don't go out on Saturday nights with boys like him. He's just so . . . *perfect*. He suggests a Chinese restaurant nearby and we leave through the back – something about Wyche and Kirby and 'avoiding all appearances of evil.' Whatever. I don't care. I'm just thrilled and flattered to be a part of it all.

In the back booth of Joy Garden is where his perfect veneer starts to crack just the tiniest bit. We're talking tiny hairline cracks . . . like, oh, I don't know, the fact that he's married.

Married?

'I've been married for three years, but I haven't seen my wife for over a year. She's living in Maryland with some other guy and they have a kid. But you know what? God told me she'd be back. He told me if I was patient and I just kept on living my life as the best Christian I can be, she'd come back to me. And that's what I'm doing.'

'So,' I say, after choking down the mouthful of tofu and rice that seems to turn into cement in my throat, 'how long are you willing to wait?' I'm thinking I'm a patient girl.

'As long as it takes.' He skewers another chunk of General Tso's and shrugs. 'A year, five years, ten years. I do what God tells me to do. I have faith.'

I wish my faith were that strong. I consider asking him if God ever changes his mind, but I keep my counsel. In my attempt to appear virtuous for this man of God, silence is one of the hardest virtues to maintain. Sure, I'm going to hope, and pray, and do everything in my power to make this work out the way I want it to – but he doesn't have to know that. I poke at my Buddha's Delight. Suddenly I'm not hungry anymore. Not for food, anyway.

'You look disappointed.'

I shrug. I don't know the right answer to this one.

'That doesn't mean we can't hang out, does it?'

'Of course not.' I force a smile.

'Good.' His obvious relief encourages me, until he adds, 'because I still have a lot of good news I need to share with you. Will you come with me to church tomorrow?'

Church? Is this what it's about for him? Am I his evangelical project this week? Maybe he gets extra points for saving a belly dancer – some sort of John the Baptist fixation? I'm no Salome; I don't want his head on a platter. On my pillow, sure – and not just once or twice, but for keeps. I'm racing for pink slips and I'm pulling out all the stops.

'I'd *love* to go to church with you, Freddie.'

'Honest?'

'Honest.' And, ulterior motives aside, I am telling the absolute truth. So help me God.

For the second morning in a row, I am up obscenely early on account of Freddie Masmoud. I tell myself that this must be *real* if I am willing to get out of bed before noon on a weekend. I put more effort into my hair and makeup than I do for a belly dancing show. I pull half my clothes out of my closet before settling on a demure cotton dress of the 'members of the school board are visiting' variety. From what I have seen on the 700 Club and in the teacher's lounge, schoolmarm *hijab* and Christian *hijab* are cut from the same cloth. I suck down two cups of coffee to cut through my Sunday haze, grab my purse, and head over to Tony and Freddie's.

When I arrive, they are standing in the driveway looking peeved. I glance at my watch; five minutes late – a triumph of timeliness for me.

'You're *late*,' Freddie growls. Tony is already getting in his car, ignoring me.

'Just barely,' I offer weakly.

'We were about to leave,' he says sternly. I am too mortified to even offer an apology. Have I blown it already?

About ten minutes into the ride, Freddie finally starts to loosen up. He chides me again for my tardiness, but adds as a conciliatory gesture, 'I look forward to church all week. That's why I'm so uptight about being on time. I can't *wait* until we get there.' He fidgets in the back seat like a puppy, peering around Tony's head at the road in front of us. Finally we arrive – not at a church, but at an elementary school.

'This is just where we're meeting until we raise money for a church,' he explains as we pull into the parking lot.

Several families are pulling in at the same time, mothers in flowered dresses and men with mustaches and sunburns, little tow-headed kids with K-Mart church clothes. I don't see anyone who looks like me. I don't see anyone who looks like Freddie, either. The vibe is seriously white and suburban.

In the school auditorium, we take our places on folding chairs. A pulpit is set up on the stage, and a full band with a drum set and electric guitars tunes up as the worshipers file in. Father Salwan would roll over in his grave. I notice that several people have 7-Eleven coffee cups and sodas by their chairs. I wish I had brought some coffee. I would have stopped at Starbucks had I known. Freddie nudges me as the band starts up.

'Do you have a pen? I might need to take notes.'

I dig a pen out of my purse. Only after I hand it to him do I realize with dismay that it's my Last Supper floaty pen I bought on Cary Street with Lee last month. Tip it one way, and Jesus passes the wine! Tip it the other way, and Judas passes the bread! I cringe, knowing that I've blown it for sure.

'Oh, *man*!' Freddie is mesmerized, tipping the pen back and forth, back and forth. 'That is the coolest pen I've ever seen! Do you mind if I hang onto it? I wanna show it to Pastor Tim.'

God and Lee may be masters of irony, but not Freddie. I now have at least one thing for which to be thankful during the service.

'He was *crying*?' Karen hasn't met Freddie yet but she now knows more about him than his own mother. I am, after all, obsessed.

'Yeah, when the preacher got to the part in the sermon about how you're going to hell if you're not saved. He told me he cried because his mother's not saved.'

267

'Well, at least somebody in the family's still got their heads on.' She loads up her pipe and takes a long puff. Come to think of it, Karen and Freddie's mother would probably get along great. 'Then what?'

'Then they did a skit about how if you watch sports on Sunday instead of going to church, you'll burn in hell.'

'A *skit*? Durin' the service?'

'Yeah, it's a "contemporary service." It's supposed to be more accessible.' I would never tell Freddie, but to me it seemed more like lowest common denominator worship. A Fox-TV version of church. And the audience ate it up.

'So when is Jethro ibn-el Bodine supposed to call you again?'

'He didn't say.' I got the distinct impression all morning that Tony was watching us closely for any appearance of evil – and Freddie was being careful not to commit any. I liked the old disco-era, pre-exorcism Tony better.

'Well, Annie,' Karen sighs, 'I got to hand it to you. You sure can pick some crazy Ay-rabs. If it ain't an oil sheik, it's a Jesus freak. But if you're happy, I guess that's what counts.'

I guess it does, but am I happy? And if I am, how long can it last?

I spend the next two weeks in a Freddie-sponsored haze of church picnics, fellowship meetings, and services. At night, I frantically read through Lee's C. S. Lewis library, trying to reconcile my barely contained skepticism with Freddie's unshakable faith. In meetings, I search my soul for the *reason*. Freddie's re-entry into my life has helped convince me that everything happens for a reason – and that 'everything,' I've decided, also includes outlying details, like Freddie's Christianity. There must be a *reason* that my perfect Lebanese Saint Anthony's man is born again. So what is it?

At a weeknight cookout at Pastor Tim's, I ignore the suspicious glares of the youth pastor's wife and corner him with a pitch about coming to minister to my students. The kids have been asking for church services for months. Youth Pastor Jay hems and haws for a few minutes before stating that it would take 'a special kind of faith' to bring the good news to teenaged sex offenders. Considering the velocity at which he departs after that statement, I can only conclude that his faith isn't that special kind.

Since my students and my dancing are my two passions aside from Arab men, and 'dance ministry' has already been done by Niran, I decide that the *reason* Freddie had to be born again was to make him a suitable candidate for me. As a rule, Masmoud men aren't good marriage material to start with – not too bright, not too faithful, not too sober, and *way* too good-looking to be trusted out of one's sight. Born-again Masmoud men may be dogmatic and sanctimonious, but they're also duty bound to be well-behaved. When Freddie pays a surprise visit to me at work to say good-bye before heading off on a Men's Alpha Group retreat ('It's Alpha because it's for beginning Christians, but I like it so much I've been three times'), Wanda at the front desk is impressed.

'Ooooooh . . . he's *cute*! And where was he going? Alpha Male?' I explain the concept, which impresses her even more. 'Our little Annie's growing up,' she says, shaking her head at me. 'You better hang onto this one.'

And I intend to.

Friday night I am sitting at the computer, sipping iced coffee, and browsing eBay for old belly dancer pinups when I hear Freddie calling my name from the front yard. I step out onto the balcony, abandoning Princess Jasmine for Juliet just this once.

'Let me in,' he calls, waving a Bible at me. 'I've got something I want you to read.'

If Jehovah's Witnesses were this cute, they'd probably have a lot more success. I go downstairs and let him in. We read a selection from Proverbs – the one about the good wife who eats not from the bread of idleness. Somehow I have the feeling that industry for this wife would not include belly dancing, eBay bidding, or writing cynical reviews of rock 'n' roll bands. I see Windex in my future, and Mop 'N Glo. But, I tell myself, the ends justify the means. After all, it says here 'her husband praiseth her.' That's what I want, right? I plan to girdeth my loins and start sewething fine linens, as soon as I figure out how to do both of them.

'Do you mind if I stay here tonight?'

'Do what?'

'They're painting my room at Tony's.' Freddie's room, a former sunporch, has maybe one wall that could be painted. It would take about forty minutes.

'Then why don't you sleep in the living room?'

'Because they're painting that, too.' I seem to recall fresh wallpaper in the living room, although that was a week ago.

'What's Tony going to say when you don't come home?'

'I already told him I was staying at Wyche's.'

Uh huh. Against my better judgment, I start making up the futon – only this time I really mean it. Unlike my dalliance with Hal, this is high-stakes dating. If I want the grand prize package complete with little brown babies, I have to prove I'm just as virtuous as the Wal-Mart Mommies at his church. I have to make him believe that I'm keeper material – and that means no fooling around. *None.* It's a good thing I've already girded my loins. I say good night to Freddie and crawl into bed alone.

At the ungodly hour of six A.M., I am awakened by Freddie, in jeans but no shirt, crawling into bed next to me. I wonder what kind of test he is planning, and hope in my coffeeless state I am up to the challenge.

'I really like hanging out with you,' he says, grabbing my arm and placing it across his chest. It occurs to me that I really like hanging out with Karen but I don't go jumping into her bed half dressed.

'Get closer to me,' he commands, a geographic impossibility since he's wrapped himself around me like the Vine of Sodom. 'Throw your leg across me,' he growls, grabbing my thigh and yanking it toward his belly. I panic and scramble over his body, out of the bed, and into the kitchen. There I busy myself making breakfast – 'She riseth also while it is yet night, and giveth meat to her household' (Proverbs 31:15). Eventually Freddie slinks in, fully clothed, and reiterates that Tony thinks he's at Wyche's. I promise not to blow his cover; besides, I have the feeling Tony would find a way to pin it on me, unvirtuous once-born belly dancer that I am. After extracting a second promise from me – to accompany him to church the next morning – he vanishes. I abandon breakfast in favor of a cold shower and ask myself, not for the first time, what Freddie really wants. It feels like Fahed all over again, only he's already been married off, a fact he doesn't hesitate to remind me of whenever he thinks I'm getting too 'girly on him,' as he puts it. I feel like I've found a store that sells everything I ever wanted, only somebody else already has it on layaway. I wonder if God is using some twisted form of aversive conditioning to tell me to eat the Food Lion ice cream? Any normal girl would be turned off Arab men for good by now. But I'm not a normal girl – although tomorrow morning I'm going to do my best impression.

As if getting up for ten A.M. services isn't hard enough, Freddie insists that I be at his house by eight-thirty so we can attend First Word. From what I understand, First Word is the sermon that will be preached at ten, broken down to an even more basic level – if that's possible. Kind of a special ed version of church. I hardly see the point, but my goal is to look teachable, so I go. This time I bring Starbucks. I settle back on a tiny Sunday school chair and listen to a lecture, complete with chalkboard notes, about separating the chaff from the wheat. Pastor Tim makes the point several times that there is chaff here among us, even today, 'sinners and scorners' masquerading as Christians. I swear I feel Tony's eyes burning into the back of my head. I can't even pretend I'm reading intently, because I didn't think to bring a Bible – major faux pas and points-loser on my part – a surefire chaff gaffe. I sip my coffee and try to look sincere. After First Word, Freddie asks me how I liked the lecture.

'That depends,' I say defensively. 'Am I wheat or am I chaff?'

'Oh, you're chaff,' he says without hesitation, 'but that's OK. We can still hang out.'

I drive home teary-eyed and dejected, angry at Freddie, angry at Fahed, angry at myself for being this fallen chaff, this *sharmouta*, this lascivious ruined belly dancer who will never be pure enough for an Arab man. I am so angry that I don't notice until I turn onto my street that Freddie has been following me the whole way. He pulls in behind my car and follows me up to the porch. I peek at him sideways from behind my glasses, trying not to show my smeared makeup and reddened eyes. He doesn't seem to notice.

'I'm not following you or anything. I'm just on my way to Wyche's. Can I have a glass of water?'

He follows me up the stairs and into the kitchen. I pour him a glass of water. He takes one sip and sets it on the table, then wanders into the bedroom. Now I'm following him, baffled. He picks a pair of cutoff army shorts up off the floor.

'Do you wear these?'

'Only around the house.' Like it matters. I might as well wear a little red suit with horns and a tail at this point.

'I'd like to see you in them.' *Huh*? I'm standing there with a big cartoon question mark over my head when he grabs me around the waist and tosses me down on the bed.

'Uh, Freddie, I don't think—'

'Don't play dumb. You know what you're doing to me.' He nuzzles my neck and tries to untuck my shirt at the same time. 'You've got *pornography* all over your apartment.' He looks up at the poster over my bed, a 1940s Arabic soap ad with a painting of a topless lady peeking out from behind a shower curtain. 'You've got all these books about sex on your shelves where everybody can see them.' I wonder which ones I missed in my sweep, but Freddie keeps talking. 'And then' – and he runs a hand down my ankle-length flowered skirt – 'you show up dressed like *this*.'

'Like *this*? I'm wearing *church clothes*.'

'You know what I mean,' he insists. Working a hand underneath me, he gropes at my butt while I try to knee him off me without ripping my skirt.

'And the way you walked up those stairs in front of me . . .'

'You *followed* me up the stairs!' I explode. 'Nobody told you to follow me home!'

'You can't wave meat in front of a starving dog,' he says, biting my neck hard.

He has the dog part right. Just as I won't be a scrapbook memento for an Emerati zillionaire, I won't play Mary Magdalene in Freddie's passion play. I wrestle out of his grasp, an involved process that leaves the mattress half off its frame, the bedclothes on the floor, and ultimately brings the draperies, curtain rod and all, crashing down on Freddie's head. While he's still untangling himself, I hustle down to the front door, where I wait, in my sullied church clothes, to lock the door behind him when he leaves. And leave he does, but not without posing the eternal question one last time:

'You're not going to tell Tony, are you?'

I don't see or hear from Freddie for four days. When he does show up again, it's to tell me that God has forgiven him. I listen skeptically from the balcony, this time feeling more like some reject Rapunzel than Juliet, waiting for a nonexistent prince and getting nothing but toads. Good-looking Middle Eastern toads, but toads nonetheless.

'I just wanted to come by and let you know that we can still hang out – but we need to do it in public, like at church and stuff, because I'm a married man.'

And I'm an idle chaff. I shake my head sadly at this gorgeous specimen of formerly Maronite Lebanese man-hood. At thirty-three, I feel like the little twerp on Arab Chat was right. I am expired, at least by Arab standards. I might as well quit waiting for Prince Ali to come. Thirty-three might be a little old to be figuring this out, but I'm starting to realize that life is not like a Disney cartoon – at least not most of the time. 'Apple core!' 'Baltimore!' 'Who's your friend?'

Me. I turn and walk into my apartment, alone.

13

Have Zils, Will Travel

*Riding on the Marrakesh Express
with Anthea*

'So are you still hanging out with that Masmoud boy?' Uncle Ronnie is pasting up a new Scariens flyer, gluing swirly hypno-wheels to a sheet of poster board in preparation for next week's show.

'No. He went crazy.' It's been a month since the end of the Freddie episode and I am still depressed over my latest dating failure, but I've learned from experience that spending time at Ronnie's will cure me, at least partially. Whether it's belly dancer politics, job stress, or love trouble, just being around people who know exactly who I am and how I work makes a world of difference. Nobody really understands Soffees but other Soffees. The Scarien persona of Arabs from outer space sometimes feels way too true.

'Well, you know we're all crazy.' Ronnie repeats this, his mantra. He shakes his head sadly – aside from me myself, no one wants me to find a good Arab man more than Ronnie. Unlike my Americanized parents, he has a deep and abiding ethnic pride that sometimes manifests itself in strange ways but is nonetheless strong and pure. He looks up from his flyer, inspired. 'Couldn't you just get pregnant and then tell him to fuck off?'

I can't say I haven't thought about it. Freddie Masmoud would be great breeder stock – between my brainy nerd genes and Freddie's big handsome ones, we could do great things for the local Lebanese gene pool. With my luck, though, the equation would end up inverted and I'd end up with a pale, dumb baby. That's not even taking into consideration the combined reaction of Freddie's father and my father to such a solution. Where my father only implies the possibility of what could happen to those who displease him, Freddie's father inflicts it in old-fashioned Catholic Dad style. Even at his age, I think he'd be quite capable of pounding Freddie into a big handsome pulp – and, as angry as I am at him, I still wouldn't want to see that.

'I don't think Tony Senior or Daddy would be too thrilled about that,' I say, and, because we are both Soffees, Ronnie understands completely.

'I remember when Tony Masmoud used to come to the Y downtown and box,' he recalls, gluing a flying saucer down over a picture of a mosque. 'We were all twenty, and he was forty.' He smiles wistfully at the recollection. 'He used to kick our ass.'

'Yeah, I think he still could,' I say, not unkindly. I arrange some cutout Arabic letters on the coffee table. 'He probably didn't kick Freddie's ass enough.'

'Well, how crazy did he go?'

I'm not sure how much of the story Ronnie needs to hear. He is, after all, still my uncle, and three hundred dollars could still put Freddie in the canal.

'Well, he's like way into the born-again thing, and even though his wife left him and had a baby with somebody else, Jesus told him to wait for her, so he's waiting. But apparently Jesus thinks it's OK for him to do whatever he wants in the meantime.' And I do mean whatever; according to Lee, over the past couple of weeks Freddie has been spotted staggering into World Cup at closing time, under the influence of something other than the Holy Spirit. Apparently Jesus doesn't hold you accountable for *staying* straight like twelve-step programs do. You can always be forgiven, after all.

Ronnie shakes his head. 'Born again Christian? Not Catholic?' I nod. He's aghast. 'You ain't just whistlin' *ya'ha sit'ti*,' he says, and I nod again. 'He must be a self-hater.' He holds up the poster for inspection. It looks good. Flying saucers and minarets, scimitars, and aliens. '*Band, show, and fiasco*,' it promises, and the Scariens always deliver.

As Ronnie sticks Arabic letters (saying Allah knows what) around the border of the flyer, Ronnie's daughter Holly drops by with her son Jidis. Named for my grandfather, two-year-old Jidis is blond and blue-eyed, the product of a marriage between Holly and Gary Bohannon, Ronnie's former business partner at the record store. 'What in the shit does he think this is, the old country?' my father had remarked when he heard Holly and Gary were getting married. Sometimes I wish it were that easy. I'd be pretty amenable to a nice arranged marriage right about now. Ronnie, proud to finally be a *ghidoo*, is working overtime to make up for the three-quarters of Jidis's background that aren't Lebanese. Besides the name, Jidis has stuffed camels in his bedroom, the *Arabian Nights* on the bookshelf, and a library of old Sinbad movies that he watches every morning before breakfast. 'My cousins,' he says, pointing proudly at the screen.

'You know, we ought to do a big show where you can dance with the Scariens,' Ronnie says. I nod; I've actually been thinking this myself for a long time. Janiece has been coming with me to the recent Scarien shows – I've all but overcome my fear of the Girls in the Corner – and from our booth behind the soundboard we've worked up a pretty good duet to the Scarien theme song. This is no mean feat considering that the Scarien theme song is a back-and-forth medley between the theme from *The Seventh Voyage of Sinbad* and 'Happy Trails.' The first part is easy.

'When's the next show?' I'm game to dance with the Scariens. Now that I've weaseled out of the Jewels, my only public appearances are at Sheva's shows at the Moose and Lucy's shows at Nick's Roman Terrace, which only add up to about a show every couple of months. If I'm going to be able to rationalize buying any more costumes, I'm going to have to get my ass onstage pronto – and there's a velvet Afifi that I've got my eye on.

'This one's on the fifteenth. We're even playing at a new place; I forget the name. But it should be better than Stop Nine.' No matter what the unnamed venue is, that's bound to be the understatement of the year. Stop Nine, the Scariens' usual venue, is located on the southern lip of Rudd's Trailer Park, a choice piece of real estate that our family inherited by way of Aunt Ida's second marriage. Given that Ronnie has taken to bringing the trailer park residents to the Scariens' shows as a sort of prefab audience, this makes it convenient in that they don't have far to stagger to get home, but Stop Nine is decidedly lacking in ambiance. The last time we were there my waitress was wearing filthy pink bedroom slippers. I ordered a Diet Coke and watched her go behind the bar, pull a can off a cardboard pallet of cans, and hand it to me, still sealed. I considered asking for a glass of ice but decided I probably wouldn't trust the glass or the ice. I ended up drinking it hot.

'Well, find out and I'll dance. I'll see if Janiece wants to dance, too.' Over the past few months, Janiece and I have been batting the idea around of starting a casual pick-up troupe just to do fun, off-the-wall shows as they come up. We organized one show on a whim last fall, e-mailing Russian rockabilly band the Red Elvises and asking if they'd like us to join them onstage at a local Yuppiefest event during their song 'I Wanna See You Bellydance.' When they took us up on the offer, we announced it at class and ended up with a half-dozen dancers who shimmied and shook to the bemusement of the khakis-and-Polo crowd. The combination of rockabilly, belly dancing, and good-looking foreign men with Elvis hairdos made it about the most fun I'd had in a while.

'Yeah, we haven't had any dancers in our show since the Mosby Court Dancers did that show.' Ronnie's job as city events planner has allowed the Scariens to slide onto the bill at more than one official city event. The show with dancers was a show in the Mosby Court Housing Project on National Night Out. As Ronnie howled in pidgin Arabic, a well-rehearsed crew of teenaged black girls in hypno-wheel T-shirts and bare feet did an African-themed line dance at the front of the stage, swinging their heads in circles and stomping their feet as the giant mechanized hypno wheels twirled. The show still turns up regularly on the public access channel, and I get a perverse glee out of calling my father up whenever I spot it, making some small talk and then casually saying, 'Hey, put it on channel nine for a minute.'

'Well, let me know where it's gonna be and we'll set something up.' I figure I can run it by Janiece this weekend. She and I are going on a road trip with the Girls in the Corner to Marrakesh – not the real Marrakesh, but the restaurant in D.C., where we hope to see some big-city-caliber belly dancin' and eat some couscous. Who needs Lebanese men when you've got Moroccan waiters who wash your hands for you in a big brass bowl and bring you spearmint tea? I wish I could bring one home with me, but I'll settle for an evening spent lounging on cushions and watching Anthea dance. It beats the hell out of guitar hymns any day.

Ronnie holds up the completed flyer for inspection. A fleet of flying saucers passes over a mosque and a tiny gray alien peeks out from inside one of the minarets. I think it looks great.

'Oh, hey, let me play you our new song.' The Scariens are branching out; after doing unheard-of things to Beatles and Elvis covers for years, they are starting to test out some original material. Ronnie slides a CD into the player and turns up the speakers, and soon his own voice is booming through the house over a Chuck Berry–style riff.

'When the word came down in 623
Mohammed told the people better listen to me
When the people got the message they took it and ran
You oughta check the record down in Afghanistan . . .'

'I wrote it this week,' he shouts over the music with a proud grin. 'Wait until you hear the chorus.'

The song continues, with Ronnie hollering over the guitar about the Taliban and the Jews and the white man. I can't make out all of the words, but I think I hear something about the undead, too. Probably so; zombies are a running theme in the Scariens' repertoire. Tapping his foot and nodding his head, Ronnie points to the speaker, my cue that the chorus is coming up.

'In the name of Allah – I will light the fuse
In the name of Allah – may he be amused
In the name of Allah – Obey the Imam
Cause it don't say blow up nothin' in the holy Qur'an!'

Jidis looks up from smiting a plastic Godzilla with a gladiator sword and shakes his head. 'Oh, for God's sake,

Ghidoo,' he says, then returns to his battle. Kids today. What do they know from culture?

'I wish I could find out where he lived; he might just wake up and find his tires slashed.' Susan makes this promise in her usual disinterested monotone. Just in case we don't believe her, she adds, 'it's been known to happen.' She is talking not about Freddie but about a local on-line journalist who wrote an unflattering article on a belly dancing workshop we'd all attended last weekend. The event had been a star-studded affair with the Ibrahim Farrah troupe from New York and was attended by dancers from as far away as Ontario. It was Sheva's first foray into workshop sponsoring in years and culminated in a professional show in the hotel banquet room with big name dancers like Phaedra, Jojouka, and Samara. The reporter didn't even attend the show, though; instead he wrote a detailed piece on how fat most of the workshop participants were and the unflattering contortions they went through during the morning warm-up.

It's this stereotype of belly dancers that makes me cringe, much more than the hoochie-coochie one or the 1970s *Cosmo* one. I don't mind if some idiot thinks I'm going to take something off, or twirl my tassels, or seduce someone's husband, because when I perform I can prove that wrong. But the idea that belly dancing is an excuse for 'fat chicks to dress up,' as someone on the belly dancing Web list once complained, really galls me. It cheapens what we do, it makes a judgment based on size that sells all belly dancers, both large and small, short, and, perhaps worst of all, it has just enough of a grain of truth in it to make it really hurt.

In the same way that one yahoo with a big mouth and a small weenie makes the NRA look bad, or one Qur'an-waving psycho ruins it for millions of peaceful Muslims, there are just enough tarted-up housewives in homemade *bedlah* to perpetuate this stereotype among outsiders. I don't mean legitimate students of the dance who attend classes and workshops and, whether they weigh 125 or 350, get out there and do their best to execute a proper hip circle, figure eight, or undulation. If you're studying the dance and doing it well, who cares how much you weigh? I mean the spotlight-hungry eight-week wonders who take one beginner class and consider that license to hop onstage as frequently and as publicly as possible, shaking all over the stage like a Maytag in need of a tuneup. Again, it doesn't matter if they're a size five or a size twenty-five; it's the motivation that makes the difference. Are you here to dance or are you here to model costumes and shake? At last weekend's workshop we were there to dance, but since we weren't all twenty years old and skinny we were treated like a bunch of desperate old fat broads with harem fantasies. And now we are pissed.

'I'm just glad Sheva doesn't use the Internet,' Janiece says, and I agree. The workshop was like some Ponce de León magic potion for Sheva. She was in her element, giving orders, collecting praise, and hobnobbing with Bobby's troupe about the good old days of bellygrams and Middle Eastern nightclubs. On Sunday afternoon she presented Phaedra with a foot-high doll with long black hair, dressed in a miniature replica of a costume Phaedra wore on the cover of an Eddie Kochak album. I've never seen Sheva as happy as she seemed onstage with Phaedra at the end of that workshop – and I didn't want to see some pencil-necked Web journalist spoil it for her.

We come up with a few more revenge scenarios before handing Tammy's van over to the valet at Marrakesh. As we step through the enormous wooden doorway into the tiled foyer, I think the same thing I thought the last time I came here: *I need to come here more often.* For a two-hour drive and the price of a much less exciting meal in

Richmond, I could be dining on couscous, grape leaves, and *bstila* and watching Anthea dance. I look around at the star-studded photographs on the wall and vow silently that from now on, I *will* come here more often. If it's good enough for Marty Feldman, it's good enough for me.

This time we are seated not in the main dining room but in a back room down a long hallway. The room has its own little bar in the corner where a man in a fez sits looking warily at us as he polishes glasses. I half expect a Brit in an overcoat to slip me a canister of microfilm before being felled by a mysterious poison dart. I love, love, *love* the Marrakesh. We sip our drinks and feel suave and belly dancerish as we lean back on the low, benchlike cushioned seats and listen to the preshow *oud* music. I look around at my surroundings, and at my company, and I suddenly feel incredibly lucky. If three years ago someone had told me I'd be spending my Saturday night at the Marrakesh in D.C. with five belly dancers, I would have been convinced they had me confused with someone else – someone with whom I'd gladly trade places. At least, that is what I think now. I wonder if, back in my tattoo parlor days, I would have been able to appreciate this as being as cool as it obviously is? Hard to say, and now I'm so deep in it that I've lost my perspective. Could it be that, to people on the outside, belly dancing doesn't look cool at all – just weird and a little cheesy? Does the rest of the world think like me and Doris and Susan, or do they think like that loser from Richmond.com?

I guess the more important question is 'do I care?' and the answer is no. Kind of like with AA. I can remember seeing it from the outside and thinking how pathetic and losery and culty the people sounded, sitting behind me and my punk rock friends at Aunt Sarah's. The recovery buzzwords floated above their table like a cloying pink cloud ... 'sobriety,' 'one day at a time,' 'keep coming back,' 'acceptance' – and I would get so disgusted that I would insist we get up and move. Now, from the other side, I realize that the rest of the world is still closer to the old me in their attitude toward the program, but I don't care. It works for me and that's all I care about. I can ignore the creepy huggers, the slogan spouters, and the people who want to trumpet the jargon over pancakes for all the world to hear and still get what I need from it. And it's the same with belly dancing. Regardless of what the babealicious babes or the eight-week wonders do, and regardless of what the rest of the world thinks of it, I am getting what I need.

A waiter comes over to take our drink orders, distributing lapcloths since we'll be eating with our hands. As he places Vera's cloth on her lap, she says in a loud voice to no one in particular, 'Well! I wish I'd brought my *zils*!' Just in case the waiter didn't know we are actual belly dancers – and just in case he cares. I think of responding, 'Yeah, well I was talking to Sohair Zaki the other day and she said the *bstila* here was great,' but I hold my tongue. I still feel like I am on probation here, like a sophomore at the seniors' table. I don't want to screw it up with my big mouth.

Soon another waiter delivers the first course, Moroccan vegetables and flat slabs of unleavened bread, and we are happily scooping up carrots and tomatoes with chunks of tasty bread. We are so involved in our dinner that we don't see Anthea right away when she comes in. Of course, she's not immediately recognizable in her bell-bottoms and glasses – but the requisite rolling suitcase she's dragging pegs her as a belly dancer as soon as we spot it. We slide over and make room for her, and she joins us at our table for some belly dancer schmoozing before she goes to change. If I felt like an insider before, now I feel like a belly dancing celebrity! The bartender sends us a round of drinks on the house – after all, we are friends of Anthea's, worthy of star treatment. Even though I have to pass on the free drink, I feel extra special and tingly. I am at least as cool as Marty Feldman now.

Anthea excuses herself to change, and we work our way through course after course of Moroccan food – lamb and chicken for the carnivores and hummus and grape leaves for me, along with couscous and *bstila* and belly dancer gossip all around. Tonight's catty comments focus mainly on Theresa, a new dancer who, at seventeen, is this year's model of the local belly dancing Next Big Thing. From the old-timers I learn that this is a regular occurrence at Sheva's – some cute young Lolita with a hint of natural talent and a flat little tummy who somehow jumps from the beginner class to paying gigs without benefit of seniority or the usual dues-paying. Unlike Jen, who moved up the ranks quickly but also took multiple classes and workshops and joined not one but two troupes in short order, the Sheva prodigies tend to consider themselves ready for the big time after one session of Monday night classes and the acquisition of a cute costume – and Sheva's tendency to favor them with high-profile paying gigs from the get-go does little to dissuade them of the notion.

Tonight's Theresa story originates from Rose and Doris's last *hafla*. Their 'Two and a Half Friends' work-shop and *hafla* series (Janiece being the half) is where local belly dancers kick back and cut loose, bringing out the fusion pieces, the ethnically incorrect numbers, and new ideas they're kicking around. Held in an old school-house on the outskirts of town, they're user-friendly and low pressure, and anyone who takes the workshop is wel-come to dance in the *hafla*. For the last one, Theresa signed up for the workshop and *hafla* but was a no-show. At Sheva's next class she approached Doris, not to apologize but to demand her money back since she decided not to come. When Doris pointed out the 'no refunds' clause clearly printed on the registration form, Theresa tossed her curls and huffed, 'What-*ever*! I don't need you or your damn *hafla*!' I am fascinated. I can't imagine being so full of myself as to tell Doris I don't need her damn *hafla* – but then again, Sheva didn't book me to dance at a black-tie reception at the Virginia Museum after two months of classes, either.

Midway through the main course, the lights dim and Anthea comes *zil*-ling into the back room for a command performance. As it turns out, the back room is usually a no-dancing zone – but, since *we're* here, right after doing her whole routine for the main dining room, Anthea jumps off the main stage, hustles down the hall, and does it all over again.

I'm so impressed with myself I can hardly eat. But I am more impressed with Anthea. I've seen her dance once before, at one of the Women of Selket's *haflas*, and I was endlessly impressed – with her *zil* syncopation, her crisp, isolated hips, and her flawless ribcage slides. More than anything, though, I was in awe of her incredible Chip and Daleness. Not since Aegela have I seen a dancer with a more inviting smile. Anthea's got a cartoon mouth – it looks like it was drawn on larger than scale, with just enough of an overbite to make her look like she's up to something. It is the perfect belly dancer mouth. Debbie West's is a close second. I am not so lucky; I have a little nerd mouth that purses into a scowl when I'm dancing if I'm not careful. I was so upset when I saw my first ever performance pictures – here I had *felt* so Chip and Dale, but in all the pictures I looked like I was about to smack someone upside the head and then deny it was me who did it. Anthea could never have this problem. Her mouth is magnificent.

Her costume, too, is magnificent – Pepto pink with little sparkly silver starbursts all over it. It's a costume I'd kill for. But it wouldn't matter if she were wearing sackcloth and ashes because what matters in the end is that Anthea can seriously belly dance. There are few things more captivating than watching Anthea dance. She will make you let your *bstila* get cold, which is really saying something. Her hips move like gyroscopes, lifting higher and dropping lower than would appear to be anatomically possible. Her shoulder shimmies are subtle and balanced, accented with sassy lifts and holds that look like she's saying 'gotcha!' with her whole torso. And she never, absolutely never, stops smiling.

We applaud raucously and *zaghareet* at every lull in her performance. We are having a fantastic time. I feel horribly sorry for anyone who is not here tonight because there is no way anyone else in the world is having this much fun. I wish that she would dance forever, or at least until closing time, but her performance is over much too soon. I think it's over, anyway – but the next thing I know, she's at our table, pulling Doris up by the hand and motioning for the rest of us to join them. She wants us to dance! In front of everybody! At the *Marrakesh*!

Needless to say, Vera is center stage in a heartbeat. She pulls out all the stops, spinning and undulating and snake-arming at every unsuspecting patron in the vicinity. The audience looks uneasy, as if they're not sure whether her schtick is vamp or camp. Vera couldn't care less; she's posing and hip-locking for all she's worth. She loves an audience, and it doesn't matter whose audience they are. Meanwhile, Doris, Susan, Tammy, and Janiece are getting into it as well, if a little less boldly. They shimmy and side-step in time to the music, throwing in the occasional arm flourish or chest lock but for the most part looking like four nice ladies who happen to know their way around a *balady*. Vera, meanwhile, looks as though she might break out the floorwork at any moment.

And where am I during all of this? Standing by our booth, frozen with fear. Dancing at a Two and a Half Friends *hafla* or a nursing home is one thing; at Sheva's show or Lucy's class party, no problem there either. Even the odd nightclub or festival, while not without its butter-flies, I can handle. But the *Marrakesh*? With *Anthea*? I feel faint. And even though I know nothing is expected of me, that the other patrons in the back room will never see me again and besides, as far as they know I am just a random nerd having dinner, I feel like my puny snake arms and soggy hips are not worthy of this venue. I have no busi-ness belly dancing here. Janiece looks at me with a scolding expression and motions me out to the floor; I paste on a smile and venture out a few steps. I try some snake hips, a couple of figure eights, a hip drop or two. I feel clunky and disjointed, like I can't find the beat. I try to copy Susan, then Doris, then I give up and go back to snake hips. I want to run away.

Later on, as we're nibbling baklava and having one last cup of spearmint tea, Anthea comes out in her caftan and thanks us for dancing with her. She chats awhile about upcoming events her troupe is having, then excuses herself to go change. As she gets up from her seat, she leans over and says to me, 'I liked your dancing. You have very good hips and nice transitions.'

I blush and thank her, but my brain doesn't let me enjoy the compliment even for a minute. Immediately a little voice says *you must have looked like such a rank beginner that she felt like she should say something encouraging to you*. This is how my mind works. Would that I were like Vera and had an ego the size of Houston and an un-flagging notion that everyone in the world was just dying to see my wonderful belly dancing up close and personal. Would that I were like Theresa and so sure of my innate talent that after a summer's worth of weekly classes I could tell Doris to stick her *hafla* where the sun don't shine. And would that I were like the babealicious babes and the eight-week wonders, concerned only about how much cleavage I could show and how often, and not whether I could do a sharp isolation or a barrel turn. But, alas, this is not to be. I am just a hapless, nerdy, Lebanese American rhythmically challenged novice belly dancer, and an insecure one at that. I spend the whole ride home reflecting on what I am sure is Anthea's pity for me and my pathetic little attempt at belly dancing.

I can't sleep that night, angry at myself for being a lousy belly dancer, angry at myself for not having any self-confidence, angry at myself for letting my petty insecurities ruin the best evening I'd had in forever. That week I look for salvation in all the usual places. My AA sponsor is unsympathetic. 'Has it occurred to you,' she says, putting the 'duh' face on, 'that maybe she said she liked your dancing because she liked your *dancing*?' Try as I might, I can't wrap my head around it. One of my therapist friends thinks maybe I should look back into my past to find the root of my self-esteem issues. She may have a point, but I don't feel like dredging all of that up just now. Vicki suggests that I join her and Janet in driving up to northern Virginia for weekly private lessons with Anthea – confronting my fear head-on, belly dancer immersion therapy. I wish I could, but my schedule doesn't fit.

In the end, the solution I settle on is the one I should have known would work all along – an evening at Ronnie's, looking at old pictures, and listening to stories about my family while the Scariens rehearse in the basement, then heading home to drink coffee and watch old black-and-white videos of Samia Gamal and Farid el-Atrache. It is just the thing I need to make me happy about who I am and what I do. I'm no Samia Gamal and I never will be – but I'm proud to be a Soffee, and I'm proud to be the amateur imperfect half-Lebanese belly dancer that I am. I might not get the black-tie bookings or the Marrakesh spotlight, but I'm carrying the Lebanese heritage torch for the next generation of Soffees. It's a small gesture, but as I watch Samia do her barely perceptible *mayas* I note that sometimes the smallest moves are the most important. One day I'll be proud to tell my children that I am a belly dancer – and I hope that if I have a daughter, she'll belly dance, too. Or a son, for that matter. I flash back to Jidis and his gladiator sword. I wonder if he'd be interested in a few lessons?

'You're playing *where*?' Talk about not being able to wrap my head around something. Ronnie has called, as promised, to invite me to dance at the Scariens' upcoming show – at the Three Chopt Bar and Grill.

'Yeah, I've never heard of it either. Some place out in Henrico.'

'Oh, I've *heard* of it,' I correct him. I can't believe my bad luck. Out of all the dives in Richmond, why would the one bar crazy enough to hire the Scariens to play have to be the Three Chopt Bar and Grill? Or should I have assumed it all along? 'It is,' I say, weighing each syllable carefully, 'the vilest, most hideous place on the face of the earth.'

'You're *kidding*,' Ronnie says, horrified. I am so not kidding. I tell him the whole story – Another Pretty Face, the heavy metal band, the prison dykes. He listens intently. I'm glad I haven't already booked Janiece for the show, as there is no way I will ever set costumed foot in that place again. My debut with the Scariens will just have to wait.

'When are you playing at Stop Nine again?' Yes, even Stop Nine is a step up from the Three Chopt Bar and Grill.

'Probably never. That place has really gone downhill.'

The concept of Stop Nine ever having been uphill is foreign to me. 'You mean it could get worse?'

'Well, they can't cook anything now. They got their gas turned off.' I don't know what is worse, a restaurant that

290

can't cook or the concept of eating something prepared at Stop Nine in the first place.

'Well, as much as I want to dance to the Scariens, I can't dance there again. I just can't do it.'

'I don't blame you. But I don't know when we'll play out again. Nobody wants us. We're too old and crazy.'

You and me both, Uncle. I hang up, disappointed. I was so sure I had found the perfect solution to my identity crisis. I know that eventually the Scariens will play again, and eventually I'll join them, but in the meantime, what's to do? I'm out of the Jewels, barely a girl for the Corner of the Room, and not babealicious enough for the Sheva gigs. Is there a place for a nerdy amateur Lebanese American belly dancer? Or am I once again hopelessly out of place in my own skin? I put on good old Mohammed el-Bakkar, prop Nejla up against the bookcase, pour myself a cup of coffee and order in falafel and hummus from Aladdin Express. Sometimes my uncomfortable skin is just a little too thin for the outside world. Thank Allah Aladdin always delivers.

14

Belly Dancer Like Me

Making Nejla Proud

'*Thaddeus?* What in the shit does he think he is, a gladiator?' This is my father's too-predictable response to my new boyfriend. The Freddie Masmoud episode turned out to be the final nail in the coffin of my search for a good Arab man. I'm starting to doubt there are any out there who aren't already related to me. Thaddeus – Tad for short – is the anti-Arab: a blue-eyed, fair-skinned former Marine. He's also classically handsome, impressively muscular, and nine years younger than I am. I'm operating on the Mary Mary theory of dating now. In the past year, I've attended both her eightieth birthday party and her racy bridal shower. Age doesn't slow down romance one bit when you're a belly dancer.

It had been two months since the Freddie fiasco, and I had sworn off dating for the whole summer when I met Tad – purely by accident. He is a bouncer at the Paper Moon, Richmond's 'upscale gentlemen's club.' By upscale they mean that the bouncers wear tuxedos while they pitch you face-first into the gravel parking lot. As irony would have it, the Paper Moon and the sex offender facility where I teach share a number of employees. Both operations are always in need of big burly guys who are capable of shouting 'You with the erection – sit down and don't touch nobody!' So there is some overlap. And it just so happened that one Saturday morning, on lunch break from a bodyguard certification course, one such burly guy happened to take a wrong exit and find himself in my neighborhood, with Tad in tow.

'I know a girl who lives around here,' he said. 'She might know where we can get a cup of coffee.' Big burly guys are masters of understatement. He banged on my door until I came storming out onto the balcony, half dressed, un-madeup, greasy hair in a bedheaded fright.

'Goddammit, Simonski, this better be *good*,' I screeched down at him. And the rest, as they say, is history.

What I thought would be a Saturday night date on a lark with a good-looking boy toy has turned into something that is showing all of the frightening characteristics of a real relationship. Who would guess that a nudie bar bouncer's idea of a great night out would involve an entire evening at my local bookstore (in the physics section, no less – be still, my nerdy heart) and a midnight lamb kebab at Aladdin Express? So it only stands to reason that, after a month of almost daily dating, I should bring him to my parents' house for Sunday dinner.

The gladiator comment is not my father's first dig at Tad's name. In fact, the first thing he ever says to him, upon introduction, is 'Tad? That's a *dog's* name.' Is it any wonder I didn't bring more of my boy-friends home in high school? My sister is also skeptical. I bring Tad to a family picnic, where she and her new husband, Kevin, eye him suspiciously from their table.

'I don't know,' she says, pursing her lips. 'He looks a little . . .' here she cocks her finger like a pistol and wiggles her thumb.

'A little what?' I know what she means, but I'm egging her on. With his USMC buzz cut, Aryan features, and mirrored sunglasses, he does look a little . . . well . . . you know. And it's not a bluff – while he may be happy to meet her, that is a gun in his pocket.

Tad takes my crazy family in stride, just as he does the eccentric AA crew at World Cup, the bust of Elvis on the mantle, and all the books and pictures I no longer try to hide. In fact when I mention Bettie Page on our first date, he genuflects, thereby earning instant points and proving himself wise beyond his years. His paramilitary political leanings and love of history make him the perfect conversational foil for Ronnie, and they eagerly debate Israeli-Palestinian relations and compare notes on Saladin while I flip through Ronnie's Roxy Music albums undisturbed. After half a dozen visits to the Scarien compound, I have yet to hear a single *ya'ha sit'ti*.

Even after four months of steady dating, Tad hasn't seen me belly dancing. Not that I don't want him to, and absolutely not that he doesn't want to, but his nightclub schedule precludes attendance at almost any dance-type event. Since we've been dating, the only place I've danced during the day has been George Wythe High School – a war zone of a public school that inexplicably holds an impressive Arts Day event every fall. At the ungodly hour of nine A.M., Debbie, Tammy, Alison, and I shimmied and undulated in the stairwell of George Wythe for a throng of lemon-faced, cornrow-wearing teenagers. Having just gotten off work at three A.M., Tad didn't attend – but he did see me on the noon news, teaching a chubby ninth grade boy how to do a hip circle.

Alison, one of Sheva's advanced students, has just started coming back to class after the birth of her daughter. She's in her twenties, quite recently married. She's a sweet girl and a good dancer. But I always feel uneasy in her presence, as if I am seeing a ghost. When

Alison comes to Sheva's class, she always wears a crinkly cotton hippie skirt and a long-sleeved baby blue top that skims her hips as she dances. Even in the hottest weeks of summer, she wears that baby blue top. The first time I saw her dance at a *hafla* I realized why. Alison is covered, chest, shoulders, back, and arms, with garishly colored tattoos. The word in the Corner is that her ex-boyfriend was a tattoo artist. Since the breakup, Alison has kept them covered and has even looked into having them removed – but apparently they're too extensive for that to be feasible. Hence the baby blue top.

When Alison dances in *bedlah*, her tattoos compete for attention with her silver sequined bra. I can't enjoy her dancing because the tattoos hurt my heart. They remind me of Chris, and Winston-Salem, and Bishop and Renée, and everything else that was a part of me four years ago. They remind me of the ragged hole that was left when Chris took it all away and sent me packing. The hole that I filled with belly dancing. I wonder about Alison's ex, who he is, if I ever met him, if he dumped her and left her heartbroken the way Chris dumped me. I think that if I had to go through what I went through with Chris's art-work staring me in the face every time I looked at my own skin, I would have jumped off a bridge. That or scraped off my own flesh with sandpaper. It would have been too much for me. Alison must be a strong, strong girl; I wish I could talk to her about it. But the wounds are still too fresh, and when I see her they hurt all over again. I don't love Chris anymore; I don't miss him and I don't want him back. But the pain is something that I don't think I will ever forget. Like a tattoo, it will always be with me.

Speaking of tattoos, Tad takes my crappy one in stride. 'That's some cool ink you've got there, *dude*,' he says sarcastically whenever it peeks out of my clothing. This places him miles ahead of Hal, who was quick to suggest laser surgery – when I mentioned the possibility of

295

scarring, he sniffed, 'A scar would be *preferable*.' Tad doesn't have any tattoos. The anti-Arab is also the anti-hipster. Besides, before we started dating, he was planning to join a mercenary group in Africa, and tattoos would make him easier to ID. Belly dancers and armed militants – they just go together.

Also, for someone who watches naked women undulate and gyrate for a living, he is surprisingly eager to see belly dancing any chance he gets – which, due to his schedule, is usually only on videos of *haflas* past. He doesn't seem to have any of that Joe Average crossover problem where belly dancers are seen as glorified strippers or well-dressed concubines. He has no interest in the dancers at the Paper Moon – a requisite for the job – and refers to them as 'product' when talking shop. But he is in awe of belly dancers, just as I still am, and that's why we get along so well.

'That's your *teacher*?' he asks dreamily when we run into Susan at the Egypt exhibit at the Virginia Museum. His eyes get misty. '*Wow*.' I decline to inform him that she is exactly twice his age – just as I decline to get jealous. Of *course* he has the hots for Susan. Everyone should. I chalk it up to good taste and continue browsing through the galleries. He puts on Middle Eastern CDs when left alone with the stereo and makes short work of tubs of hummus and *m'joudra* left in the fridge. If he wasn't the poster boy for racial purity, I'd swear there was a *kaffiyeh* in the woodpile. I suppose there is something to be said for youth and potential over age and experience; if you get them while they're young, they're still teachable. Tad is nothing if not eager to learn.

And learn he does – sometimes more than I realize. One Saturday night – or Sunday morning, to be more precise, at three A.M. – I go down to answer the now-familiar pounding knock to be greeted with this indignant proclamation: 'You're not going to believe this, but one of our new dancers got up onstage in one of those things you wear and started belly dancing!'

'Impossible,' I counter, calmly blinking the sleep from my eyes. 'It couldn't be.' Probably just some two-bit floozy in a Frederick's of Hollywood harem outfit. Happens all the time. I don't say it, but I am just a little disappointed that we are even having this discussion. I thought he knew better.

'No, this was really a belly dancer,' he insists, following me up the stairs to plead his case. 'Her costume had beads and stuff just like yours. And she was *belly dancing*. I wanted to go up there and throw my jacket over her and tell her to stop.' I thank him for his concern but continue to explain that this girl is no more a belly dancer than a girl who strips out of a police uniform is a cop. A beaded bra does not a belly dancer make. 'But,' he argues, lifting one arm above his head in a perfect Arabesque, 'she was doing *this*.' He breaks into a studied hip circle, with all the accents. Them's fightin' moves!

Wide awake now, I storm into the computer room and fire up the Internet. Enlarging the group photo from Sheva's recital, I point out the likely candidates. Was it her? Her? How about her? I'm secretly hoping it was Theresa – a fitting comeuppance for snubbing Doris's hafla. But Tad doesn't recognize any of them. And his descriptive skills leave something to be desired, anyway; he is always insisting that my light brown hair is black.

I finally give up the search, but not before dashing off a quick e-mail to the Girls in the Corner to let them know about the sighting. Something must be done – we have a reputation to protect, after all, and it's hard enough without some bimbo in *bedlah* perpetuating the myth that so many people already believe. Tad promises to call immediately the next time she works so we can form a posse and surprise her. Unescorted women ordinarily aren't allowed at the Paper Moon – one too many angry wives

297

have caused one too many scenes – but with as many friends as I have on the crew, I doubt we'll get bounced. Besides, as I continue to be reminded each time we venture out, a group of belly dancers is welcome almost anywhere.

Unfortunately, after we go through the trouble to form a phone tree and designate a driver and photographer for our covert mission, the mystery dancer vanishes from the Paper Moon's roster. What's that about the best-laid plans? I suppose we should have suspected it all along; the half-life of a Paper Moon dancer is roughly equivalent to that of a fruit fly. Sad, yes, but more important, it helps the women of the world who don't take it off for a living feel a little less resentful about the fact that those who do take home a couple of grand tax-free every night. A couple of grand a night would go a long way toward new *bedlah* – something Dancer X could probably use. It seems she left the top half of her costume behind when she disappeared. Ever eager to add to my dance wardrobe, I ask Tad to bring it home. But I am too late. That night, the abandoned bra is found in a stall in the ladies' room – submerged.

'I guess the other girls didn't like her too much,' Tad explains. Either that or someone from our posse made it there after all. The Belly Dance Code Arbiters have agents everywhere. At least we know that, wherever she has gone, she won't be doing her belly dancer impression – unless she does it Nejla style.

My life continues on in a comfortable rut – dating Tad and going to dance class, meetings, and work. I dance out every few weeks at *haflas* and class parties, spend stress-free Saturdays at the bookstore and the coffee shop, and report weekly for Sunday Snacks with my dad without fail. It's not exactly a glamorous existence, but I'm happy. One regular Monday morning, as I'm quickly scanning through my e-mail before work, a brief note from Jen pops up on the screen.

From: jen@mindspring.com
To: Samirasafi@aol.com

Call me when you get a chance. I have something about Selket I want to ask you.
—sw

My antennae perk up. Something about Selket! I am moving up in the gossip hierarchy. No more speculating on the babealicious babes for me! I fire back quickly, telling her I'll call from work. And call I do, but unfortunately Jen is one of those dark-agers who still connects to the Internet via her home phone line. It figures from a Saint Catherine's girl; that set clings to the old as if their pedigree relies upon it. *Q: How many Richmonders does it take to screw in a lightbulb? A: Three. One to screw it in and two to talk about how much better the old one was.* Determined, I shoot her another e-mail asking her what it was she had to tell me. I can't imagine, but I certainly try. Selket gossip! This should be good!

After a day full of teaching Shakespeare and correcting rowdy teenagers and an evening full of Sheva and Dr Mendez's *doumbek* and good old scratchy George Abdo, I have forgotten that I am even waiting for Selket gossip. My brain feels like one of Sheva's belly dancing records, crackly and fuzzy and barely still usable. I come home and see Jen on the caller ID, but I have no message. I try to call her; still busy – gotta talk to her about that. But first I've got to reach her. By this point, though, it's almost a relief, because in order to talk I'd need to form sentences. I file it away for tomorrow. And when I log onto the Internet for my evening nerd session, it comes as a complete broadside to find the following in my mailbox:

From: jen@mindspring.com
To: Samirasafi@aol.com

Well, I was hoping to catch you on the phone, because e-mail is so impersonal, but anyway, here goes: The Women of Selket would like to cordially extend an invitation to you to audition for the troupe. Let me know if you would be interested and I'll fill you in on the details . . . and keep it under your hat. . . .
– jsw

I am Chip and Daleing my little heart out, alone in my computer room. Invited to audition for Selket? *Me?* For real? Maybe I'm not as hopeless as I was feeling tonight as I stumbled around the ficus at the Hunt Club Apartments. I jump up from my chair. I've got to tell someone! No, wait – I'm supposed to keep it under my hat. But that's not fair! This news is too big to sit on. OK, I have to keep it under my hat to other belly dancers, but I can tell regular people. It's a Catch-22, though – regular people won't care. I could call Karen, or my parents, or Tad, but nobody would realize what a big deal this is except another belly dancer, and I'm not supposed to tell any other belly dancers. What the hell?

I look around the room, grinning like an idiot.

'Hey, Nejla,' I say to the album propped up against the bookcase. 'I got tapped to audition for *Selket*!'

Nejla doesn't answer, but I know she's proud of me. I'm proud of me. I e-mail my sincere thanks to Jen and crank up some celebratory el-Bakkar. Insomuch as it is possible to 'arrive' as an amateur belly dancer in Richmond, Virginia, I have arrived.

* * *

On Christmas Eve, with the Paper Moon mercifully closed, I invite Tad to accompany me on my yearly pilgrimage to Saint Anthony's. I'm fairly confident that we won't encounter Freddie Masmoud, as I'm sure he has something much more showy planned for the biggest Christian holiday of the year. We attend with my parents; regretfully, I am the only Soffee of my generation to come to Saint Anthony's even on major holidays. That is, I am the only Soffee in name. My great-aunt Jackie's daughters, my grandfather's nieces, have always been super-active in the church – teaching Sunday school, working at the food festival, raising hordes of little brown babies who spend their summers climbing on the big green box. But the Soffee name is no longer there. I am, as it were, the great white hope.

Of course, this belies the fact that, in order to keep the Soffee name alive at Saint Anthony's, a) I would have to attend church more than twice a year, and b) I would have to reproduce – and we're not even going to touch the fact that, were I to reproduce in the sanctioned Saint Anthony's fashion, my name would no longer be Soffee anyway. The fact of the matter is that, sitting here in my uncomfortable church dress and Ann Taylor wool coat liberated from the Paper Moon dressing room ('If they leave it, we toss it – but you should probably wash it really good'), I find all of the familiar insecurities creeping up on me like old ghosts. I'm too pale, too outspoken, too quirky, too rebellious to ever be a good Saint Anthony's girl. In the pew in front of me, Leyla Hawad's children clamber over each other, stuffing their little brown fists into a Ziploc full of Cheerios as Father George chants the Syriac portion of the mass. Leyla fell in love with a student priest from the old country who came to study with Father George. He left the priesthood to marry her. Their first son, Sharbel, was named after the Maronite church's first official saint. This is what I'm up against. With competition like that, what hope do I have? Half white already and a total Arab dating failure. And a belly dancer, no less! My Aunt Frances was right. My daddy ought to smack my face.

As usual, my visit to Saint Anthony's just convinces me even more that I ought to pack it in. After all, I've got other options. Be like my sister and embrace my whiteness – join a Protestant church and move to the suburbs. Bag the whole ethnicity question and go back to the way I was five years ago – hip and funky, retro nerd girl; I've already got the apartment in the city and the lounge CDs. Abandon the Catholic side of my family for the Muslim side – join a mosque and try to get a teaching gig at the American School in Bahrain. I could ditch the kitsch, join Selket, and defect to the Ethnic Police; that would mean no more fusion or Sheva-style cabaret harem fantasy shtick, but plenty of basket dances and Persian arms. Or – and I always forget this last option, because it's the one that makes the most sense – make the most out of what I am: a sober, nerdy, rock 'n' rolling, coffee-drinking, school-teaching, erotica-reading, kitsch-loving, Lebanese American belly dancer. And a Scarien. With a twenty-five-year-old would-be mercenary of a boyfriend.

All things considered, it's not a bad gig. As Lee would say, 'life is not boring.' And by writing my own ticket I stay one step ahead of all of the various factions that I would no doubt run afoul of otherwise – the Maronite church, the Ethnic Police, and the avatars of hipness, to name just a few. So far as I know, there are no other rock 'n' roll nerd kitsch half-Lebanese belly dancers around; at least none in the general vicinity. So I am free to do as I please without fear of reproach. I can dance at spots that would be scorned by the Ethnic Police, carouse in ways that would make the Ladies' Auxiliary blanch, and embarrass myself so thoroughly that true hipsters will pretend they don't know me when we pass in the aisles at Plan 9. And I will have fun.

Tartaji min yawmika l-ati s-alah, W-al-amani fil-a'ali ta'irah. You expect goodness from your coming day and the hopes are soaring high. My fortune *mamoul* is coming true. And I ain't just whistlin' *Ya'ha Sit'ti.* My future is brighter. When Father George begins uttering the Syriac prayer of thanksgiving, I pray along, and this time it's not to impress anybody. I really am thankful. I'm thankful to be the half-breed amateur nerd belly dancer that I am, thankful for my crazy family, my checkered past, and my mercenary boyfriend. I'm thankful for my Lebanese half, but I'm thankful for my other half too, since without it I'd probably be making baklava for the Ladies' Auxiliary and I never would have had any of the rock 'n' roll adventures that made me who I am. As it turns out, being not enough is just enough. Any more might be too much – and too much is never good.

Father George and the little brown altar boys lead the procession down the aisle to the back of the church, and a flood of unibrows and hook noses follow. Mass is over. I scoot down to the end of the aisle, genuflect one time with feeling, and throw in a little upper-body camel on the rebound. You can take the belly dancer out of the *hafla*, but you can't take the *hafla* out of the belly dancer. Father, forgive me – I didn't mean to sin.

I was only belly dancing.

EPILOGUE

My Ya'ha Just Gets Sit-tier

*With a Few Snakes and Guns
to Balance Out the Schmaltz*

It's been five years since I took up belly dancing. They've been a big five years. I've danced a lot of shows, dated a lot of Arabs, taught a lot of hard-knock kids, and eaten a lot of Aladdin Express takeout. I've bought my first house, I'm publishing my first book, and in a few short months, I'll be embarking on yet another first.

Last November, as I was nerding out in high style, with Cheb Mami on the stereo and eBay on the monitor, Tad pulled up a chair and suggested we see what ebay had to offer in the way of engagement rings. No biggie – we'd talked about it before, casually, over falafel. I figured he was just trying to keep me from spending another forty bucks on old Nejla Ates head shots. I had nothing against knocking back a few cups of coffee while we compared the merits of various styles of engagement rings. How about this one? Too busy. How about this one? Too mall-bunny. How about this one?

Which one? The one he just pulled out of his pocket. Princess cut, with a snag-proof setting, 'so it won't get

304

hung up on your veils when you're dancing.' Is he the perfect belly dancer boyfriend or what? So now he's ready to become the perfect belly dancer *husband*. I can't say I was exactly the perfect proposee . . . I froze. Froze and cried, because I didn't know what the hell else to do and, besides, I was wearing a flannel shirt and a ponytail and shouldn't this moment somehow be really glamorous? Tip to other potential proposees: Don't freeze and cry. It makes the proposer really, really nervous.

'Um, well, if you don't want it,' he said, fumbling with the box, 'that's OK. I can take it back and get a Glock.'

Bless his little gun-toting heart.

So anyway. We're trying to plan a Middle Eastern-style wedding. If only Aladdin was bigger, we would seriously have it there. Tad has already decided that Susan will dance at the reception. And I am still lobbying for a Beirut honeymoon – something that makes Mister International Threat Awareness absolutely crazy with apprehension. We'll see. In the end, I usually get what I want.

We went to the Richmond Wedding Expo this weekend to scout for deals. Not a lot of baba ghanouj being offered, but we did run into one familiar face in the photography aisle . . .

Stan. The photographer from the mall. And he *gave me his card*! He wanted to *photograph my wedding*! I didn't ask him if he wanted to do it without the top. I actually don't have any hard feelings about the whole top incident . . . he did a good job on those pictures. I might even go back to him for more belly dancing pictures. But I don't think we'll be using him for the wedding.

On the subject of old faces, I haven't seen any of my potential princes since each made his own personal gallant exit. Actually, I *did* catch a fleeting glimpse of Freddie through the crowd at Saint Anthony's Lebanese food festival, but I was able to dodge him. I'm not exactly eager to reminisce about the good old days or the Good News –

though just for a moment I was tempted to ask him if he'd had a chance to climb up on the big green box over by the concessionaire. I hear from Mariane that Hal got married less than a year after our mismatch. And Fahed vanished completely off the radar when he drove off that night in May . . . although I must admit, a little guiltily, that I did look extra closely at the faces of the hijackers that were broadcast after September 11. Yes, we even do it to ourselves.

And Chris? He called. He called my parents' house, about six months ago at one-thirty on a Wednesday morning. He told them that he was calling to tell me that his boss at the tattoo parlor, Bishop, had died. And he left a number for me to call him back. Bishop Walker was pretty much the only *good* part of that whole chapter in my life. He was funny, and tough, and generous, and honest. He was a hell of a good guy. And I don't need to call Chris back to remember that. I told my dad to throw the number away.

In dance developments, I have yet to dance with the Scariens because the Scariens have yet to play out again. I also haven't auditioned for Selket yet, either. I tell myself that it's because they're more of a folk dance troupe and I'm more of a cabaret girl, and I tell myself that I can't afford the costume requirements, and I don't have the time to do the traveling, but it would probably be closer to the truth to say that I'm more than a little petrified about the audition process. You have to demonstrate your proficiency in everything from stage makeup to choreography to *zils* to costuming in front of the whole troupe. It's like the LSAT of belly dancing. I think it's the *zil* requirement that gets me. I get nervous and my *zils* go clonky. So I'm currently a free agent. And I'll probably be a lot freer after this book is published. I'll never *taqsim* in this town again.

But, hey. If it happens, it happens. I'm one of those

naive optimists who believes everything takes place for a reason. If Chris hadn't dumped me, I wouldn't have discovered belly dancing. If Simonski hadn't taken the wrong exit, I never would have met Tad. And so on and so forth. I can do some mind-boggling rationalizations around this stuff to make me feel like every little setback has a silver lining. For instance, this past summer, a series of NA-related events transpired involving a scumbag loser who ran off with a junkie stripper, leaving a houseful of pets orphaned and starving. And guess who got to nurse two boa constrictors back to health?

Samira el-Safi, aka Serpentina the Snake Dancer . . . coming soon to a midway near you!

Other Hip Shimmy Stuff

I'd like to open this section with a big fat jingling disclaimer – this is *not* a how-to book, an educational tome, a reference guide, or anything of that ilk. I've written a book about myself in which I happen to belly dance. My editors suggested that I include some resources for anyone who is interested in trying belly dancing after reading my book, and that's great – *but* – and I don't think I can say this enough times to mollify the Ethnic Police – *this is not a reference book!* This isn't even the Cliff's Notes. Maybe it's the Classics Illustrated comic book version. Yeah, that's probably close. That or the *Mad Magazine* version.

If you're looking for a real, credible, last-word-on-belly-dancing reference guide, check out Tazz Richards's book on my Reads list or Shira's site on my Links list. They're chock-full of good stuff. Me? Heck, I'm just a nerdy little hipster who happens to belly dance. Don't quote me on *nothin'*.

Belly Dancers

THE GREATS IN BLACK-AND-WHITE
The Grande Dames of the Danse *Back Then*
Tahiya Carioca
Samia Gamal
Badia'a Masabni
Sohair Zaki

KITSCHY KITSCHY KOO
Belly Dancers for the Masses, Circa 1970s
Nejla Ates
Boubouka
Ozel Turkbas

MODERN GODDESSES
Some of Them Are Still Carrying the Torch 'Over There'
Fifi Abdou
Dina
Nagua Fouad
Nadia Hamdi
Lucy (not my teacher Lucy, but Lucy from Cairo)
Mona Said

FROM BROOKLYN TO THE NILE
A Very Incomplete List of Big Names from Right Here at Home
Amaya (New Mexico)
Cheri Berens (Massachusetts)
Dalia Carella (New York)
Cassandra (Minnesota)
Delilah (Washington)
Fat Chance Belly Dance (California)
Laurel Victoria Gray (Washington, D.C.)

Jasmin Jahal (Illinois)
Mesmera (California)
Morocco, aka Aunty Rocky (New York)
Shareen el Safy (California)
Suhaila Salimpour (California)
Nourhan Sharif (New York)
Suzanna Del Vecchio (Colorado)

Check out Shira's site in the Links listing for a comprehensive list of dancers here and abroad.

Musicians

OLD SCHOOL
(Straight Out of Sheva's Scratchy Stack!)
George Abdo
Farid el-Atrache
Mohammed el-Bakkar
Umm Khulthum
Eddie "the Sheik" Kochak
Gus Valli

MIDDLE SCHOOL
(Musicians Who Won't Steer You Wrong; Sturdy Stuff)
Anything on ARC's Best of Bellydance series of CDs
Chalf Hassan
Hossam Ramzy
Mostafa Sax
Emad Sayyah
Susu and the Cairo Cats

NEW SCHOOL
(Try These On If You Like It Funky)
Hakim
Hanan

Cheb Mami
The Supreme Orient Series on Sony
Tarkan

For my money, the best bet for upbeat Arabic pop is Pe-Ko music. Check them out in the Links list!

Reads

The Belly Dance Book, by Tazz Richards, Backbeat Press, 2000.
A great reference on everything from history to costuming to working with a snake. A great starting place for the beginner and a must-have for any dancer's shelf. Where was this when I was an obsessed beginner?

The Compleat Belly Dancer, by Julie Russo Mishkin and Marta Schill, Doubleday, 1973.
I'm including this mainly for historical reasons. It's out of print at the moment, but rumored to be heading for a reprint. Call me a skeptic, but I don't see how you can learn belly dancing from a book. I dunno.

Looking for Little Egypt, by Donna Carlton, IDD Books, 1994.
Ahhh, the midway! Speaking to a subject near and dear to my heart, Carlton investigates the mysterious identity of the real "Little Egypt," the dancer who caused such a stir at the Chicago World's Fair in 1893. No definitive answers, but lots and lots of facts and photos.

Serpent of the Nile, by Wendy Buonaventura, Interlink Books, 1995.
Another must-read, though I've seen some nits picked

with the accuracy of some of her facts. Gorgeous pictures and plenty of good stuff nonetheless.

I'm starting to sound like one of Sheva's skipping records, but Shira has a much more comprehensive list on her Web site. Oh, what the hell. Here you go . . .

Links
(Yes, including Shira's site)

Anthea's Web site
http://www.kawakib.com
See the pictures Susan (aka Zara) took the night we ate at Marrakesh!

AOL's Arab Chat
Itching to meet your own Prince Ali? You won't find him here, but if you simply must check it out, it's listed under 'Chat' in the member-created message boards and it's usually full. Wait for an opening, jump in, and flirt away.

Aziza Sa'id
http://www.zilltech.com
Even though she outbid me on half of the cool stuff I wanted on eBay, I have to admit she has a great Web site. Lots of info here.

Belly Dance New York
http://www.bellydanceny.com
Stay up-to-date on New York shows, workshops, and so on.

Boulder Bellygrams
http://www.boulderbellygrams.com

Maria, the cool lady with the Bettie Page 'do, has been so kind as to catalog a list of movies that feature belly dancers!

Bhuz
http://www.bhuz.com
Discussion boards, directories, and articles.

Farid el-Atrache
http://www.faridelatrache.com
Arabic musician who starred in many movies along with Samia Gamal. A lot of nice pictures and a surreal caption contest on this site.

The Gilded Serpent
http://www.gildedserpent.com
A great on-line magazine with a lot of 'back in the day' articles from the golden age of belly dancing.

Joy of Belly Dancing
http://www.joyofbellydancing.com
A lovely site by Yasmina of Arizona.

Mediterranean Dance Listserv
Which is populated by a lot of the dancers mentioned on the above list (yes, you can mingle with Aunty Rocky and the gang). To subscribe, send an e-mail to Majordomo@world.std.com with 'subscribe med-dance' in the body of your e-mail. Then watch the sequins fly! If you join quickly, you can probably watch yours truly get roasted over a slow fire for God knows how many in-accuracies, half-truths, and just plain belly dancer no-nos they'll find in this book. I'm gonna bring my own marshmallows!

Mohammed el-Bakkar
http://www.el-bakkar.com
The man, the myth, the legend!

Morocco's Web site
http://www.tiac.net/users/morocco
Aka Aunty Rocky, Commander-in-Chief of the Ethnic
Police.

Pe-Ko International
http://www.pe-ko.com
For all your Arabic music needs. I was so stupid when I
lived in L.A. I lived right around the corner from them
and never went in! What did I know?

The Scariens
http://members.aol.com/scariens
My life in music.

Scheherezade Imports
http://www.scheherezadeimports.com
My teacher and the lady with the costumes!

Shira's Site
http://www.shira.net
Did you skip straight to this? You know you did. Don't
worry; my feelings aren't hurt. Everything you need to
know is there, not here.

Baba Gha-Who?
The Words You Didn't Know

aiwa 'Yes!' Sometimes used as an exclamation of appreciation, as when seeing a particularly pretty girl or engaging dancer.

akh laa 'Oh, no!' A cry of dismay.

baba ghanouj A dip made from eggplant and sesame paste. The name means 'Old Spoiled Daddy'; ostensibly it refers to a toothless old baba whose daughter mashed his eggplant for him since he couldn't chew.

balady A folksy, improvisational type of music. The term itself means 'country', and *balady* (or *beledi*) can refer to the style or the specific beat of the music.

bedlah The traditional cabaret costume of a bra, fringed belt, bare midriff, and skirt or harem pants. Singular or plural; *bedlah* is *bedlah*.

beledi dress The covered garment worn for certain Middle Eastern dances – usually the ones done in – you got it – *beledi* style.

bris milahs In the Jewish faith, the circumcision ritual and gathering/reception.

bstila Moroccan pie with chicken, nuts, and pastry.

chiftetelli A beat used in Middle Eastern music. Often refers to the part of the show where some floor work might happen.

choli A long-sleeved midriff-baring top worn in tribal-style dance (also a traditional Indian garment).

danse orientale The Ethnic Police's preferred term for belly dancing.

debke Traditional folk dance of Lebanon. A basic line dance that's easy to pick up from those around you, it's frequently seen at weddings and family gatherings.

derbickie What my family has always called a *doumbek*.

doumbek A Middle Eastern hand drum. What my family has always called a *derbickie*.

fatwa Interpretation of Islamic law.

fatayer A meat-filled pie, folded into an origami-like triangle and baked.

felahin An Egyptian peasant.

ghawazee A dancing tribe of Egypt that flourished in the eighteenth century.

ghidoo Grandfather.

habibi 'Baby' or 'sweetheart'.

hafla Party. Also called *hafli*, or, in my family's always questionable pronunciation, *huffly*.

haram Forbidden. This is where the term *harem* originated, as it was *haram* for men to enter the womens' quarters.

hijab The loose clothing and head coverings worn by some Muslim women. Might, but does not necessarily, involve a face veil (*niqab*); *hijab* translates as 'modest covering'.

hummus A dip made from sesame paste, chick peas, and garlic.

Imam A recognized teacher or spiritual leader in Islam.

Insh'Allah 'If Allah wishes it'. Used the same way my aunts always use 'God willing'.

khaleegy "Gulf"; that is, from the Persian Gulf area.

kibbe nayee A Lebanese raw meat dish, traditionally made from lamb, cracked wheat, and spices. At my house it's made with beef.

mamoul A cookie filled with mashed dates, figs, or nuts. The date ones are extra tasty.

Marhaba 'Hello', 'welcome'.

Maronite A Lebanese Catholic religion founded in the fifth century by Saint Maroun.

m'joudra A dish made of lentils, rice, and onions.

muezzin The person who makes the call to prayer for Muslims.

muttawa Muslim religious police.

oud A stringed instrument played in Middle Eastern music. Looks kind of like a pregnant banjo.

pappadom A thin lentil-flour wafer served with Indian food.

Pharaonic Dance inspired by Egyptian paintings – very stylized, often with lighted globes in hands.

Raks Sharki Belly dancing.

Raqsat Shemadan Egyptian wedding dance performed with elaborate candelabra worn on the head.

Saidi Upper Egyptian folk dance done with a stick or cane.

Shamadan The headpiece used in *Raqsat Shemadan*.

sharmouta A woman of ill repute, whore.

shisha Freestanding water pipe use to smoke fruity tobacco mixture through a tube. The smoking of the *shisha* is a social affair.

souk A marketplace.

sukhthange 'Eat up!'

tabouli A salad made with finely chopped vegetables and cracked wheat.

taqsim The snaky slow part of the music or the dance. The term actually means 'improvisation'.

thobe A long, loose garment worn in the Gulf area.

vegetable biryani A traditional Indian rice dish.

Wallah 'Dude' in chatroomese. It's an Indian greeting, but over at 'Arab Chat' it just seems to mean, well, 'Dude'.

wubbid The layer of grease that forms on top of the *yuknhee*.

ya'ha sit'ti Loose translation: 'May his future be brighter'. Looser translation: 'That piece of shit!' I've never heard anyone but my Uncle Ronnie use this one, so who really knows.

yalla 'Let's go!' Often used as an exclamation along the lines of the Ramones' 'Hey, ho, let's go!'

Yehud A Jewish person. Probably not the most politically correct term, but then again it must not be too bad judging from the traffic on www.yehud.com.

yukhnee A meat and vegetable stew – it's almost got a pot roast thing happening; it's just enormous chunks of meat, carrots, tomatoes, and potatoes.

zaghareet The high-pitched ululating sound made by wagging the tongue quickly back and forth while shrieking. Right now there's a lot of debate on whether or not its use as an audience appreciation sound is appropriate; some factions of the Ethnic Police hold that it's strictly a wedding thing.

zar Ceremonial trance dance of North Africa. Involves a lot of head swinging and a really sore neck the next day. My zar hangover feels exactly like my old Morbid Angel concert hangover used to feel, but the Zar head motion is swirlier and less headbangy than the heavy metal one.

zils Finger cymbals (also *zagat*, *sagat*).